4.20

'Brian Staley is a political idealist, realist and activist. As a young man, during the Vietnam War, while those from more privileged educational backgrounds marched and carried banners, Brian took himself to the front-line in Vietnam. There, supporting himself by ad hoc journalism, he befriended and earned the trust of many on all sides of the conflict. This book tells the remarkable story of the one-man peace mission of a young British man in which he helped, very nearly, to broker a political way out of the impasse. Later, back in Britain, Brian was involved in domestic Liberal Party politics and played a courageous role in uncovering the moral rottenness within the party during the Jeremy Thorpe era. More recently Brian has been providing much valued support for the Gurkha Community living in Britain. The book might read like fiction, but extraordinarily, it is all true!'

TED HARRISON, Former BBC Religious Affairs Correspondent
and Presenter of *Does He Take Sugar?* the campaigning
programme for the disabled.

'I have known Brian Staley since 2003 and he has always been hard working and kind. He is one of the pioneers of the Gurkha Justice Campaign and has worked tirelessly for the community. He has held the position of chairman of the Gurkha Peace Foundation and is currently Vice President. He has worked beyond the call of duty, is one of the most genuine of men and is universally loved by Gurkhas.'

BHIM RAJ, Chairman of the Gurkha Peace Foundation and
a leader of the Campaign for Gurkha Justice.

'Running like a thread through this book is evidence of Brian's total commitment to peace, justice, and the upholding of what is right. I am so glad he has drawn together here proof of a life lived in single-minded pursuit of those objectives.'

MARTIN VYE, Liberal Democrat County Councillor 1989-2017.
Former Lord Mayor of Canterbury.

My Road from Saigon

Brian Staley

My Road from Saigon

Published by The Conrad Press in the United Kingdom 2020

Tel: +44(0)1227 472 874 www.theconradpress.com info@theconradpress.com

ISBN 978-1-911546-78-8

Copyright © Brian Staley, 2020

Typesetting and Cover Design by: Charlotte Mouncey, www.bookstyle.
co.uk Cover design created with authors own images and: Saigon - AO DAI
(Bicylces)- Photo by John Post 1967-68 from Flickr CC BY 2.0; Vietnam War
protestors march at the Pentagon in Washington, D.C. on October 21, 1967
cortesy of The Lyndon B. Johnson Library; Air Force HH-3E Jolly Green Giant
helicopter by Expert Infantry Flickr CC BY 2.0

The Conrad Press logo was designed by Maria Priestley.

Printed and bound in Great Britain by Clays Ltd, Elcograf S.p.A.

Foreword

*M*y *Road from Saigon* describes three dramatic periods of my life: the Vietnam War and subsequent peace negotiations; working with Jeremy Thorpe and Cyril Smith just as the scandal was emerging and setting up the 'Campaign for Gurkha justice' and the 'Gurkha Peace Foundation.'

My testimony and dialogue may not be verbatim but it is as accurate as memory allows and much is verified by previous articles, statements and publications.

As a political based memoir contentious views are mine alone but may reflect upon those seeking a greener ethical foreign policy and the need for community values.

Brian Staley
January 2020

Contents

Acknowledgements

First, I must pay tribute to my long-suffering family and friends who provided moral strength during a turbulent life. Any achievements described in this book are not mine alone but built upon a foundation of a faith in the innate goodness of the human spirit.

Those I was able to confide in strengthened my resolve to overcome adversity. They include Ted and Helen Harrison, Dr Adrian Pointer, James Cameron, Frank Allaun, Fenner Brockway, John Holmes, Sheila Kesby and numerous others. I recall a conversation with Leonard Cheshire, V.C. who encouraged me to create the first of two charities that I was to help construct. The first was for Vietnamese orphans and the second the Gurkha Peace Foundation.

I would like to thank the Hanoi Government for agreeing with my suggestion to release the names of American P.O.W.s held in north Vietnam through Ted Kennedy. This led to meaningful talks which led to the eventual withdrawal of Americans from Vietnam. The inspiring story of Vietnamese neutralists such as Professor Nhon who risked their lives on numerous occasions for peace and reconciliation is revealed in this book.

Last but not least the 'Band of Gurkha Brothers' plus their supporters is an on-going story that I am proud to be involved with. Bhim Raj, Gopal Giri, Deb Pun, Prem Limbu, Peter Carroll, Joanna Lumley, Virginia McKenna, Charlotte McCaul, James Walker, Pat Todd, Angela Maxted, Amanda Cottrell, George Koowarree and Stanley Jones are the nucleus of a growing number of supporters for the Gurkha Peace Foundation. Twinning schemes with projects in Nepal including the handicapped and blind schools are now linked by Skype and the hope is that the fact that Gurkhas serve in eight out of sixteen United Nations Peace Keeping Missions will receive the recognition that they richly deserve.

A huge vote of thanks is due to those who have helped me bring these revelations to light in this publication. John Parker, Geordie Hayward and his team at Hayward Design & Print and James Walker are due special mention in proofreading, editing and design.

Indochina

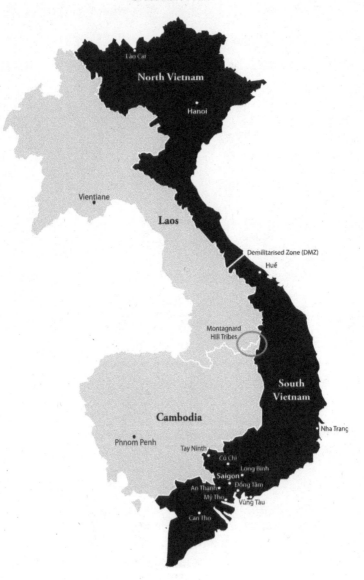

My Travels Around Vietnam 1968 - 1973

Saigon: capital of South Vietnam until 1975 and then renamed Ho Chi Minh City

Long Binh: largest American base in Vietnam east of Saigon and close to Binh Hoa

Can Tho: city in centre of the Mekong Delta near the jungle base where I kept my head down while I was reported missing November 1969

My Tho: city south of Saigon where I was blown out of bed by a Viet Cong rocket May 1969

An Thanh: south of Saigon where I and a colleague survived an attack by the Viet Cong and on this road from Saigon I experienced gas for the first time December 1968

Cu Chi: the American base where I experienced gas for the second time. After the war it was revealed that the VC had tunnels and bunkers underneath the American Base October 1969

Dong Tam: the American base six miles inland from My Tho

Vung Tàu: favourite coastal resort eighty miles from Saigon

Nha Trang: coastal city north of Saigon and main base for training officers of the South Vietnam forces. April 1969

Tay Ninth: city on the border with Cambodia east of Saigon which has a cathedral for the Cao Dai, a religion similar to the Bah Hai, amalgamating all the leading religions

Border area with Vietnam and Cambodia and Laos in the north where the Montagnard hill tribesmen used to live and the area known to Americans as the Ho Chi Minh Trail

Hue: just south of the DMZ which was the traditional capital and scene of one of the bloodiest battles in 1968

Hanoi: capital of North Vietnam and from 1975 capital of a unified Vietnam

Vientiane: capital of Laos

Phnom Penh: capital of Cambodia

Personal Timeline

1939 - Brian Staley Born in Deal

1962 - Joined Liberal Party

1964 & 1966 - Became parliamentary agent for
Canterbury Constituency

1967 - 1968 - Elected to national policy forum of
Liberal Party

1968 - Flew to Vietnam in September for first visit of
18 months

1970 - Returned to Britain in March

1970 -1975 - Involved with Paris Peace talks in London,
Paris and Vietnam

1970 - 1973 - Two further visits to Vietnam

1974 - For one month of February worked professionally for
the Liberal Party as the Kent coordinator preparing
for the General Election.

1975 - After the fall of Saigon in May worked for the Liberal
Party and became the Membership Director of the
National Liberal Club.

1979 - Withdrew from professional politics after the

acquittal of Jeremy Thorpe. Became founding chairman of the Federation of Small Business in Canterbury and District and chaired large public meetings for some of Mrs Thatcher's ministers.

1990 - 1993 - Became Liberal Democrat constituency chairman for three years

2003 - Started the Campaign for Gurkha Justice by introducing the Gurkhas to Peter Carroll, thus starting 16 years of involvement with the Gurkhas.

Proposed motion at Regional Liberal Democrat Conference which was passed; the essence of it was to create a community bank from the Crown Post offices and develop a network of agencies with the post offices' proprietors to strengthen the role of small businesses and local charities. Royal Mail would have become a full blooded co-ownership scheme similar to the John Lewis Partnership.

2007 - 2015 - Served as Liberal Democrats Councillor

2008 - 2013 - Created the Gurkha Peace Foundation by first building resources and opening the day centres

2013 - Made trip to Nepal to identify projects worthy of twinning with schools and colleges in the U.K.

Vietnam

1941 - Indochina (Vietnam, Cambodia and Laos) was a
French colony until the Japanese invaded

Ho Chi Minh fought an insurrection against the Japanese
who were supported by the Vichy French.

1945 - Japanese defeated and French began to return.

1954 - French war ends with demarcation and agreement to
unite the country with elections two years later.

After 1956 - war gradually develops with American
involvement as US "advisers" increase in number.

1963 - Following assassination of President Kennedy war
escalates with American ground troops peaking at
600,000. Casualties mount and after the American
invasion of Cambodia millions were to be killed
throughout Indochina.

1968 - Start of Paris Peace Talks

1973 - Kissinger/Tho Agreement

1975 - War ends and Vietnam is unified by the Communists

UK Events relevant to this book

1939 - World War 2 starts

1945 - World War 2 ends

1956 - Jo Grimond elected Leader of Liberal Party

1967 - Jeremy Thorpe elected Leader of Liberal Party

1978 - Jeremy Thorpe Committal Proceedings

1979 - Jeremy Thorpe Old Bailey trial

1979 - Jeremy Thorpe defeated in General Election

Nepal

2008 - Mao insurrection ends when despotic king is over thrown and attempts are made to create a parliamentary democracy.

Gurkhas serving in the Indian Army play an increasing role in United Nations Peace Keeping Missions. (Currently serving in 8 out of 16)

2014 – Nepalese Earthquake

Introduction

I was once blown out of bed by a Viet Cong rocket; apart from my ears feeling as though a needle had been thrust in them I escaped unscathed. Within two or three years I found myself with beer in hand chatting to Le Van Sao one of the leaders of the Viet Cong Government. We were joined by a doctor friend with a wicked sense of humour. He related the story in a facetious way by saying that his rockets were far more effective than an alarm clock. Le Van Sao had a frown on his face as he put a consoling hand on my arm and said 'You know it was nothing personal.' Such has been the topsy turvy experiences in my life.

The war in Vietnam was unlike any other. More weight of explosives was used by the Americans than by both sides in the Second World War. All those of military age were compelled to fight for one side or the other. Each had a little gun in his hand and a larger one in his back. Brother fought against brother and South Vietnam was full of intrigue and espionage. The Vietnamese longed for peace even more than the Americans. The political machinations and regime changes remain an untold story and till this day lies and deception still live on in America and Britain.

I was asked to write something good that the Americans were doing in Vietnam by the features editor of the Sun. A blank piece of paper was all I could produce. A fact finding tour that I intended to last three months became a first trip of almost two years. In this time I came to know leaders on both sides and my involvement lasted for seven years in which I came to meet or communicate with many world leaders including U Thant and Ted Kennedy. I worked with Professor Nhon the Vietnamese Pasteur who tirelessly attempted to end the war and eventually became the architect of the Kissinger Tho Peace Agreement. As a personal contribution I was able to negotiate the release of names of American POWs held in North Vietnam which led to meaningful negotiations for the departure of the Americans in Vietnam, Laos and Cambodia.

The war would have ended within a year if President Kennedy had not been assassinated and would have ended in 1969 if Nixon had not been elected as he ruled out any neutrality or accommodation with the Communists. Millions of people died as a result and non Communist Vietnamese were killed by the American side. British assistance was given to the Americans without the consent or knowledge of the British Government. Until the fall of Da Nang the war could have ended far more satisfactorily and prevented the tragedy of the Killing Fields and the Boat People.

After the Communists took over in Vietnam in 1975 I worked professionally with the Liberal Party. If I had hoped to escape the covert political machinations in the safety of the National Liberal Club I could not have been more wrong. A clash with a paedophile who could not be sacked because of his friendship with the man who hired the hit man for Jeremy Thorpe ended my professional political career. Sadly it also ended the National Liberal Club as a members' Club. Working with Jeremy Thorpe and Cyril Smith is a sad reflection that so much idealism should end in their personal disgrace.

Before entering the third dramatic political act when I triggered the campaign for Gurkha Justice followed by the creation of the Gurkha Peace Foundation perhaps a few salutary points should be made about my personal motivation without entering a detailed auto biography. I was born into a working class family; my father was a Christian Socialist and both my parents were hard working with a rather puritanical approach to life. I was too young to know my godfather who was the son of a Tory alderman and was killed in the RAF during the war. It is an interesting point that though my father was the secretary of the local Labour Party it did not detract from his respect and sometimes friendship with political opponents. This is a philosophy that I have always tried to follow: fight for issues that you believe in but never be malevolent to those who don't agree with you.

One memory when I was a five years old I remember well was when my parents were unable to arrange a child sitter for me as they were determined to see a full length film of the newly liberated German concentration camps. As I entered the cinema in my father's arms the steward said 'He shouldn't see this' my father replied 'He will fall asleep as soon as we get inside.' Rest assured I was determined to stay awake and watch. As a young man I witnessed dreadful scenes of carnage and suffering first hand so perhaps this was a preparation for such experiences. I was curious and always faced up to unpleasant situations including wandering into an uncle's slaughter house when I heard the sound of squealing pigs.

I was a horrible kid (no change there) and as a teenager I needed a personality transplant. In my late teens and early twenties I worked long and hard in partnership with my father to create a small but thriving company. I also became involved with the politics of the newly emerging Liberal Party. In the first General Election that I was old enough to vote I became the agent and acted in the same capacity eighteen months later producing the ninth best result for Liberals in Britain. Just after this I was elected to the national policy making forum of the Liberal Party.

Many of those who attended these meetings were more erudite and academically gifted than I could ever be yet it was interesting to meet so many young activists with a future in politics or law. I was enjoying some success writing articles at this time and so much information about what was happening in Vietnam made me curious as to the truth. After numerous conversations with Labour as well as Liberal leading activists I decided to make a fact finding trip to Vietnam. I was grateful for very good advice from a veteran journalist Brian McConnell who was soon to move from the Mirror to the Sun as Features Editor. Calculated risks had to be taken but there was a spirit of adventure and curiosity and a little altruism but certainly no death wish. Ironically, though Brian gave me sound advice on comparative safety in a war zone, he was later shot in the Mall trying to defend Princess Anne.

On the last Liberal Council meeting I attended, in both morning and afternoon sessions Jeremy Thorpe sat beside me. He had just become the Leader of the Liberal Party and I was blissfully ignorant of his private life.

Many years later a chance meeting with an ex Gurkha told me just how badly they were being treated; after serving a full term in the British Army they were being sent back to Nepal with inadequate pensions and healthcare. This included those who had been injured or those who had young families with children who had never known any country but this one. Contact with my colleague Peter Carroll and later Joanna Lumley led to the start of the Gurkha Justice Campaign which was supported by brilliant lawyers such as Martin Howe and Company. Later the Gurkha Peace Foundation was created to continue the work started by the Justice Campaign. This work is ongoing and I am very proud that Gurkhas in cooperation with the Indian Army serve in eight different countries in United Nations Peace Keeping Missions. They mediate and strengthen the agencies providing education, healthcare and food production.

Many of us who have experienced the horror of war are the most powerful advocates for peace. Perhaps deprivation in childhood or witnessing injustice can lead to a desire for social justice. In a recent reunion of doctors and nurses who had served in Vietnam, we discussed why we put ourselves in harm's way. We were adventurers with a great deal of curiosity and perhaps a little altruism.

Gandhi once said 'There is enough for everyone's need but never enough for every one's greed.' Brazen affluence alongside dismal poverty does not equate with a healthy democracy. We have a global economy but the world cries out for global justice. Far from free trade we have a kind of corporate fascism with large multinational corporations seeking refuge in tax havens and destroying thousands of small and medium sized businesses as a result of the lack of parity in taxation. There is money in war with huge fortunes made in the arms trade. Even American Presidents are unable to stop the gun lobby which bankrolls many Senators and Congressmen.

Somewhere between the slothful state capitalism of Marx and the corrupt imperialism by proxy from Chicago and the Pentagon there must be a third way to develop democratic politics? Schumacher wrote 'Small is Beautiful' believing that medium term technology could best develop economics based upon human need. Community values with small companies and the profit sharing co ownership schemes for where economy of scale led to larger units could be the way forward.

Many politicians are selfish and elitist throughout the world not listening to the voices of the most vulnerable. The West has created its own enemies and now faces a cruel suicidal form of terrorism. The only way to overcome an alien ideology is with a superior one. Our forefathers provided us with some of the answers from the founding fathers, habeas corpus, and human rights legislation.

Dreadful atrocities occur in war but in 1945 few countries were more revered by friends and respected universally than Britain. After enduring the most grievous sacrifice of military conflict there began a transformation from Empire to Commonwealth. I believe that Britain still has a unique role to play in international affairs as a champion of freedom and reconciliation in a troubled world. Humanity cries out for a moral compass that restores dignity and justice and recognises that freedom is of value in proportion to its universality and the first freedom is the freedom from want.

My journey of life has taken me through the satanic hell of war and the corruption of domestic politics to the promised land of hope and glory. I have been privileged to meet some great and inspiring men and women who tirelessly work for altruistic causes. Amongst these are the Nepalese Gurkhas.

Emerging from a poor country struggling to build a parliamentary democracy, their courage and empathy with the poorest and most desperate in the world is an inspiring story that I am privileged to be associated with. Their foundation of Buddhist, Christian and Hindu faith is humbling and should strengthen a belief that politics is the art of the possible.

Chapter 1

Welcome to Saigon 1968

Please fasten your seat belts, we are about to arrive at Tan Son Nhut Airport, Saigon.'

The purring feminine voice repeated the request in Vietnamese then French as the giant 707 juddered and began its descent. For security purposes, landing in Saigon in 1968 was an unusual experience: moving in a tight corkscrew, the aircraft nose-dived at an angle of around thirty degrees, bringing the ground, pockmarked with overlapping shell holes reminiscent of Emmental cheese, hurtling up at alarming speed.

Armed with a visa, a vaccination certificate for smallpox, cholera and malaria pills, I had finally arrived in Vietnam. Immunisation against the 'black death', a strain of bubonic plague more prevalent here than in the whole of the rest of the world combined had also been advised, but for some reason the jabs could only be obtained within the country. The journey from London had been long and tiring, a change of aircraft in Paris and stops in Rome, Athens, Tel Aviv, Teheran, Karachi, Delhi, Bangkok and Phnom Penn, offering at least a regular leg stretch in the airports and breakfast in Bangkok. It was late afternoon in Saigon, and stepping out of the plane felt like entering a cucumber house. My glasses steamed up and there was a strange and pungent aroma of vegetation. U.S. soldiers were milling around in the airport, along with a group of young

Vietnamese women. Clad in flimsy pastel-coloured silks, with jet-black hair reaching to their waists, pouting mouths and dark flashing eyes, these, I was informed by a man with an American accent, were 'show girls'.

After a bevy of Vietnamese porters had rushed to carry my cases and secure a tip, I was whisked off in a taxi towards the Caravelle Hotel. The road was swarming with cycles, peculiar three wheeled taxis in which the brave passengers sat in front of the driver, and a variety of other strange looking vehicles. I was amazed by the number of Honda scooters carrying up to four passengers, with tiny children clinging on for dear life. Approaching central Saigon on the increasingly congested highway the air grew thick with pollution, and though the heat was stifling I was reluctant to open the window. I had also been warned about explosive devices being thrown into cars. Against a scenic backdrop of massive roadside billboards advertising toothpaste and baby food, were numerous reminders of a country at war: sandbag and barbed wire forts manned by diminutive, morose looking figures carrying disproportionately large guns, American and Vietnamese troops in trucks and on foot, amputees striving to cope with their newfound disability. There were also reminders of Vietnam's colonial history in the ornate dilapidated villas, presumably built by the French long before the wars.

The road rose in a slight hump as we crossed a stagnant river, where primitive dwellings made from strips of tin, the material originally intended for beer cans, stood on wooden stilts over the water. With no sanitation the inhabitants were living on an open sewer. Women wearing large conical straw hats and rather drab tunics which resembled black pyjamas could be seen balancing twin baskets across their shoulders. They were selling food items, soup and other wares on the pavements. Girls and younger women wore bright coloured tunics - the traditional ao-dai, consisting of two flaps that flowed from the waist both back and front down to the ankles. Fluttering gently in the breeze above delicate silk pants, the ao-dai were a variety of pastel shades, with blue and purple predominant.

The Caravelle Hotel was then the tallest building in Saigon, towering up to nine stories plus a roof garden. Entering the foyer I embraced the welcome rush of cool air conditioning and changed a travellers' cheque to pay for the taxi driver. It was impossible to purchase the piaster outside Vietnam. A well-meaning American, having observed my arrival, came over with advice, 'always barter with the driver before you get in the vehicle, and never change your money in a hotel or bank: you've just been screwed.' An Indian porter showed me to my room on the fifth floor. Such luxury would not last, as after a few days I would need to find a cheaper domicile. In the meantime I could make the most of the air con, plus a shower, flush lavatory, a clean bed, ample cupboards and a writing desk. I stripped off, took a refreshing shower and flopped on the bed. I was woken a few hours later by a rumbling sound. Dusk was approaching. The bombing had begun.

After an enjoyable dinner and a Tom Collins cocktail in the hotel restaurant, I made my way up to the roof garden. The night air was pleasingly fresh. As I stood by the railings gazing down at the ant like figures on the ground, a large affable American, bourbon in hand, introduced himself. As a newcomer to Vietnam I was in a listening mode, and interested in what he might have to say about the place. It transpired that he was an arms dealer, so naturally what he had to say was all about the war, the benefits of which he proceeded to wax lyrical upon. We had sat down and were facing Cholon, watching slow parachuting flares light up the sky for the dive-bombers. My new friend told me precisely how much each flare and bomb cost. 'Western economies would collapse if we didn't have an arms industry,' he pronounced, going on to explain how the trickle down effect of this trade would help the local population. He had just flown in with some more 'toys' for 'our boys'. One could hear no irony in his evangelism and it seemed that he really meant what he was spouting. Many years later I would repeat his words. I think few people believed that anyone would actually say such things.

Sipping our cocktails in comfort we were three miles away from people being killed. The Caravelle was in a relatively safe part of Saigon, although a Japanese journalist had died in a rocket attack while staying in the hotel. Despite the constant shudder of bombs I slept soundly that night, roused, oddly I thought when the noise abated at sunrise. Breakfast consisted of papaya followed by bacon and eggs, a pleasant surprise though the bacon was very salty. It was now time to explore a little of Saigon. Armed with a street map I stepped out into the morning heat and strolled down Tu Do Street, the Vietnamese name for freedom, changed from Rue Catinat, as featured in Graham Green's 'The Quiet American'. Once famed for the gaiety of its French nightlife, the street now reflected the human misery resulting from war. The pavements were strewn with beggars, men, women and children so thin they reminded one of the images of concentration camps. Worse, many were mutilated. One emaciated woman held a small baby, mother and child both looking close to death. 'Give me money eat, chop-chop' she repeated continually, waving an upturned straw hat. I had to zigzag to avoid falling over another heap upon the pavement, a legless man whose torso and arms were nothing but skin and bone. A ragged little boy approached, tugging at my sleeve to follow him, 'You like girl, very cheap.' Then a well-dressed man accosted me and whispered, 'You like change money? You have dollars?' Despite my repeated 'no thank you' he persisted until turning his attention to another westerner. Further down the street were numerous bars, outwardly like terraced houses, with small windows and wide open doors. The painted signboards in bright garish colours were designed to register with the mostly American customers - the 'New York Bar', the 'San Francisco Bar'. Even at this time of the morning, girls in mini-skirts, white smocks or tight trousers cut so low that they failed to cover the bottom were already at work, inviting passers by in for a cool drink and to buy them a Saigon tea, which would pay for their company.

Weaving between children trying to sell me peanuts, I passed Maxims, the upmarket nightclub offering floor shows and an opportunity to dance with some of the most beautiful of Vietnamese girls, and came to the riverfront. The My Lanh, a floating restaurant, was doing a brisk trade despite as I learned later, being blown up twice and sustaining numerous American casualties. Crossing the wide river were a number of packed motorboats steered by tiny girls looking no older than ten. These small craft were so over laden that the decks were almost at water level. The passengers were mostly elderly women with baskets hoping to buy food in the market.

Moving along the riverfront I came across the fish market, which with the heat and lack of refrigeration gave off a sickly odour. Close examination revealed that this was not the kind of seafood I was used to seeing in Britain. Alongside fish of every shape, size and colour were the most magnificent shellfish, with giant crabs, prawns, lobsters and large quantities of squid, smoked like kippers. Lost in the thronging market I found myself the centre of attention. Children were particularly intrigued by my presence, but with so many pairs of eyes staring at me I became a little uneasy. Looking around I realised I was the only foreigner, and for reassurance I longed to see another westerner. I had been warned that with the ferocious guerrilla war underway in the country, Vietcong snipers could be anywhere, and might easily take me for an American.

Leaving the fish market I followed the street map to a square that would eventually lead back to the hotel. The area appeared to be more cosmopolitan, which brought a sense of relief, until the shrill sound of a whistle made me look round in alarm. A white-uniformed police officer was stopping a youth on a motorbike. I had heard how the police were prone to fire their guns over someone's head if they wished to question them, and if that didn't work the next shot would be aimed at the torso. This youth had been riding the conventional way, but to deter Vietcong guerrillas throwing explosives and making a fast getaway, it was now compulsory for pillion riders of Hondas and motorcycles to be ridden side saddle only.

The sun was strengthening as mid-day approached. I passed by the huge city centre, seeing on one side a large police compound protected by sandbags and barbed wire. Opposite was the entrance to the enclosed market and bus and cycle terminus, where the former dictator Ky had executed prisoners regularly in full public view. On either side of Le Loi, a broad dual carriageway with cycle tracks, the pavements were lined with stalls selling every kind of commodity from clothes, books, records and tinned food to condoms and pornographic magazines. Standing groups of girls and women broke into giggling chatter as I passed, a few words of English were offered in case I might be interested in buying something. Vietnamese music blared out its five tone language strange to my western ears. Sweat was dripping from my brow when I reached the hotel, and I was keen to jump under the shower and enjoy a brief rest before venturing out again.

My destination for that afternoon was the nearby press centre where I was due to attend my first briefing, popularly referred to by ex-pats as the teatime follies. Arriving at the large room, which was guarded by three armed U.S. marines and a pair of Vietnamese policemen, I was allowed in with no request to see my press credentials, which I had yet to collect. A big table was laid out with various press releases from the three American armed forces and one from the Vietnamese military. A Vietnamese civilian tapped the microphone and opened the proceedings by introducing a major wearing the uniform of the Republic of Vietnam. The major read a document in Vietnamese followed by an English translation: 'During the twenty four hour period ending 0600 hours today Communist units caused seventy four incidents. Military region 1 Thua Thien: Yesterday at 08-45, an infantry position located about twenty kilometres west of Hue City received eighty six rounds of mixed mortar and recoilless rifle fire and was attacked by Communist troops. The attack was repulsed. Four enemies

33

were killed and two weapons were seized. Three Arvin soldiers were killed and two wounded due to the attack…'

The briefing continued, naming districts in all four regions. When the major had finished a smartly dressed colonel in the United States Air Force took the rostrum. A map of Vietnam was spread on a board and the colonel used a wooden pointer to indicate locations as he spoke. 'Forty six sorties were flown over North Vietnam in the panhandle… four ammunition supply dumps, an oil installation and two anti-aircraft guns have been destroyed. Five bunkers in the Demilitarised Zone have been destroyed.' The delivery was dry and laconic, and when answering questions the colonel was almost monosyllabic, and departed swiftly from the rostrum. Next an American civilian approached the microphone. He was diplomatic and presented his news in a slow and somewhat weary manner. One battle was described as having a 'good kill ratio'. Search and destroy missions were reported as killing and neutralising so many men. A number of Viet Cong sampans were reported destroyed and the Americans had lost three gun ships, shot down and the crews feared killed or missing. The casualty list for the week was given as eighty Americans dead or missing and one hundred and five hospitalised. Sixty-five South Vietnamese or Arvin were reported dead. The number of Communists reported killed for the week was four hundred and sixty-seven. One American reporter whispered that the numbers reflected a rather quiet time, as during the Tet offensive casualties had been six times higher.

Leaving the press centre I felt an Orwellian chill. Figures had been banded about quite detached from the human misery inflicted. I had introduced myself briefly to the press officials and told them of my intention to collect my press passes the next day. The passes would give me the rank of major with the authority to travel or eat in the officers' mess. I bought an English language paper from the eager boys waiting outside and followed the majority of the reporters making their way to the Continental Hotel. In the bar of the Continental I spoke with the English journalist whom Brian McConnell had told me would be a positive contact and mentor in Saigon. The man greeted me however with some indifference, seeing me I think as a potential rival rather than a colleague. Two Americans were far more helpful and we were able to exchange views and ideas. Chewing on peanuts and drinking a Tom Collins, which cost little more than a beer, I read the local paper. The news was heavily slanted, referring to Formosa as China and mainland China as Red China. Some of the advertisements were not calculated to please feminists: 'Villas, apartments, cars and temporary wives available. Come to Miss Lee of Cong Ly.' The bar of the Continental was open on two sides, allowing patrons to enjoy the shade along with the open air. It also allowed unwanted beggars and street sellers to wander in and try their luck, before being chased out by the staff. As we sat there a group of ragged looking boys came in asking to clean our shoes. Given the hot dusty streets of Saigon they could usually do quite good business. The Americans present were sympathetic and offered up their shoes, while most of the English contingent lunged hostile kicks at the boys. One of the Americans explained that these were street children with no parental support. Some were orphans and some simply abandoned out of sheer poverty. 'Where do they live?' I enquired. 'In a sewer pipe' said the American. Apparently, some large concrete pipes intended for a sewage scheme that had been abandoned for lack of funds, was now their proud home. 'It's waterproof and cool in the heat of the sun.' I was also told that the older boys took a paternal role in this makeshift community, and looked after the youngest members.

As dusk approached with the now familiar rumble of bombs I retreated to my room at the Caravelle and began a plan of action. The next day I would visit the two press centres and then the British Embassy. I realised that the big stories of battles and catastrophes would be dealt with by the big news agencies. Unless I was close to an incident I simply couldn't compete. But the street children sleeping in the sewer pipe or the children's hospital where British doctors and nurses worked with Vietnamese counterparts were surely equally important human stories. I also thought of writing about the plight of the girls compelled to earn their living in the vice trade. I resolved too, to visit some of the American bases, and to try to glean an insight into U.S. thinking and strategy behind the conflict.

The next morning I found the Vietnamese spokesman particularly talkative and helpful. The American press officer was complimentary about freelancers that went foraging for stories, but spoke in disparaging terms of journalists who lived in Singapore and sent despatches claiming to be from Saigon. He said that many of their stories had been plagiarised from the English language papers during their occasional visits to Vietnam. He spoke of one particularly idle journalist that had phoned to ask about the commotion outside his hotel when a Buddhist monk had set himself on fire in protest at the war. My next destination was the British Embassy, situated just opposite the new large American one. An elegant three storey building standing in its own grounds surrounded by a tall iron barred fence, the British Embassy had an armed Gurkha on duty, who smiled politely as I walked past. Once inside the glass doors it was even cooler than the hotel. I was soon met by the press attaché who escorted me upstairs to his office. He began an official brief of the current situation. 'The Vietnam War is both a guerrilla war and a strategic war fought with mobile fronts. Most of the population of South Vietnam lives by the coast in the larger towns; plus of course the agrarian population scattered throughout the Mekong Delta. Communist troops bring their supplies down the mountainous jungle covered corridor, which borders Laos and Cambodia. In fact their trails and supply bases are increasingly found over the borders well inside Laos and Cambodia. Most of the population is now under the control of the Saigon government but the rural areas tend to be under the control of the Viet Cong. No road outside the towns is safe after dark, when the Communists come out of hiding and blow up bridges and capture villages.'

I decided to venture some blunt questions: 'Who was going to win the war?' 'How corrupt is the Saigon regime?' and 'Ky once said that South Vietnam needed thirty Hitlers and they only have me; is there a legitimate government with local support?' The attaché sighed and there was a lengthy pause before he attempted to answer. 'The outcome of the war,' he told me, 'will depend upon the resolve of the American people. It's an election year and anything can happen. The Pentagon will want to get through this year as uneventfully as possible, after which there will be less interference from politicians. The military establishment believes that the Tet offensive was a big mistake by the Communists. Their losses were enormous: it could be the beginning of the end for them. As for corruption, that is endemic in this part of the world. Considering the pressure that they are under the Saigon government is no worse than many others.' When I pressed him on the role of Thieu he gave a stout defence of the regime. 'The President was elected, and if you add the votes of Hoang the Prime Minister, they have a mandate to govern.'

'Even when Dzu his opponent in the Presidential Election is now in jail and more than half of the population wasn't entitled to vote?' I said, 'It's very difficult to hold an election during a war. We didn't even try in Britain.'

'From the military perspective,' replied the attaché, 'Thieu is now firmly in the saddle. He has strengthened his position by ensuring that all the Commanding Officers are personally loyal to him. Anyone who has the slightest link to Big Minh is kicked out. The last bastion of support for Ky is in the Air Force but the Americans have put him in place so he poses no threat to Thieu. He is a Catholic and his government and military infrastructure is entirely Catholic and they are the most anti-Communist, especially those who come from the North.'

I then asked, 'Are the Buddhists happy that Catholics, who are less than twenty percent of the population, should control the whole government and military forces?' The attaché never answered this question clearly, for it blew a hole in his argument. For me, the moral dilemma was: what do the people of South Vietnam really want? My instincts told me that above all they wanted peace and there was no way that they should want to continue with hell on earth. Did they really vote for a policy of perpetual war? The argument about dominoes was that if Vietnam should fall to the Communists, everywhere from India to Australia would also fall. If that was true, was there something attractive about Communism? Did the government of South Vietnam ask the Americans to enter the war, and was the Presidential Election legitimate? I believed then and now, that the most natural instinct of any people is to fight against foreign invaders. We British did so for a thousand years, even when we were ruled by tyrants.

I was informed that there were nearly three hundred British nationals living in South Vietnam. Some worked in the Embassy and some were members of the medical team at the children's hospital in Saigon. A Save the Children team was located in Qui Nhon, some Brits were serving in the American or Australian armies and a dozen were police advisers. A small number worked with charities and the media. Before leaving the Embassy I discovered a small waiting room where back copies of English newspapers were kept. Glancing through them I felt more than ever before what a great deal of dross filled the papers. I found cricket scores the most interesting ingredients. Front pages of the tabloid press were filled with news and photographs of celebrities: the lead story was of a pop star fornicating with a new bimbo. There was news of an impending strike and nothing at all about Vietnam. I had already heard Americans on the point of departure saying that they were going back to the world. I began to understand what they meant.

The Nhi Dong Children's Hospital was situated just inside the Cholon area. When I found the location and walked towards the entrance I saw piles of refuse all around and two of the largest rats that I have ever seen in my life scurrying along. The hospital building was dirty and depressing but there was a great deal of noise and activity. I met the team leader Dr McCauley, a mild mannered man from a Quaker background. He told me that the twelve nurses and eight doctors concentrated on medical treatment, whilst patients' mothers that came into the hospital to care for their offspring often brought their other children. There was therefore a great deal of havoc with so many little ones running around. After Dr McCauley had given me a tour and introduced me to the staff I was free to wander around at will. Several babies were suffering from malnutrition with undeveloped limbs and bloated stomachs. Some were covered in sores, but despite their obvious discomfort looked somehow tranquil and resigned to their fate. I took a few photographs and joined some of the nurses and medics when they took a break. I was handed a glass of iced green tea, which was an acquired taste but quenched my thirst better than anything else in the hot climate. After a brief chat with the staff, one of the doctors invited me to a party being held at a villa in Cach Mang Street that evening. Nurses and doctors alike were soon hauled back to their duties, and I said I looked forward to meeting them in a more relaxed setting later.

Cach Mang Street was the main artery from the city centre to the airport so it was easy to find. Reaching the three-storey villa I was shown up to the roof garden, where from a well stocked bar someone handed me more than an ample rum and coke. I was disappointed that the nurses were not present, but the male doctors were high-spirited, colourful characters with a wide dichotomy of ideas and opinions. From the nearby streets came the shrill, intermittent sound of police whistles followed by shots. 'Don't worry about the rifle fire unless it comes from both sides of you, in which case you get your arse out of there,' advised one doctor. 'Police are prime targets so they're nervous and trigger happy.' The medics talked about the work that they were doing with Vietnamese children, and differing views on the war. Unlike similar all-male gatherings back in Britain, sport played no part in the conversation, but occasionally it became obvious that some were seeking solace in sex. Dr John Bass had a glint in his eye as he described the huge surplus of attractive Vietnamese girls. Dr Adrian Pointer spoke at some length about the children that he was treating, describing how that day he had removed an American bullet from a wounded child. When two U.S. guests became annoyed and questioned his assumption about the origin of the weaponry, the doctor replied pointedly, 'I know an American bullet when I see one! You can't expect me to not mention who is responsible when I spend my life treating the youngest and most vulnerable victims of war.' With a heated argument brewing, I tried to concentrate the discussion on the specific injuries and diseases being treated. Some said that the children had the same health-care problems as those in other third world countries. Adrian maintained that the big difference here was injuries from war such as napalm and lazy dog. When I enquired about the latter, Adrian described it as a weapon dropped from aircraft, which on landing, exploded two or three feet from the ground, sending hundreds of L-shaped razor blades spinning through the air. The effect was to maim rather than kill instantly, causing amputations often followed by gangrene. The lazy dog was designed to tie up medical services and generally drain enemy resources, and was used extensively in North Vietnam or identified Viet Cong villages. It was generally agreed that war often inflicted high numbers of indirect casualties too, for example by causing food shortages and destroying healthcare provision. One interesting point made, was that both sides in a war had a vested interest in underestimating the numbers of casualties, rather than risk demoralising combatants.

As the evening wore on and the drink flowed, some became the worst for it. Being probably one of the more sober members of the party, I was shocked to see one doctor climb on to the perimeter wall of the roof garden and perform a balancing act. Reminding him that there was a very long drop the other side I shouted, 'Get down you silly bugger'. As he did so a colleague tried the same trick, but instead of landing safely, he lost his balance and disappeared over the other side of the wall. Hearing a crash we rushed forward and saw him clinging to a broken fanlight on the adjoining building, about to fall through onto some bicycles parked three stories below. Bracing myself against the wall I managed to grab him and pull him to safety. He was cut badly by the damaged fanlight and needed hospital treatment. Though the risk to me had been minimal, he would thereafter always introduce me as the man who had saved his life.

Chapter 2

Dangerous Encounters

With the help of Melvyn Bowler, a technician with the British medical team, I relocated from the comfortable but expensive Caravelle Hotel to a more affordable room. Melvyn also had access to a Red Cross truck, which would be useful until such time as I could afford to hire my own car, and one evening he invited me for a drive around Saigon. It was gone ten o'clock, and a curfew was now in operation, meaning only the military and emergency services were allowed out on the streets. Anyone disobeying this order was liable to be shot. Melvyn drove at incredible speed, and it wasn't long before we were challenged by a shriek of whistles and the dazzle of searchlights. From a mobile wooden barricade with large rolls of barbed wire strewn across the road, a number of crouching figures emerged aiming their weapons at us menacingly. Melvyn shouted 'bac-si', Vietnamese for 'doctor', in a nonchalant tone. It was the magic word. The barriers were swiftly drawn aside and we were waved on. The knowledge that at any time a rocket or random street fire fight could materialise gave me an adrenaline rush of excitement.

After a circular tour of Saigon we reached the military complex at Tan Son Nhut Air Base. Melvyn drove in and stopped outside an all night cafeteria run by Americans, catering mainly for servicemen that had just come off duty. The self-service establishment offered hamburgers, milk shakes, chilli, coke and ice-cold milk or coffee, prepared by Vietnamese girls who took payment at a cash desk. The girls were adorned in clean white smocks and exchanged chit-chat in Basic English with their customers. To counter the black market a specially printed military currency was used, the notes easily obtained and valued somewhere between the Vietnamese piaster and the American dollar.

A jukebox was playing 'My World is Blue', the air conditioning was full on, and for a while you might almost forget you were in Vietnam. Suddenly an almighty sound rocked the building, followed quickly by another, this time making my ears pop. 'Rockets?' I asked Melvyn. I could now distinguish between the various loud noises that were a regular feature of life in Saigon. Bombing by Americans in the outskirts of the city and the incoming shells of the Viet Cong produced a thud and a shudder, while outgoing artillery was a sharp crack. Melvyn nodded, 'A mile or so away,' he said laconically. Being a new boy still, I asked what might have seemed a stupid question to a seasoned ex-pat: 'If a rocket attack is really close, is there a procedure we ought to follow - head for an underground shelter, cover our ears, dive into the foetal position?' Melvyn shook his head, 'There's no point in Saigon, because it's all over in a flash. They say you never hear the one that gets you, so if it's really close all you can do is shit yourself.' With these reassuring words we left the cafeteria to find the night sky much lighter, illuminated by flares descending on the other side of the airport where some military action was taking place.

The next day I agreed to meet up with Dr Adrian Pointer. From our earlier encounter I felt he had a great deal to get off his chest, and I had decided I would like to despatch a story based upon his experiences. Adrian hailed from Maidstone in Kent and had arrived earlier in the year during the heavy assault on Saigon. He described his work treating children burned by napalm: 'Napalm sticks like glue and is difficult to extinguish. Victims are skinned alive! Children cry out in perpetual pain. We do what we can to ease the suffering, but often the percentage of burns is such that they die from their injuries.' The Lazy Dog, the cluster bomb that exploded close to the ground scattering hundreds of L shaped pieces of metal, also came up again. It was said Adrian 'a dreadful weapon,' the metal pieces 'spinning like propellers until they make impact. In an agrarian society, gangrene sets in and the only way we can help is by amputation of a limb, if the patient is lucky.' He added that large areas of Cholon were bombed indiscriminately and many innocent people had died. 'I have removed numerous bullets from wounded children and we are swamped with children mutilated by the bombing. There is also an increase in the number of abnormalities from Agent Orange.' This was the chemical defoliant used extensively throughout Vietnam to kill off jungle areas, providing a greater firing line for American base camps. 'The Vietnamese often refer to monster babies being born with increasing regularity,' said. Adrian. He then spoke passionately about the treatment of the Montagnard hill tribesmen, who had inhabited the rainforests for centuries. Still wearing loincloths, civilisation had passed them by and they lived an entirely separate existence to the Vietnamese people. Sadly their traditional homeland was the jungle area close to the Cambodian border, known to Americans as the Ho Chi Minh Trail. Heavily bombed, the area was now designated a 'free fire' zone and the Montagnards had been told to abandon their ancestral burial grounds. Adrian remarked that for them to move would be like going to the other side of the moon.

When I had despatched Adrian's testimony, the response from London was disappointing; apparently the material was too subjective, and I was asked instead to write something good that the Americans were doing in Vietnam. In hindsight I could have described the efforts of one G.I. to help street children or the work being done to educate the hill tribesmen. There were good Americans here, people who were driven by altruism. But these were the shining lights in an otherwise very grim scenario, and I did not believe that the American presence overall was in any way beneficial to the people of Vietnam. I therefore returned a blank piece of paper to London.

Adrian Pointer was to become a lifelong friend, though much later our communications would rely on email or Skype as we would frequently be living thousands of miles apart. Small in stature, Adrian was blunt, even courageous in his views, including when talking to American military personnel. Never comfortable among the cocktail set of western diplomats, he was a brilliant linguist and had not only learned Vietnamese but also addressed those from the North in a separate dialect. He believed in treating everyone with equal human dignity, and was befriending a growing number of intellectuals and dignitaries. A year or so later his contacts would lead me into the machinations of Vietnamese politics.

Despite the close proximity of war and the depressing evidence of its effects on the population, life was not always gloom and doom in Saigon. I soon made new friends in both the British and American communities and if I tired of

Vietnamese food I could always eat in the American officers' mess. The most senior officers dined and drank or occasionally watched movies in the Brinks of an evening, and it was here that Dr John Bass, one of the most colourful characters among the British medics, after inviting me to see his work in the refugee camps, asked me to join him for lunch. The refugee camp was an enclosed community of those displaced by the war, and though residents were free to come and go, a ten-foot high fence surrounded the place. After Dr Bass had dealt with a long line of children waiting for a medical examination we were on our way to the centre of Saigon. Arriving at the Brinks, we were greeted by a Vietnamese girl, signed the guest register and entered the dining area. Dr Bass had a mischievous look in his eye as he scanned the room for the most senior general with a space at his table. Spotting his mark, he led me to the vacant seat and asked the officer politely if we could join him, introducing himself with his usual modesty, and me as the man who had saved his life on the rooftop that night, making me sound like some latter day Ernest Hemingway. 'How's the war going General?' Bass asked boldly. The general was taken aback by the direct question, but once assured of the company he was keeping he began to converse.

When I first arrived in Vietnam there was some speculation that negotiations might produce a peace settlement. Talks in Paris had first stalled over who should be represented at the discussions. The North Vietnamese insisted that the Viet Cong be there while the Americans wanted the Republic of South Vietnam to play a role. So that neither side lost face a round table was suggested. Our conversation came just as the

American Presidential Election was approaching. Rumours had spread that Big Minh would become head of state in a form of neutrality similar to the Laos agreement but I believed that this idea was fading as Nixon was growing in strength.

After the General had departed speculation continued with Dr Bass. Many years later the veteran BBC journalist Charles Wheeler was to uncover a plot by Nixon, who had sent a secret envoy to Thieu, urging him not to sign any kind of agreement and promised that if he was to win the pending presidential election he would be more supportive of his government and help him to build up his armed forces.

Unbeknown to me at the time, U.S. Vice-President Hubert Humphrey was starting to back away from the Paris peace talks and concentrate on the election campaign. I had already felt however that there was no big political settlement in the offing here, and our conversation with this particular general seemed to confirm the impression, likewise discussions with American journalists and diplomats, who gave no indication of expecting an imminent resolution. It is easy to start a war, far more difficult to end one. Meanwhile an opinion poll of civilians and servicemen in a Saigon English language paper showed a large lead for Nixon and strong support for the far right candidate George Wallace. The psychology of survival dictates that people living in a war zone, regardless of politics tend to support the side that is defending them. This instinct was what the Americans were counting on in South Vietnam. If the majority of those drafted into the armed forces were fearful of the Communists they would soon become loyal to the American side. Each man with a gun in his hand would thus have a bigger one in his back.

After enjoying a good lunch at the Brinks I parted company with Dr Bass and met up with a handful of American journalists to discuss the stories they were working on. To gain a better understanding of the situation I decided it would be useful to take a flight over Saigon in a helicopter and enquiring at the press centre was given the name of a Vietnam Air Force officer based at Tan Son Nhut. Melvyn asked if he might come along for the ride. Sure, I said, if we could get permission. Wasting little time Melvyn drove me to Tan Son Nhut, where, at the tightly guarded military base we had to ask several times for directions before finding the right building.

Inside the complex the atmosphere was relaxed. Several young servicemen were sitting around awaiting their next deployment orders, and Melvyn and I received a friendly, smiling welcome. When we told them the purpose of our visit, several of the pilots invited us to join them on their various upcoming trips. Having expected some degree of official resistance to shadowing the military I was surprised at how easy this all seemed. I asked if we might accompany a reconnaissance mission during the daytime. It was no problem it seemed. We were given a time to report and advised to wrap up well, as at high altitude it would be cooler and we would be taking a gun ship, flying with the doors open. After the sweltering temperatures out here I found myself looking forward for the first time in my life to feeling chilly.

Suitably attired, Melvyn and I returned to Tan Son Nhut at the appointed hour. Boarding the helicopter, the engine already running, I felt a rush of excitement. One of the crew told us that more helicopters were deployed out here in Vietnam right now than in the rest of the world put together.

It was easy to believe. All around us we could see and hear the drone of one helicopter after another departing or landing. They came in a variety of shapes and sizes, from small single seat craft - sometimes referred to as pregnant Easter Eggs and used for reconnaissance - to massive flying cranes for transporting mobile bridges after the original structures had been blown up. Most numerous were the type we were on, medium sized machines that ferried troops to the latest hotspots, cruising with open doors and machine guns at the ready – the gun ships.

The whirr of the rotor blades intensified as the helicopter moved forward and left the ground. As we climbed steeply, radio contact directed the pilot towards the outskirts of Cholon, the scene of prolonged skirmishes the previous night. Swooping low, there was nothing to see now but the usual daytime bustle and congestion on the streets, while the sky around us seemed full of various aircraft heading in all directions. The strong draft from the yawning mouth of the helicopter was cool but not unpleasant. Wearing no harnesses and apparently oblivious to danger, the South Vietnamese servicemen peered out at the terrain far below us. I looked out too, but having read a few weeks earlier about a Japanese journalist being sucked out of an aircraft, I kept a tight grip on the overhead straps. Once dubbed the Paris of the Orient, Saigon was now a sprawling conurbation, the population having swollen rapidly in recent years with so many trying to escape the war in the rural regions. I noticed the crew taking particular interest around the perimeter of the city and the airport, where a few days earlier a mobile rocket launcher had fired shots as aircraft were landing and taking off. The elusive perpetrator, nicknamed 'One shot Charley', was thought to have struck elsewhere, but there was no discernable pattern to his activity.

On return to the base I asked if we could follow up by going on a night patrol. I was interested among other things in seeing exactly how the flares were deployed. Again this was readily agreed, and after an evening meal Melvyn and I reported once more and were this time shepherded aboard a C47 aircraft. This too flew with the doors wide open, but in place of the fixed machine guns were small flare shoots. The C47 travelled faster and higher than the gun ship and there was a continuous blast of night air into the cabin. This was refreshing at first but after a while, despite the extra clothing I was uncomfortably cold for the first time since arriving in Vietnam.

The pilot had been directed to the outskirts of Cholon, and on receipt of the given radio signals the cylindrical flares, about four feet long and a foot in diameter, were released down a slide. Having watched the devices descending from a distance I was fascinated to observe the operation from the air, tracing their descent until they burst into light and floated down on their parachutes until extinguished on landing. The Viet Cong tactic was to strike by night and escape the massive firepower of their opponents by disappearing among the local population or into the rain forests. The objective of this mission was to verify intelligence reports and identify any movement on the ground. I watched impassively as the South Vietnamese airmen placed and released the flares one after another into the dark void, again working dangerously close to the open gap.

Growing bolder, on our return I requested a flight on a dive-bombing mission with a Vietnamese pilot. I was told to report the next day and to wear dull or camouflaged clothes in case we were shot down. In the sudden awareness of this possibility, my enthusiasm turned to apprehension. Waking the next morning and placing a new film in my camera, I felt rather as a condemned man is said to, with all sense of time swept away. Greeted at the base by the officer I had met the previous day, I was introduced to a pair of dashing young pilots in their early twenties and told they were two of the best and most experienced in the Vietnam Air Force. Why did the word kamikaze have to flash into my mind? This time I was advised to wear a safety helmet, but after trying several it seemed likely that the Vietnam Air Force simply wouldn't have one big enough for my English head. The choice was stark: I could try again the next day when they could borrow a helmet from the Americans, or fly without one.

Seeing the indecision on my face, one of the young pilots said, 'We don't plan to get shot down, you'll be alright with us. We are only going to bomb some Viet Cong bunkers that have been sighted about 100 kilometres north of Saigon.' These reassuring words of Lieutenant Thang convinced me to go sans helmet, and I followed him and his colleague Lieutenant Vinh towards two A1 G Sky raiders waiting on the runway, and after being fitted with a parachute, climbed up the slippery wing and into the cockpit.

Everyone around me seemed calm and relaxed. The aircraft was about twenty years old but a popular type in this kind of war. Seated alongside the pilot I found that there was dual control for training purposes. I was shown a little yellow handle between my legs and told on no account to touch it other than in an emergency: it was the ejector seat; if we needed to evacu-ate it would flip up the roof and hurtle me out. 'Don't forget,'

Lieutenant Thang impressed upon me, 'if we do get shot, pull the handle and bale out, because I'll have gone. If you land safely, run like hell to avoid being captured.' I nodded my head as my earphones and a microphone were fitted to provide radio communication. Each of the two aircraft flying the mission carried ten 150lb bombs under the wing and could fire eight hundred rounds from a twenty millimetre cannon. A moment later the aircraft roared into life, accelerated at immense speed down the runway and we were airborne.

The first task was to fly low over the Saigon to Vung-Tau road for any signs of Viet Cong activity. There was a wonderful aerial view of the paddy fields but when we came to the rubber plantations and strips of rain forest there was little to see but a veneer of green as the Sky raider skimmed the treetops. The road appeared to be secure and traffic was flowing normally. 'Here, you have a go. Just take the joystick and you can fly the plane,' invited Thang, releasing his hold. Reluctantly I grasped the joystick, but the aircraft was soon veering alarmingly from side to side. I appealed for him to take over again. When he did so I glanced down to see people peering up at what must have appeared to be an aircraft out of control. They were right. Thang laughed loudly, 'Half of them down there think we're going to have an accident.' I replied, 'Half the people up here have already had one.' My attempt at humour was lost in the engine's roar.

Approaching the outskirts of Vung Tau we ascended higher and flew northwards. Our destination was Tuc Trung not far from Xuan Loc. Below was impenetrable jungle until Thang pointed excitedly to an area close to a river tributary. Through the trees and undergrowth I could just make out tiny specks of glistening steel: the target, a cluster of Viet Cong bunkers, was in sight. The two Sky raiders circled high as the pilots checked their coordinates then turned and plunged dramatically earthwards. The jungle grew suddenly large and I tried to blot out the thought of being blown to pieces at any second. When the bunkers came into sharp focus I also felt a stab of conscience, and in those few brief seconds said a little prayer that no one would be killed. The sense of responsibility was bound inextricably with fear. Petrified, I pledged that if I survived I would do something towards trying to end the war. This was no revelation on the road to Damascus, but a wretched, terrified man trying to cling on to life. How I would fulfil my pact with the Almighty I had little idea, other than the vague vision of going to peace rallies and making a few hapless speeches. I certainly never dreamed that within a few years I would be talking to leading world statesmen or negotiating to obtain the names of American POWs held in North Vietnam.

Somehow I managed to photograph the bunkers just before the bombs struck, and at this point we were so low I thought we must surely crash. But Thang yanked at the joystick and not a second too soon the Sky raider's nose lifted and the trees got smaller again. The sensation seemed ten times more violent than a fairground switchback and I could feel my head still going down even as my knees were going up. A cloud of smoke rose from the ground as the bombs exploded. As we circled higher I peered back to see Vinh replicating our actions in the other Sky raider. Our aircraft then repeated the exercise. I photographed the destruction until the film was used up. Then suddenly a clatter of cannon fire shook the plane, and amid the noise and confusion I was convinced it was incoming and we had been hit. The tension eased as we re-ascended to a safe altitude. Thang then made a third dive with more cannon fire from the Sky raider strafing the ground. After the second aircraft had followed suit, it was a moment of immense relief as we ascended for the third time and Thang gave the thumbs up before executing a victory roll.

On the flight back to Tan Son Nhut Airport we switched to Radio Saigon and listened to pop music. After a smooth, almost perfect landing, the roar of engines abated and I climbed out of the cockpit to hear that the mission had destroyed four Viet Cong bunkers and damaged three. I was astounded that such a precise report could be given almost instantly. There was however no mention of casualties. War in the air is such an impersonal mode of armed conflict, clean and clinical, and so easy to forget the human misery involved. In future years, if politicians are to be spared the sight or sound of any suffering whatsoever and can minimise their own side's casualties, it might be possible to wage war purely for financial gain while hiding the truth. If the media were to be controlled entirely by vested interests such an Orwellian situation could easily arise. It has happened to some degree already. The role of a free and diverse media is essential to retain an ethical dimension in politics, particularly in foreign affairs. This was and still is my view; that the west, particularly the Anglo-Saxon races has a special responsibility to build upon our proud heritage of the Founding Fathers and Habeas Corpus in the pursuit of truth and in building a fairer world, free of colonialism and all forms of exploitation.

The two young pilots shook me warmly by the hand and said how pleased they were that I had flown with them. I was presented with a metallic badge of an aeroplane in appreciation of my trust in their competence. Apparently very few reporters had accompanied them on missions. They then invited me to join them for a drink. I politely declined but promised to do so on a future occasion.

After the press conference the following day I received an invitation to work with an American news agency. This would at least pay a regular income, enabling me to hire a reliable looking Austin mini with a slightly extended body. The agency was headed by Steve Tyler a recently retired U.S. Air Force colonel, who now combined writing with business interests, and with whom, despite my expressing strong misgivings about the morality of the war I seemed to strike a chord. Steve offered to take me to some of the American bases and to meet the officers. He was a man of huge charm, which he used to some effect upon women, whether they happened to be eighteen or eighty. But though a shameless flirt and sometimes over the top in his conversation, it was always delivered with good humour. And as I soon discovered, the strength of his personality combined with his considerable military experience could inspire trust and enable conversation with men of all ranks. I looked forward to accompanying him into the Mekong Delta.

While the routes between most of the cities and towns outside Saigon were by now too dangerous to navigate other than by air, the road to My Tho was considered reasonably safe. The downside was the unbearable heat and fumes on the outskirts of Saigon. As we sat in the chronically congested traffic, Steve, who was driving us in his Volkswagen, issued regular reminders: 'If you do want to open the window, get ready to bat anything away.' It might have been a premonition on his part:

later that year while giving a lift to an American in uniform, an explosive device was thrown into his car. Successfully deflected, it exploded on the roadside.

Approaching a tall Buddhist pagoda that stood on the edge of the urban squalor we saw the first sign of open country. Steve put his foot down while I poured some bottled drinking water into a beaker, opened the window slightly and began to relax in the clean, cooling breeze. Passing an American base, a loud crack of artillery made me jump, drenching us both with the water.

On a similar trip a few weeks later when I had been driving with two American colleagues, without warning came a sensation like lighted cigarettes being thrust in my eyes, the air was sucked from my lungs and I felt I was drowning. As the car wobbled and slowed we gradually regained our breath and sight. 'What on earth was that?' I asked anxiously. One of my passengers explained that it was a type of gas used to kill the Viet Cong in their tunnels and underground shelters. This was the first indication I had that the Americans were using gas in this war.

On that previous trip Steve drove over several narrow bridges guarded by U.S. troops, who every so often would drop a grenade into the river. Steve stopped to ask if there was any trouble and was told that this was routine to deter Viet Cong frogmen blowing up the bridge. One of the soldiers remarked that they never lacked a good supper as the explosions always left a few dead fish floating on the surface. I was relieved to see the road fairly busy, as it was generally known that when local traffic was sparse it meant the Viet Cong were around. The flat terrain looked fertile enough, with men and women toiling in paddy fields, harvesting rice as their ancestors had done for centuries. Rivers and tributaries were channelled into dykes and small ditches irrigating several acres of land. Beside roadside dwellings, children offered small piles of pineapples and watermelons for sale. I was just beginning to appreciate the rural tranquillity when we saw a large American car lying cannibalised and rusting. It was also riddled with bullet holes. This stark reminder of conflict made me think just how perilous life must be for the Vietnamese, with many such outlying areas controlled by Saigon during the day and the Viet Cong at night.

About half way to My Tho we came to a small town called An Thanh. The place was heavily fortified and there were numerous white faces mingled with the Vietnamese. Pulling in for a break we were invited to lunch with some officers and friends of Steve. Among our hosts was a senior general who was studying some computer data with a look of dismay. 'We've lost a village,' he exclaimed. 'Whereabouts?' I asked. 'On the computer,' he replied. Steve and I laughed but the general was in earnest. 'If we've lost a village on the computer, it means we really have lost a village,' he insisted, and explained how each day the whole of South Vietnam was re-photographed and all the information fed into a computer. He was adamant about the accuracy of the system, and this development had left him somewhat distraught.

After lunch Steve went off to find a mechanic, as he had been having some problems with the Volkswagen. On returning he advised that to allow time for the repairs it would make sense for us to stay overnight, and promptly arranged accommodation in a house used by police training officers. I made a facetious remark about Volkswagen's advertising claim that you never hear of people breaking down in their vehicles: this was the first time I had ridden in one and it had happened. I also mentioned facetiously that my father often referred to the VW as Hitler's car!

I felt relaxed about staying in the town, but had overlooked the fact that it was situated next to a bridge, a favourite target for the Viet Cong. Some time after midnight all hell broke loose, the thud of incoming rockets quickly accompanied by the crack of outgoing artillery as the bridge was stoutly defended. A few minutes into the cacophony Steve came into my room and said gravely, 'I've looked around and the only munitions in the house are a few hand grenades. If the Viet Cong break in here they'll assume we're with the police and we'll be prime targets for assassination. We must be prepared to defend ourselves.

Chapter 3

Revelation and Rebellion

The possibility that the Viet Cong might break through filled me with dread. If so they would be sure to check out the house, and as Steve said, automatically assume we were their enemy. Would my desire to survive overcome a deep-seated aversion to violence and the moral dilemma that I had come as a neutral observer who had pledged not to take up arms? The idea of killing another man was bad enough, but the effects of using a hand grenade to do so did not bear thinking about. I also had a slight handicap in the shoulder, limiting my capacity to throw.

Steve and I remained in the house on high alert listening to the gunfire rattling though the night air, and with each fresh burst I looked at the hand grenades, wondering when the fateful decision whether or not to grasp one might be needed. The fighting was intense and prolonged but with the first glimpse of daylight the noise began to diminish, eventually bringing silence and much relief.

By mid-morning, the mechanic having completed the repairs to Steve's VW we set off again towards My Tho. Once on the open road the traffic became sparser, just the odd Lambretta buzzing past or an occasional tuc-tuc chugging along like a small milk float. About eight miles from My Tho Steve turned off to take a short cut directly to Dong Tam, the large American base in the Mekong Delta. I was soon to learn that this road, narrower and flanked by jungle on either side, had been nick-named by the Americans as 'ambush alley'. Within a few moments a dark figure emerged from the undergrowth ahead, and to our alarm appeared to throw something towards the car. Tensing in anticipation, we then saw a young boy grinning at us. It was his idea of a joke. Steve pointed out that if we had been armed soldiers trained to react in a split second to potential threats the boy could have been killed. Despite the relief, I remained apprehensive. 'I hope your car doesn't break down here,' I said. Steve was sanguine, 'It's much safer now with gun ships flying regularly overhead and they've even got some ferocious dogs patrolling the rain forests. Anyway, we'll soon be there.' As we joined the My Tho to Dong Tam road the landscape changed, dividing into intensive smallholdings where here and there a water buffalo could be seen plodding through the fields, a tiny boy perched on the animal's back to guide a plough or cultivator.

Arriving at Dong Tam, the largest American complex in the Mekong Delta, Steve and I stopped off and made our way to the Provost Marshall – the 'hooch' - where we were quickly engaged in conversation by several officers, all very friendly especially when they learned that I was English. They were also curious as to why I was in the country and what I thought of the situation. Still being early days for me in Vietnam, I replied that as an independent journalist I wanted to learn about the root causes of the conflict and that I had an open mind. This was met with approval by most of those present. One name I recall from that group was John Kerry, destined to rise to prom-inence in the U.S. As I was leaving the hooch, one of the young

61

officers followed me out and enquired where I would be staying that night. 'In My Tho, at the hotel where the river meets the canal,' I told him. Steve had arranged a room there for me, as he had been offered accommodation with an old friend here in Dong Tam. The young man then asked if he might visit me that evening. He said he wanted to talk to someone outside the military and to get something off his chest. I was intrigued.

In the intervening hours I met more of the Dong Tam servicemen and learned their custom of greeting one another by announcing the number of days left of their mandatory one-year tour. When close to demob they simply raised the relevant number of fingers to indicate their happy day really was nigh, assuming nothing untoward happened in the interim; the phrase uttered when saying goodbye to those left behind, 'take care', was not perfunctory. It seemed every effort was made to provide for the men's morale, from the excellent quality of the food to the murals on the walls of the hooch depicting scenes of the American landscape. Along with the cinema, regular live shows featured Filipino and Vietnamese singers and musicians, with strippers and American performers usually the most popular acts. Phone lines were also available for the men to call and talk for a few minutes to their loved ones back home.

Inevitably perhaps the GIs existence was somewhat detached from the Vietnamese. Many never once sampled the local cuisine. For most Americans, contact with the locals meant chatting to the women who cooked and cleaned for them, and if venturing into Saigon or one of the popular coastal towns, conversation with a taxi driver or bar room girl. Although disillusioned with the war most of them believed that they were fighting for their country in repelling Communism and they had all been told that they had been asked to help by the government of South Vietnam, and that it had been elected democratically. Local radio blared out from the sleeping quarters while television was piped continually in U.S.O. cafeterias. A popular diversion was tuning into Hanoi Jane's sweet and seductive voice broadcasting North Vietnamese propaganda. Men of all ranks could not be friendlier and I was offered more drinks than I could possibly consume.

In the evening I was taken on to My Tho. The hotel was full of American civilians, many of them working for a construction company building wider roads into the Delta town of Can Tho. The Vietnamese owner of the hotel introduced himself and showed me to my room, which, I was pleased to find, was clean and with a shower and loo. Right on time the young American captain pulled up in his jeep and I was soon sitting in the shade over a cold beer ready to hear what he had to say. He began by telling me that he had been the youngest officer commanding in the U.S. Army, and that Nixon had used this fact to present him as a patriotic icon or poster boy - the young American hero. He revealed how disturbed he had been when interrogating a Viet Cong woman, who had asked him what he was doing in Vietnam and wanted to know how he would like it if his country were to be occupied by foreigners bombing his people and endangering his family. This intelligent young man had soon realised that the ordinary Vietnamese wanted the war no more than the American people, and that they loathed the government that was being imposed upon them. He then described the search and destroy missions that he led penetrating the jungles looking for the Viet Cong. 'We would follow a track but rarely come across the Viet Cong. However we would invariably suffer from a booby trap that would kill or seriously injure one of my men. This happened on a number of occasions and my men asked me: what are we achieving? My men believe in me and in my judgement but I no longer believe what Nixon is saying. He is claiming that once we hand over to the South Vietnamese army we can withdraw and leave them to it. But that policy won't work as they don't want the war. And if we gradually withdraw without an agreement it will become more precarious for Americans who remain.'

I listened impassively. The young man had a faith and a firm belief in the highest principles of the Founding Fathers. He was in a most difficult position and wanted to know what he should do. I also understood from him that he was not alone in his thoughts. A growing number of soldiers of all ranks were already playing a positive role in the peace process, with a minority that had felt strongly enough to refuse to fight and had settled in Sweden. However it was far more difficult for a serving officer to extricate himself and his men from a morally reprehensible war, but as he put it, to do nothing and continue to obey orders would make him no better than the Nazis. What were his options? My first thoughts were that he should communicate with the democrats in the Senate and Congress who were beginning to revolt against the perpetual war policy – Ted Kennedy, George McGovern and even Fulbright.

After a couple of hours spent exchanging ideas the young officer left to return to his base in Dong Tam. Within a few months of our conversation a company of black GIs tasked for a search and destroy mission would refuse to obey. They agreed to defend their position but would not venture into the jungle to achieve only amputations or death. The word spread and a second company likewise refused. When a third contingent was ordered in, the colonel was willing to lead but his men would not follow him. The rebellion gathered strength throughout the United States Army and there were no more search and destroy missions into the Vietnamese jungle.

The bombing that night in My Tho was much louder and closer than in Saigon. As I was trying to sleep an almighty blast of shrapnel hit the building next door and threw me out of bed. As I lay on the floor curled into a foetal position with my hands over my ears, which felt as though needles had been jabbed into them, a rocket landed in the street followed by a third thud from the nearby canal. I counted the seconds, waiting for the regular Viet Cong pattern of hit and run to play out. Apart from ear and headache I was unscathed and eventually got off to sleep. Next morning I heard that two men in Dong Tam had not been so lucky.

After breakfast I took a stroll along the riverfront. Passing a market I saw a shop with the words Hot Tok painted garishly above. Needing a haircut I entered and was ushered into a large chair by a smiling barber. I watched with amusement and fascination as a young girl took off my shoes and socks and placed my feet in a bowl of warm water, and after washing my feet clipped my toe and fingernails. At the same time the barber was massaging my neck and shoulders before eventually attending to my hair. It was certainly different to the English experience and very refreshing.

Thanking the barber and his assistant I walked a little further along the river in search of some cool refreshment. A friendly female street vendor offered a choice of three drinks: crushed sugar cane, which tasted like condensed milk, coconut juice or

Soya milk. On this occasion I was keen to try the sugar cane juice. I was missing fresh milk and the good old English cuppa, though these were available in the American cafeterias, but I would soon begin to enjoy the acquired taste of iced green tea.

Back at the hotel Steve turned up in his VW and beckoned me to jump in. 'I want you to meet a couple of my friends at the C.O.R.D.S building.' He drove to the other side of My Tho and pulled up at a barbed wire surrounded complex guarded by two military policemen. The barricades were about ten feet tall, the wire razor sharp. 'If anyone knows what's going on in this district these guys do,' said Steve. 'Listen and you may glean a great deal of information from them.' There was much greater emphasis in his tone than before our visit to Dong Tam.

In an office towards the rear of the building I was introduced to two Americans. One was a large bulky black man who spoke in soft, mild tones but sounded articulate and informative. The other was a middle aged bespectacled white man. Ample cups of coffee were poured as the four of us exchanged news and information. A C.I.A controlled organisation, the role of C.O.R.D.S was to build the infrastructure within the South Vietnamese government's control. This meant working with civilian and military leaders in the strategic hamlets on building housing, small business plants and other projects. Security and economic aspects were also important, and above all intelligence gathering.

Our hosts invited Steve and I to lunch in the canteen where some fifty civilians were partaking of roast chicken and vegetables followed by ice cream. Conversation with these field operatives was quite different to the political hype that pervaded most of Saigon. From their tone there seemed little enthusiasm for the long-term objectives of the various projects these people were embarked upon. As the dining hall emptied Steve and the white man left the table leaving me to chat with the black man.

'Do you know we train the God-damn Viet Cong?' he said. This comment startled me and I waited for an explanation. 'There's no problem with the reserve youth army,' he continued, 'but when men are drafted into the regular army at eighteen we prepare them for battle; they undergo intensive training and we show them all the tricks of the military trade. When the time comes for positioning them to a base of operations they're due to go home for their first leave. We never see around forty percent of them again. They just disappear, unless we capture them as prisoners or find them amongst the dead after a battle. What's more, they're often the brightest and best forty percent.'

'That's incredible,' I replied, 'and do you think all of those forty percent join the Viet Cong, or do some just vanish?'

'A few may desert but the great majority change sides. You can imagine how much heart that gives me for my job.'

'Pretty devastating for you I should think.'

'You can say that again; and do you know that a few of the Vietnamese officers here in the Delta must collaborate with the enemy so that each side avoids engagement in battle. 'Of course, we're supposed to flush out the Communists from South Vietnam otherwise we can never win. Charlie knows that time is against us. We're gradually pulling out; we like to get our wars over quickly. We've no stomach for fighting in this goddamn place year in year out.'

'That's a different story to the one Nixon's telling,' I said. He's telling the world that you're pulling out because the war is virtually won.'

'That son of a bitch isn't here, but he must read all the intelligence reports that we send him. He lies so much that he believes his own propaganda.'

I paused for a moment to reflect on the enormity of what I had been told. I then asked, 'If so many men defect to the Viet Cong surely there are some who opt to remain with the South Vietnamese Army for intelligence purposes, to become spies in other words?'

'That's right. And the more we hand over to the South Vietnamese Army the more precarious our position becomes.' Looking around the room to ensure that no one was listening the officer then emphasised, 'What I've told you is off the record. I could have my arse shot off if they knew what I've just said, but hell, people should know what's going on. It's our lives that are in the firing line.' I gave him a reassuring nod. With servicemen like this eager to reveal the truth about the war surely the lies of Nixon and Kissinger would be exposed.

When Steve came to collect me he pumped me for information but what I relayed came as no surprise to him. I was pleased to spend another day in the Mekong Delta and we returned to Dong Tam for the remainder of the day. When Steve dropped me back at the hotel in the evening he told me that it would be good for me to chat to some of the American civilians who were living in the hotel. Most of these guys carried guns but behind the tough exterior they simply wanted to earn a good wage and relax with a beer at the end of their shift. This was always the best time of day, sitting in the shade over a leisurely meal. They were a friendly group most of whom worked building the road to Can Tho. They reassured me that after the noisy and dangerous night, security would be stepped up and we would probably have a more peaceful night. I was told that the usual fashion was for several weeks to pass in relative peace until without warning a Vietcong attack shattered the tranquillity.

Dawn was heralded by a loud chorus of cocks, geese and assorted jungle sounds, and I was pleased that the night had been more relaxing, without the familiar rumble of bombs. After devouring a breakfast of papaya, ham and eggs I wandered beside the river to take in some reasonably fresh air before Steve came to take me back to Saigon.

My next invitation with Steve was to fly to the coastal city of Nha Trang to view the large officers' training centre, a project at the heart of Nixon's policy of expanding South Vietnam's armed forces. It was on this visit that I was pleased to meet Don Tate, a Pulitzer Prize winner for his reporting of the battle for Hue. A good-looking American, Tate was about my age, a good conversationalist and an interesting travel companion. Our journey would begin outside the Vietnam Press Centre where a coach was waiting to take us to the airport. Most of the journalists present were from neighbouring South East Asian countries together with a few who worked with local newspapers and radio. Our host for the trip was called Lieutenant Binh, a stocky, crisp mannered Vietnamese who spoke English with clear diction. We had all been told that we would be shown around the training grounds and introduced to those training each of the three services. Binh could not hide his disappointment that a number of American reporters, most of which relied on agencies for their representation and information, had also been invited on the four-day event but declined their invitation.

Bundled into a military aircraft with uncomfortable seats set around the sides of the fuselage, as we flew north I peered down at the dense green jungle and reflected on how such a view afforded a perspective on the war: one side with total air superiority, the other digging into the bowels of the earth in an attempt to avoid the most intense bombardment in the history of human conflict. Steve interrupted my thoughts with another mordant observation: 'You can measure the relative position of safety that you're in by how many men are sitting on their helmets. No one is bothering on this trip but if there was the slightest chance of being shot at everyone sits on their helmets to protect their balls.' I replied that we had no helmets, and in any case wouldn't sitting on them be pointless if we were shot down. 'Probably,' agreed Steve, 'but it's a psychological act. No one wants to be killed or injured but one fear that exists in the minds of everyone under fire is the thought of losing their balls or their eyes.'

The Vietnamese amongst us spoke highly of Nha Trang as a beautiful resort and as the aircraft descended and I caught a glimpse of this city by the sea. We landed smoothly and were escorted onto an old military bus with the now familiar wire frame in place of glass windows. Soon after leaving the airport we took a coastal road for two to three miles to our final destination, where Lt Binh directed us to a delightful rambling villa on the seashore. The view was breathtaking; the horizon where sky and sea met, twin shades of perfect blue, the gold of the sun before its evening departure blending like molten butter into the sand. The villa had an exotic allure with colourful creepers climbing the walls and railed steps that led down to the beach. This was truly a fairytale setting, a place of peace and enchantment where the idea of war seemed worlds away.

Lt Binh divided our group into pairs and showed us to our rooms. Don Tate and I were given a room with two ornate four-poster beds enclosed in mosquito nets. The nets were to prove invaluable. Tate, quietly spoken but ambitious, was fast building a reputation in journalism. I discovered that his views were somewhere in the middle of the American spectrum but he had an open mind and could be light hearted with a dry wit and was altogether good company. There was still time for a dip before sundown, and once unpacked most of the party left the villa to walk over the sand and jump in the sea. Even at this time of day the temperature was that of a warm bath, comfortable and refreshing. I entered with caution however, not knowing what dangers lurked beneath the surface; the sea was a transparent blue and I could see various shapes moving around, jellyfish or octopus perhaps? Our Vietnamese colleagues meanwhile were splashing about without a care in the world, and seeing my trepidation one of them tossed something playfully in my direction. It was a sea snake though dead; I made a tactical retreat and sat on the sand, cool enough now to enjoy the glorious vista.

As the others finished their swimming and dried themselves in the setting sun I joined a small group including Don Tate and a South Vietnamese officer attached to the Military Press Centre. As war stories and reminisces of life in Vietnam were exchanged I asked them which experiences had made the most impact. Don was the first to answer. 'It had to be Hue that made a lasting impression upon me. Not just the ferocity of the battle and the enormous slaughter but one particular feature.

Bodies were blown into the citadel wall making a giant imprint. The head, torso, outstretched arms and legs were smashed into the walls as though some giant had stamped upon them. Other bodies fall and are out of sight but these stayed erect to haunt us.'

It was the turn of the South Vietnamese officer to offer his most striking anecdote. 'Perhaps this story epitomises the Vietnamese tragedy. I met a fellow officer in a bar in Tay Ninh who was trying to drown his sorrows. Wearing his heart on his sleeve he needed to tell someone his troubles. He was leading a search and destroy mission when his platoon came across a small group of guerrillas who had not heard them creep up on them. There were just four Viet Cong laughing and drinking together. They were in such close proximity that he instructed his other men to hold their fire in case there were any more enemy about whilst he mowed them down with his automatic weapon. He cut them in two with his fire, waited for a brief moment to ensure that they were alone then triumphantly advanced to identify the bodies of his victims. With a great sense of shock and horror he discovered that he'd killed his own brother.'

Don Tate then brought Ho Chi Minh into the conversation, and voiced criticism of the Communist leader. Expecting the Vietnamese officer to agree with him, he and I were amazed at the man's response:

'Oh, but we Vietnamese do like Ho Chi Minh, even though in the south we fight against the system. He fought against the Japanese and the French and is the father of the nation. It's the Communist system that we don't like, not the man. He is a nationalist first and a Communist second.'

Tate challenged this: 'How can you say that, he's the Communist leader.'

'He's mistaken about the system,' replied the officer. 'Power lies within a village or district and the people may decide that a businessman is making too much money out of them. Sometimes they have a people's court and sentence a man to be executed. The leader at the top has nothing to do with what happens within a village.'

I was intrigued. 'What you say is incredible. Your complaint about the system in North Vietnam was probably made about the early settlements in the United States - mob and lynch law in a primitive democracy founded by the principles of devolution and power to the people.'

The South Vietnamese officer had the last word; 'It can be a very unfair system, for if a man's unpopular for any reason he may be condemned.'

As the night air brought swarms of mosquitoes the beach party retired back to the villa. That evening we explored Nha Trang. I loved the seaside atmosphere and the charming French ambience of our accommodation. The only down side was the midges that followed us around and settled repeatedly on the arms and face. Malaria pills were supposed to be taken every three weeks but by now I had forgotten when I had my last one, and reflected that inoculations might have been better. Once in bed though the mosquito net and the sea air ensured sound sleep.

Over a continental breakfast washed down with plentiful coffee, Lt. Binh's sharp military manner began to mellow as he advised us not to eat too much during the day, as later on a banquet in our honour was to be held. It was now time to take a short bus ride to the official purpose of our trip, to visit the U.S. sponsored officers' training establishment. On arrival we watched a group of NCOs practise scaling a cliff, climbing a rope ladder at great height, performing bayonet drill and firing live ammunition. The pace was unrelenting and as soon as one task was completed the men ran straight to the next, their stamina impressive. We were told they ate three meals a day, more than most of them could hope for as a civilian. Boys were drafted in part time at sixteen with full time service beginning at eighteen. Each recruit undertook three months training before seeing action, and those selected as NCO material trained for five months, the first three in the lecture room before practical experience living under canvas. The final phase was learning to live underground and being subjected to battle conditions.

Major Hoang the Chief of Staff at Nha Trang briefed the visitors: 'Before Tet the students were trained up to eight hours at a time but we increased this to fourteen hours and now we train them to sustain a twenty four hour period of activity. In this type of war the first five minutes of a battle may be crucial. A squadron leader decides the battlefield and his reflexes can determine the course of the battle. There are two academies in Vietnam for training to the rank of NCO and above. These are Dalak and Nha Trang. Here alone we have trained more than 11,000 men in the last year. Those who plan to further train and specialise in intelligence are flown to Malaya to be trained by the British. Our strategy in the next few years is to build an army of a million men and have an air force bigger than the RAF.' Announcing this goal the major's tone was ebullient.

We watched the training routines for several hours and when dinner was flagged up I whispered to Don Tate, 'I'll just be pleased not to see any more bayonets being stuck into plastic dummies. There's only so much testosterone and sweat one can take in one day.' Lt Binh led us into the dining room where we were joined by more than a hundred trainee officers and instructors. My initial impression of Binh had been of a tough, no-nonsense military man but the brusqueness hid a gentler side, which came out more during the meal. The banquet was an event we really enjoyed. There were an amazing seven courses of food, all of them excellent including a banana, mango or custard apple served in sequence around the table. I received the custard apple, a first for me, while Don Tate sitting next to me was given the humble banana. The name for the custard apple varies throughout the world, and in Vietnam is referred to as a Blue Dragon. After the dinner Lt Binh's military mask dropped further when he amazed us all by standing up and singing a love song in the most beautifully soft and lyrical voice. Before leaving we were also treated to entertainment from performers in the Vietnam Air Force and Navy.

Arriving back in Saigon I was scolded by a nurse who said, 'I don't know how you can write about military expansion. Just one day's budget for the war is greater than one year's spending on social and health care for the whole country.' This rebuke led me to Phu My and a large room where three nuns were trying their utmost to look after 170 babies, one of which, malnourished and very underweight was handed to me. I was also given a bottle of milk. The nuns told me that if I could get the infant to feed it might just save its life. God knows I tried but the poor soul was so weak it could not even drink and died in my arms.

Chapter 4

Suffer the Little Children

'Phu My is one of the better orphanages and a centre for all men's ills.' It was the Reverend Michael Counsel speaking, who with his wife Elaine had escorted me to their Protestant church opposite the British Embassy. In Vietnam it was a surprise to find an English couple in such a location. I had now taken part in their worship a few times and found a congenial atmosphere amongst the congregation of mostly American servicemen. There was always a cold drink available and often an invitation for everyone to join the Counsels for lunch. They told me that my presence made for more stimulating debates, especially when I stoutly defended Jane Fonda.

The orphanage in which the child had died in my arms was on the road to Bien Hoa just on the outskirts of Saigon. I had previously visited another orphanage that was a place so bereft of resources that the nuns who ran it had appeared thoroughly depressed and suffering from malnutrition as much as the infants in their care. Being told that the death of children was an everyday event had not eased my distress.

I was assured that Phu My was far more inspiring and attracted more sponsorship from diplomats' wives. 'But why don't any of the babies cry?' I asked. The reverend's wife replied, 'Babies cry when they want something. It's their first attempt at communication. Here if they were to cry there would be simply no response so it would be a waste of effort. They have never been shown that love and care for which every child craves. Still, here there is an attempt to help. Look at those children playing real mothers and fathers. Even the boys and girls of no older than ten are trying to feed the babies, and they wash, clothe and nurse them as well.' I noticed that under each naked baby was a strategically positioned hole that led directly to the sewage system.

We left the babies' room and entered the toddlers' section, where the response was quite different. Every child approached us and wanted to be touched or picked up and cuddled, all yearning for the individual attention they so seldom enjoyed. It was almost impossible to walk without a pair of little hands clamouring around our legs in a desperate effort to find love and affection. I felt like the Pied Piper as we made our way slowly through this sea of clutching hands towards a third room. Entering we found a slightly older age group, much noisier and more animated. In one corner blind children were being taught Braille by one of the nuns, while at the far end victims of polio were being helped to use crutches.

A man patiently encouraging a child with spindly legs to walk was I realised English. The child was clearly in pain and finding the challenge difficult. The nuns introduced the English man to us, 'This is Doug Grey.' Doug had pioneered the building of a hydrotherapy pool here, begging for the materials and recruiting several American civilian and military men to help him in the construction. It was, claimed the nuns, a little miracle that such a stranger should have come to them and pioneered such valuable work. Doug was a Cornishman, originally from Plymouth, who had begun his career as a Marine and then worked in nursing, gaining similar qualifications to that of a sister. Much of his life had been dedicated to charity and he had raised the money to come to Vietnam by his own efforts. About five foot ten and in his early forties with a small goatee beard, Doug spoke softly about his experience of nursing children with polio before arriving in the country. On one point he was emphatic however: he was convinced that many of the children in the Vietnamese orphanages would die without more help. The mortality rate was horrendous, and with so little food to go round the weakest had to rely on the generosity of the strongest when it came to mealtimes.

Over the next two or three years Doug was to become a legend to all those who knew him. With no financial resources of his own, he begged and scraped for the cash to rent, staff and equip a large villa, which he filled with polio children from the various orphanages, then persuaded visiting American doctors to perform operations and sometimes arrange for medical treatment abroad. From that first meeting I kept in contact with Doug and tried to support him and his work in whatever way I could.

At Phu My there was a sense of hope for the most vulnerable, from babies to the frail and elderly. As I bid farewell to the friendly nuns, the memory of the child that had died in my arms in the babies section of Phu My would often return to haunt me.

Having promised to visit an American friend suffering with an oriental illness I made my way to the large Third Field Hospital run by Seventh Day Adventists. The hospital was often the first destination for wounded soldiers, providing assessment and patch up before sending them back to the

States. My friend was fast recovering and looking forward to being released, but around him large numbers of patients lay in a clearly serious condition, many of them sedated. As we were talking an orderly approached and said that the staff were under great pressure with a number of critically injured soldiers needing urgent treatment; could we pacify the soldier in the next bed? We looked at the soldier, his face swathed in bandages and just regaining consciousness for the first time since being injured. 'His parents have been informed,' said the orderly, 'and we will have another look at him as soon as we can.' The orderly then explained the specific nature of the soldier's injuries. How could we ignore such a request? But equally how does one tell a nineteen-year-old boy that he has gone blind? My friend and I sat by the bed and assured the young man that he was in hospital and being looked after, that his life was no longer in danger and that his family had been contacted. Meanwhile he should try to rest and not worry. Keen to relate what had happened to him, he told us that he and his platoon had entered a village when there was an almighty flash of light and he had lost consciousness. I said goodbye and left my friend deep in conversation with the young man. His time here was over; one more whose life had been irrevocably damaged by what seemed increasingly to be an endless, utterly illogical and cruel war.

Prompted by my boss I began to investigate the plight of the indigenous girls that earned their living from offering 'personal services' to the large number of foreigners in Vietnam. They were not hard to find; bars and massage parlours were everywhere. Together with a male friend I entered a few of the bars and spoke with some of the girls. Their command of English varied but the first thing they requested was a Saigon tea. The men they entertained generally drank beer or spirits, and the girls would ask them what they were doing in Vietnam, whether they had a girl friend, and so forth, very similar to the scenes described by Graham Greene during the 1950s insurgency against the French. The girls appeared sexually assertive and in control but in reality, their position was one of desperation; they were simply trying to survive. The higher infancy mortality among males meant many Vietnamese women remained unmarried and having to fend for themselves, a situation exacerbated by the loss of men in conflict. The parentage of some of the girls may have been influenced by the French tradition of courtesans, but one got the impression that the majority had yearned for a conventional marriage to a Vietnamese man and the chance to have children. Sadly, with the cultural life in the villages destroyed by the war, their hopes had been shattered. Consequently the population of the large cities and towns had doubled, or in the case of Saigon trebled, as girls drifted in looking for work. Some found employment in markets, shops and cafes, or as seamstresses or cleaners, the whole economy increasingly built upon servicing the military machine. The most congenial job would be in an office or restaurant, but for those who could speak some English and were reasonably attractive there was the lure of the bars, where girls could survive sometimes without having to sleep with the customers.

But with a natural desire to love and be loved, many of the Vietnamese girls looked to the Americans for something more than a meal ticket. Though the chances of any of them finding a lasting relationship were slim, affairs sometimes went on for a year or so until the serviceman left for home, leaving the girl alone. More prolonged attachments tended to be with older civilians working in an ancillary capacity with the military. I recall being invited to a wedding between an American officer and a girl from a traditional Vietnamese family, and on another occasion I attended the wedding of a British doctor and nurse. Despite the difficulties presented by the military officials many Vietnamese girls did become G.I. brides and settled happily in America. For the great majority of Vietnamese girls however, romantic encounters were at best fleeting. The expectations and behaviour were to an extent a reflection of the shift in Western culture at the time; the sixties and early 'seventies was the age of the pill, flower power and the permissive society. It was also the era of filmic fantasy, in which James Bond made love to beautiful girls of all races at the drop of a hat but no one ever got pregnant or caught venereal disease. Indeed there was a belief that science had made such diseases a thing of the past, a mindset that would only be rocked by the emergence of Aids in the early 1980s.

Wherever there were American bases, bars and brothels had sprung up nearby. Some were crude and grimy, but others were cleaner and well managed. The aptly named President Hotel, five storeys high with several hundred bedrooms, each occupied by a girl and surely one of the largest brothels in the world, was run by the United States military. Every girl that worked there was given regular health checks and there was never a lack of customers among servicemen with a few days rest and recreation to spare. Sauna and massage parlours were popular particularly with those that had lived close to rural bases, many claiming that only the heat of a sauna could clean the pores of jungle sweat. Having seen the discoloured water that came out of most Vietnamese hotel showers this was not so surprising. When I tried a sauna bath for myself I found the experience unusually relaxing. After emerging from the sauna I was instructed to lie on my back and asked if I would like the massage to be soft and gentle or hard and vigorous. Choosing the latter I had two girls walking on my back, paying special attention to my spine and using the balls of their bare feet. After an hour or so of being thus manipulated I felt that my spine was stronger and my whole body invigorated. A Vietnamese man claimed that though most people could not afford a doctor, the positive effects of a sauna and massage was beneficial for health. Some establishments of course were less about medical or health benefits, and more about providing stressed out soldiers with masturbation and oral sex.

One day while browsing in the reading room of the British Embassy in Saigon I had a chance meeting with a smart and articulate public school educated Englishman. He claimed to be the highest serving non-American in the United States Army, and wished to tell of his experiences in the war. However he did not want his story to be published while he was still in Vietnam as it would be very dangerous to do so. I told him that if he was not prepared for me to cover his personal information from Saigon then I could provide him with relevant contacts in Britain. Adjourning to a coffee shop a short walk away from the city centre we resumed our conversation. He told me that he was serving in Special Forces, the American equivalent of Britain's S.A.S. Much of his deployment involved being in jungle patrols in platoons of around a dozen men. Intelligence gave them the locations of small hamlets where the men folk were known to be away on active service with the Viet Cong, leaving their women and children at home. His platoon would approach the village by night and spray it with napalm. He described in chilling terms the screaming women and children running from their huts in flames until they fell in dishevelled heaps on the floor. 'I did this for Jesus' he said calmly. 'It gave me a great buzz seeing this spectacle'. I had also heard claims by some Americans of throwing prisoners from helicopters and heard from a diplomat working within the British Embassy of how an unfortunate Viet Cong prisoner had his legs tied to two jeeps, which drove slowly in opposite directions and split him down the middle.

For me this was Satanic but I kept my composure and encouraged the Englishman to tell his story. I put him in touch with Brian McConnell and my friend James Cameron did the research and presentation and the story made the front page of the Sun newspaper. This was the first time that I heard details of what was called the Phoenix Operation and the role within it of the Provincial Reconnaissance Units. These covert actions were designed to terrorise local residents, making them too frightened to support the Viet Cong. In fact those Vietnamese whose relatives became victims were so revolted that they joined the opposition to the American backed regime. It came as a shock to me that the Pentagon should sanction terrorism and the breaking of the Geneva Convention. I believe the cruelty towards the Vietnamese people gradually eroded the support of Americans at home and in Vietnam, turning around those who had begun as enthusiastic supporters of the war against Communism. Numerous officers who had served in Vietnam and those like Oliver Stone changed their minds and started to support the peace movement. They were confronted by a huge propaganda machine, which insisted that the fight was between a cruel Stalinist force and enlightened freedom and democracy.

After this grim conversation, the idea of spending a day by the seaside escorting a group of children was welcome. The invitation to this excursion came from Dr Adrian Pointer, who was planning to drive the children in a Red Cross truck to Vung Tao. Understandably he wanted to maximum the time spent by the sea and was keen to start the journey early in the morning. I persuaded him to wait for an hour later than he wished, and even then I deliberately held the party up. From experience of travelling out of town I felt it was never wise to be first on the road. Such caution was justified; as we reached the huge military base of Long Binh we passed the body of a Viet Cong who appeared to have tried to enter the base. A little further along the whole convoy of vehicles was stopped by American troops. To the left of us we could feel the heat of a rubber plantation that was being burnt by napalm and was engulfed in thirty-foot flames. A little further along the road we passed four more bodies, which we assumed to be Viet Cong. They had been laid alongside one another and were being guarded by a South Vietnamese soldier who objected to my attempt to take a photograph. We were able to move about a mile further before being stopped again. A bus carrying Vietnamese passengers had been blown up as it crossed a small river. There had been several fatalities and the traffic had been diverted alongside the river bridge to a smaller bridge, where the first vehicle over was blown up. Waiting for clearance we alighted from our truck to take a closer look at the carnage. Two Vietnamese men had been killed and I can still recall the sight of blood and the grey of brains pouring from their wounds.

The children in our party were eager to inspect the site and to my bewilderment appeared excited, even exhilarated by what they saw. While we adults recoiled and walked quickly back to our truck, the children made it clear they thought this to be the reaction of wimps. I was very glad that I had insisted that we should never be the first on the open road in rural areas.

The rest of our journey was uneventful and we were soon to arrive at the seaside resort of Vung Tao. This was to become a favourite place for me, to which I would make several trips during my time in Vietnam. Being a peninsular it was one of the safest places in South Vietnam and a favourite destination for servicemen with a few days off in country. I was to learn that it was also popular with American deserters, who could survive for several months if they had the support of a Vietnamese girl friend. Days spent by the shore bathing in the warm sea was a far more attractive proposition than going back to their jungle base to face the constant threat of incoming shells and booby traps. Golden sands and a warm, inviting, almost transparent blue sea was a great way of relaxing, and after splashing about with the children I lay down under the shade of some palm trees. Perhaps the constant adrenaline rush of being in a war situation deepened the sense of batteries being recharged, until roused from slumber to partake of the snacks we brought with us, along with a glass of cold beer.

Glancing further along the beach one could see the wreck of a Japanese ship left high and dry after a military engagement during the Second World War. I never learned the details of the battle but it reminded me of a book by Tom Driberg, in which the M.P. described the surrender of the Japanese in 1945. Receiving the order to lay down their arms the Japanese handed their weapons and the government offices to their opponents the Viet Minh. The Vichy French had collaborated with the Japanese, and complained bitterly, insisting that power should be handed back to the French. A small contingent of British troops was sent to South Vietnam to handle the surrender together with a number of Chinese Nationalists who had a similar task in North Vietnam. Though the Americans at that time wanted ex colonial countries to become independent as happened with the Philippines, Burma and Indonesia, Britain still had an empire and perhaps a guilt trip after destroying the French navy. The British rearmed the Japanese who were ordered to kick the Viet Minh out of the government offices and helped the French to return to Indochina. This would eventually lead to the war between the Vietnamese and the French.

The trip to Vung Tao motivated me to go and see the Australian military bases, one of which was nearby and another a little further inland. I felt it would be interesting to learn the perspective of the officers and men serving in Vietnam for I knew that their presence here was hotly contested back in Australia. I also was aware that enormous pressure had been exerted on Wilson when he first became prime minister in 1964 to send at least a battalion of British troops to Vietnam. This pressure came from the Americans and a number of British military leaders, but was resisted by some members of the British Labour Party. Ann Kerr, a member of the Tribune Group told me that twenty two MPs sent a round robin letter directly to Wilson stating that if he did concede to the request by President Johnson to send a token force to Vietnam they would bring down the government at the first opportunity. Labour only had a paper-thin majority at this time. My first impressions on entering the Australian base was that there was far more emphasis on sport than in comparable American bases. Despite the heat men were energetically playing basketball, cricket and Australian football. Also noticeable here was the high wall of sandbags shielding the sleeping quarters, minimising the dangers from incoming Viet Cong rockets.

The Australian servicemen were cheerful, rough and ready, and after some initial pommy bashing I was invited to join them for their evening meal. The after dinner entertainment was a series of boxing bouts between an inexhaustible number of keen and sometimes inebriated volunteers. Unlike many of the Americans they seemed to seek solace in sporting endeavour rather than sex. Indifferent to their situation, they gave the impression of neither knowing nor caring whether the war was right or wrong. Casualties were much lower than with the American forces, which may have reflected the fact that their bases were not so close to the fiercest fighting near the Ho Chi Minh trail or the D.M.Z. Nevertheless when patrols penetrated jungle areas there could be losses and injuries and the same feeling of futility in a war with no end in sight. Responsible for their zone, despite the dangers however, they seemed reasonably content in that they could escape easily for a few days rest to nearby Vung Tao and participate in an endless number of beach parties and BBQs with large juicy steaks.

After returning to Saigon I was required to visit the Mekong Delta again. I drove to my usual small hotel by the canal and early the next day went to Dong Tam and caught a flight to a small base just outside Can Tho, the centre city of the Delta. Without penetrating too deeply into the dangerous jungles, one could still appreciate the colourful and exotic birds and butterflies and a curious cacophony of natural sounds. Hitching a ride into Can Tho I was received warmly by some U.S. soldiers. They also warned me that the situation in the vicinity was turning nasty and strongly suggested that I stay with them. I didn't need much persuading; I had heard frequent bangs and blasts in the surrounding area, along with news of some Viet Cong attacks that had killed several Americans. An abundance of alcohol, good food and a comfortable bunk to sleep on convinced me that I had made the right decision. Following a series of night attacks on the base perimeter I stayed several days longer than planned in Can Tho. I felt relatively safe and it was good to chat with the men about their experiences. When the attacks subsided I made my way to the airbase to travel to Dong Tam and managed to get a seat on an Air America plane with five other passengers. One was a very nervous Italian, who held up the flight by predicting that we would crash into the neighbouring trees as we took off. These planes were used to flying low over the jungle however, dropping supplies to hill tribesmen in Laos. It was an open secret that Air America was fully owned by the C.I.A. When we arrived at Dong Tam my little car was soon to take me back to the hotel in My Tho. Here I was taken aback when the hotel owner told me it was thought that I had gone missing and perhaps met with disaster. Another Englishman had been killed, and as my car had been seen parked in Dong Tam and I had not booked out of the hotel there had been a hue and cry. I immediately informed the British Embassy to pass on the news that I was safe and well. Apparently some newspapers had even reported that I had disappeared in the Vietnamese jungle and was feared dead, while the local M.P. in Britain had contacted my family to ask if he could do anything to help, which must have been distressing for them until I could get word through to them.

Driving back to Saigon late in the afternoon via Cong Ly I called in on Dr John Bass, who lived down a small cul de sac. I was hoping for a cool drink and a catch up on news before returning to my lodgings close to the airport. John informed me that New Zealand's prime-minister Sir Keith Holyoake was about to hold a press conference just a hundred yards along the road. Sir Keith having just flown in from talks with Nixon in Washington I hoped that he might have something interesting to say about the latest peace talks with the Communists. Downing my drink I made my way to the conference and was in good time to see the special guest resplendent in black tie approaching the rostrum, where he delivered a diplomatic presentation to around twenty five to thirty reporters. When there was an opportunity to ask a question I enquired if the Americans would be prepared to allow internationally organised elections within South Vietnam in which the Viet Cong could participate. Sir Keith paused before answering in diplomatic language. However he did not make the usual excuse that Thieu was the elected President and that therefore there was no reason to hold another election.

After a few more questions Sir Keith announced that he had to leave as he was expected at the palace for dinner with the President. Then as he left the rostrum, to my surprise he walked straight towards me. 'You know I couldn't answer your question publicly,' he said. 'If you talk to the Communists and they indicate that they would be interested in pursuing such strategies do let me know. Both sides need to find a way out of this nightmare without losing too much face.' He was genuine in his comments and told me that he had instructed his relatively small contingent of New Zealand forces to focus on supporting humanitarian resources such as hospitals and centres for refugees and the handicapped. He told me that he had been overwhelmed by what he had seen of the dreadful social disaster in South Vietnam and that from this point on his troops would concentrate solely on protecting people. Placing an arm on my shoulder he then led me towards his limousine. We shook hands before he climbed into his car. I looked round to see that he had taken me past a Presidential Guard of Honour; two lines of men in ceremonial white uniform all saluting. All I could do was walk back up the line acting as if I were a regular participant in this kind of grand protocol, despite being dressed in short sleeves and, having driven all the way from the Delta, smelling like a skunk.

A few days later I called in on some New Zealand friends I had made recently, among them Robin, an attractive fair haired girl who lived in a villa with her brother and worked for I.B.M. Visiting them that day was the wife of the military commander of the New Zealand forces serving in Vietnam. As we chatted over coffee she mentioned that the next day she planned to show Sir Keith Holyoake's wife around the Saigon market. I replied by urging caution and not telling too many people of their plans. Although the Viet Cong leadership would not be interested in harming them in a guerrilla war, someone on the end of the trail might have a grudge to settle and seek a soft assassination target.

Shortly afterwards I went to see Dr Adrian Pointer who had just returned from a few days in Hong Kong. Adrian had brought back a number of photographic magazines that were propaganda for the Viet Cong. With him were four young Vietnamese men, whom I was amazed to see were reading the magazines with great enthusiasm, clearly indicating their support for the Viet Cong. There was a strange dichotomy in Vietnam in that foreigners like Adrian or a G.I. on rest and recreation in Hong Kong could buy and read such material but any Vietnamese caught with it would be in serious trouble. Outsiders like me were also in a privileged position in that we could talk with different political leaders and factions who could not or would not talk amongst themselves. After residing in Vietnam for about a year I sensed that people had developed a growing trust in my views and integrity. My friendship with Adrian and with other doctors would also lead to a series of introductions to senior political activists, including former Presidents and Chiefs of State.

Chapter 5

Vietnamese Democracy

The International School in Saigon was a prestigious institution to which both President Thieu and Vice President Ky sent their children, alongside those from the diplomatic community who were foolish enough to bring their offspring to Vietnam. I was to learn in the next few months that it was also a hotbed of political intrigue in which teachers from a wide political spectrum earned their living. The school provided a basic education in Vietnamese and English together with a comprehensive introduction to several languages and subjects including Japanese. Limited space precluded out door sporting activity but fencing, judo and keep fit was keenly encouraged and students enjoyed music lessons. A pleasant evening in the home of the music teacher who played guitar and sang in both Vietnamese and English was my first introduction to the International School. Xuan was a jovial man who lived with his wife, four teenage daughters and blind father-in-law. It was a happy household despite obvious poverty. At one point I needed the loo and was directed to the back of the living room where a three-foot wall was the only privacy. Needs must and I could see the teenage girls giggling as they peeped at my activity.

Music was once described as the language of the soul and during my time both in Vietnam and when I first returned to Europe I believed that it reflected a longing for an end to suffering and the insanity of war. Whether it was the sorrow-ful sound of Vietnamese girls or globally the singing of Joan Baez, Julie Felix or Nancy Griffith or later the songs from Hair, particularly Aquarius, there was a message that went beyond mere words for even the most hardened militarist.

Within a couple of days Xuan was to introduce me to the school principal, an impeccably dressed dapper man in his thirties who spoke excellent English. Tran Toung Nhon and his wife Sophie were the inspiration and the administrative centre for the enterprise. I was intrigued to learn more about this remarkable couple and I knew that it would take more than one conversation to glean all there was to know about their activity. They were from the small Protestant Church and their division of labour was that Sophie dedicated herself to charity work whilst her husband had so far survived involvement in politics. Nhon told me that he had worked with Thieu when Ky was the powerful dictator. He had helped to create the Freedom Democratic Party and held the position of Secretary General, and believed that the creation of a grassroots Democratic Party could lead to eventually inviting the Viet Cong to enter elections and end the bloodshed. The autocratic tendencies of Thieu were a disappointment to him and there had been no significant overtures for peace as he had hoped. When the Presidential Election was held in 1967 he broke with Thieu and became a nominee for the Presidency. Like some others who wished to challenge for the Presidency his nomination had been rejected on a technicality. After this as a Pasteur of the Protestant Church he had managed to make some broadcasts as the voice of Christianity in which he had emphasised that Christ was the Prince of peace.

Until this time I was unaware of a Protestant Church and had assumed that South Vietnam was 20% Catholic and 80% Buddhist: but that was an over simplification. There were smaller but significant groups such as Hao Hoa which I was told was linked to the Buddhists and the Cao Dai which was similar to the Bah Hai in that it was influenced by several other religions. With their own Pope and guided by spiritual séances they practised a kind of humanist theology but their influence, particularly close to the Tay Ninh border with Cambodia, was very powerful and at one time they even had their own army. The gathering of large groups of people particularly of the left or centre was dangerous and even top lawyers who had defended dissidents would sleep in a different place each night. That included those who defended Dzu who was allowed to stand against Thieu in the presidential election but was imprisoned just afterwards. The secret police had eyes on anyone who was in any way involved with politics. The way round this obstacle was to be involved within religious gatherings and numerous dinner parties. To a visiting journalist who usually stayed in South Vietnam less than a month there would be a veneer of democratic respectability. There was a presidential election together with elections for a Senate and a House of Representatives but the real power was always with the military and the police.

Nhon would introduce me to several members of his staff: one was the Japanese teacher who was related to Big Minh who was a popular general who had just been allowed back inside the country after a long exile in Thailand. Big Minh was the Chief of Staff within the military under the Catholic dictator Diem who ruled from the departure of the French in 1954 to

November 1963. Big Minh was a Buddhist at the time when they were being persecuted and Diem had asked him to convert to Catholicism. After this he led the coup against Diem and it was hoped that he would try to accommodate the Communists within a form of neutrality. It was rumoured that just before Nixon became President a peace deal might be struck leaving Big Minh as the titular head of South Vietnam. He had now been allowed back inside Vietnam but forbidden to play an active role in politics.

As light relief I was also introduced to a man called Duc, who as well as teaching had his own film production company. Duc was a mercurial character and I was impressed by the quality of his films portraying the wonderful variety of colour and texture of the Vietnamese flower markets and girls in bright coloured ao-dais. Understandably Duc was invariably surrounded by beautiful young actresses all hoping to be the next starlet. A well-publicised story was that President Thieu had asked Duc to produce a film to project the image of South Vietnam. Duc had replied 'What do you want, bodies, bodies and more bodies?' Needless to say Thieu never asked again. On one occasion a small party of friends including Duc and a few of his young actresses and teachers were eating al fresco in a popular Vietnamese restaurant by the river. The highly eccentric Duc could be dangerously indiscreet for a Vietnamese and quite loud with his opinions but knowledgeable about what was happening and the role that each was playing. Between courses he would sometimes break into song much to the amusement of those nearby. Late into the evening a Vietnamese man of stocky build aged about sixty staggered towards the diners. I had seen him before make an appearance at similar restaurants around Saigon. He was known as the Nutty General. He would usually break into a loud diatribe in Vietnamese. I was told that he was a former general who had been destabilised mentally after one of the coups. He had the reputation of being the only man who could swear at the President without being arrested. His particular target was restaurants frequented by GIs with their Vietnamese girl friends, his message along the lines of 'Americans go home!' As our group had few Americans the General spent less time ranting and cursing and once he saw Duc he appeared to recognise him and immediately shut up and left the throng. Duc leaned close to me and said quietly 'The General is no more mad than you and I but by pretending to be either inebriated or mad he is uninhibited in what he says; he enjoys his little rebellion!'

My abiding positive memories of Vietnam would always be the love of communal dining al fresco in the cool of the evening or first thing in the morning when everything was fresh and clean before the fumes would pollute the atmosphere. I was lucky to have acquired a room not far from the airport that had both a shower and a French style water closet. Each morning before sunrise I would look out and see elderly Vietnamese living in the cul de sac eating a humble breakfast seated at little chairs and tables, the food I was told, provided by an elderly widow in exchange for a small payment. In a land without pensions or social benefits this was the Vietnamese way to look after those who had no other means of support. This sense or shared resources became relevant as my socks were gradually lost in the communal wash. When I complained that I was now down to my last three pairs I was told not to worry and as if by magic another three pairs appeared. I later was told that it had been a mistake to reduce my socks to three pairs as everyone should have six pairs. In a hot climate that was just about adequate.

An upcoming assignment was some research on the American soldiers who were absent without leave in Vung Tao. Mixed in with the high number of Australians living there it was difficult for American MPs to question suspects as there had been several incidents of Australians reacting abrasively when approached by military police with no authority to do so. I always enjoyed my time spent in Vung Tao so set off in my mini Austin in a carefree mood. About three quarters of the way as I approached a large bridge over a river a number of men in black pyjamas appeared from nowhere and quickly surrounded my car. Believing them to be members of a rural military unit I exchanged some pleasant banter. They wanted to know who I was, where I was going and what I was doing. After looking at my press credentials their leader grinned broadly and waved me on my journey. At the International Hotel in Vung Tao I was greeted by the manager, who asked me if I had come across the Viet Cong as they had captured the bridge and held it for a while. I was then told that American astronauts had landed on the moon. Only then did I notice groups of girls and customers listening intensely to radios in the hotel lobby. I reflected later that I must be one of the few people who learned about the moon landings as a secondary item of conversation.

By a kind of coincidence within a couple of months Nhon introduced me to an American girl who was teaching English in his school; it was Corinne Collins the niece of Michael Collins the third man to go to the moon. Corinne was a sweet natured, fair-haired blue-eyed girl and had only just flown to

Vietnam. She told me of her experience of downward thrust when her aircraft flew over the thermals. Later I experienced something similar when it felt as though we were about to descend suddenly from the sky. Corinne had brought with her a box containing six round moon rocks which she was to present to President Thieu as a goodwill gift from President Nixon. She handed me a couple of them for a feel before carefully putting them back in the box. In hindsight I realise that space flight led to great advances in satellite communication links but back then my thoughts were somewhat cynical as there was speculation about spreading military might and talk of future star wars. I believed then and now that humanity should concentrate on finding a way to stop killing and live in peace and harmony on Earth before putting weapons in space. Of course I kept these thoughts to myself as I had no intention of upsetting Corinne. After all I had huge respect for young ladies who ventured to Vietnam regardless of their motives: this included the doctors, nurses and charity workers and many others who risked their lives and I believe must have faced criticism from families and loved ones. This must have been my Freudian slip for I was to learn that the sight of a dying attractive girl could be more upsetting than that of a dying and injured child.

Nhon guided me to meetings with leading members of the Vietnamese community through several leading intermediaries. First was a Catholic named Ninh who as a young man served as an adviser to the Diem government. Nhin told me how many government advisers wanted them to accept the direction of the Geneva Conference and prepare for an election in 1956 to help bring together the two governments of Vietnam. Alas, the Americans who were now beginning to financially support South Vietnam were very much against this, believing that following the war with the French, Ho Chi Minh had become the national hero and would win any election in South Vietnam hands down. Foster Dulles and Vice President Nixon were the powerful advocates of ignoring the Geneva Conference chaired jointly by Britain and Russia and painstakingly put together by Winston Churchill. This was to be the last contribution for peace made by Winston Churchill and helped to let the French depart from Indo China without losing too much face.

Nhin arranged a meeting with Monsignor Bhin the leading Catholic prelate in Vietnam. It was important to know what he was thinking, as the backbone of the American backed government was comprised almost entirely of Catholics. Catholicism was introduced to Vietnam by a man who combined religion with a soldiering career and was later defrocked by the Pope. In recent years the Catholics became the most powerful influence against the Communists and one priest even led his village battalion. As we strode towards the Monsignor, Nhin threw himself on the ground and kissed his hand. I simply held out my hand to shake his in the customary way. The reception that I was given was far more positive than I had expected. Ninh told me that his Holiness the Pope had instructed him to work for peace and reconciliation and he expressed an interest in talking with leading Buddhists and other religious leaders if only to share the burden of charity and relief work. I promised to pass this on and in the years ahead Mrs Nhon was to help in bringing the religions together. I remember seeing on television screens in the early sixties the dreadful sight of Buddhist monks pouring petrol over themselves and setting themselves alight in a protest against the war and the way that Catholics persecuted them.

I looked forward to meeting the former Chief of State of South Vietnam, Pham Khac Suu, who had been the civilian head during the time of the Kennedy assassination. I was ushered into an upstairs room where a dozen or so men were assembled. We were soon joined by an elderly man in traditional Vietnamese dress, which to my western eyes resembled an elaborate dressing gown. Pham Khac Suu was introduced to me with great solemnity and I knew that he was a greatly respected elder statesman. Diplomatically I questioned the historical role that he and his government had played. 'Surely this was when President Johnson began an escalation of the war and introduced the first American ground troops?'

Suu shook his head nonchalantly before replying. 'That was never the policy of me and my government. We wanted to begin talks with the Communists and after the removal of Diem this had become a reality. President Kennedy had acquired a neutrality deal in Laos during the previous year and we all hoped for something similar for South Vietnam. Alas within four days of President Kennedy's assassination the policy was changed and the Americans began an escalation of the war with complete contempt for the views of the South Vietnamese government.'

I then asked 'So what made you so confident that the Communists would agree to a form of neutrality if you were able to pursue your policy?'

'Communists are human too,' replied Suu, 'and I have a good old friend in a senior position in the North. Thaung who has just succeeded Ho Chi Minh as the President of North Vietnam once shared a prison cell with me during the French rule.'

'What happened next?'

'My government was out of favour with the Americans and so another coup was arranged to kick us out and replace us with a more subservient one for their military policy.'

Our conversation moved on to some of the nuances but what I had heard was quite incredible. The whole world was being told by the Americans that they had been invited by the South Vietnam Government to defend freedom and democracy and I had heard directly from the Chief of State at the time that this was a complete lie. It was a lie duplicated by the International Community including Britain. The knowledge that the moral impetus of the bloodiest war fought since the Second World War was based upon such a lie came as a great shock. The enormity of it was something that I needed to think about. I had no confidence that any media outlet outside the Communist world would repeat such information but I always believed that truth must come out. My conscience was troubled as I departed from Pham Khac Suu and his associates but I thanked them for entrusting me with such information and promised that I would pass it on in some beneficial way.

Immediately after this meeting it was arranged for me to meet with Nguyen Than Vinh the former Chairman of the Constituent Assembly, the equivalent to the Returning Officer for the Presidential Election in 1967. Vinh was a chemist by profession and I went to see him above his shop.

We were joined by a small group of his supporters as Vinh spoke of the events leading up to the Presidential Election in 1967. 'The Americans scraped the bottom of the barrel when

Air Marshall Ky became the dictator of South Vietnam. The Americans wanted some sort of respectability to legitimise the war both for within the United States and its close allies. Once Ky had blurted out to a journalist that South Vietnam needed thirty Hitler's and they only had him, this became too much for the Americans to bear as it was combined with public executions in the main street. They had to persuade Ky to accept Thieu and enable him to stand for a Presidential Election. Thieu would be the candidate for the Presidency of South Vietnam and Ky would stand as the candidate for the Vice Presidency. All this was beyond my brief but I hoped that a popular candidate would campaign for a rational solution leading to negotiations that would lead to universal approval. Alas military administrators found technicalities to prevent more than half of the population from standing. Popular figures that might have rallied the people such as Big Minh and his running mate Tran Ngoc Lieng were ruled out of standing and at one point there may have been no opposition candidate at all. This would not help the Americans who wished to proclaim their stand for democracy, so they approached Troung Dinh Dzu a lesser-known lawyer to stand on a peace ticket. The intention of the White House was to measure just how much opposition there was to the war but at the same time ensure that the military leadership stays in place. Even so it was necessary for the police to stack ballot boxes so that Thieu could be assured of defeating Troung Dinh Dzu.'

'What was your position?' I asked. 'I thought you were supposed to be the equivalent of the Returning Officer.'

'I was supposed to legitimise the Presidential Election but I did construct a dossier of malpractices throughout the country and it did state that the election was fraudulent and its result democratically wholly invalid. We even had evidence from Catholic nuns who witnessed some of the irregularities. Brazenly Ky told Dzu during the election that he would be flung into prison immediately after the election where he now remains. On the day I was going to present the findings of the Investigation Committee to the world I was arrested by Thieu's secret police and a revolver was placed to my head. I was told that if I ever spoke of the election again my brains would be blown out.'

I realised that by telling me what had happened Vinh had risked his life and possibly the lives of his associates. Yet by entrusting me with such information they had done so for a reason; they wanted me to find a way to pass it on but I did not want to cause the death of this man. I spoke of this dilemma to my journalist colleagues. Their view was that Vinh might be in greater danger if such events remained covert but once in the public domain if anything happened to him the point of suspicion would point to Thieu and his secret police. I was unsure of this and reminded of Dzu being placed in prison after giving an interview with a British reporter working for the Times.

During my first stay in Vietnam which lasted almost two years (1968 - 70), life was made bearable by a romance with a French Vietnamese girl. She had been educated in France, spoke very good English and resembled the Eurasian TV presenter Myelin Klass. I never mentioned politics to her except in a very general way as this might endanger her life. Though this is not an autobiography it reflects other aspects of my life, which was not all gloom and doom. Indeed hearing the reflections of a Vietnamese girl strengthened my understanding of her people and the dreadful plight that they were in. It was also a source of comfort and reassurance to return from trips to the tiny embrace of a lover.

Reporters from all over the world occasionally visited Vietnam but of course a large number came from the United States. The most famous ones tended to be based in more pleasant locations such as Singapore and would make their stays as brief as possible. The ones that I respected more than any others were the war photographers and film and television camera crews. They were incredibly brave, often seeking the latest battles and venturing towards the middle of conflicts. One such war photographer was Catherine Leroy; Brian McConnell told me to try to meet her as she had taken the most dramatic pictures that were published in Paris Match. I had no direct contact with her but at a little party held by Australian friends in a villa on the coast of Vung Tao she was pointed out to me. She was not at all what I expected; she stood staring out of the window to the coast below completely alone. I expected an ebullient cocksure girl with possibly an Amazonian physique. Instead she stood barely five feet with a slender figure, a tiny French girl who was rather shy and my lasting impression was one of great sadness. Perhaps that was not surprising, as she had spent so much time witnessing death and dying. Yet the impact of her and her colleagues was profound in demonstrating the sheer hell of war and bringing it into drawing rooms across the world in a way that thousands of words could never do.

Three war photographers that I greatly admired were I was told great friends and nicknamed by those who know them as the 'rat pack'. They were Larry Burrows, Shaun Flynn, the son of Errol who had turned his back on a movie career to become involved with Vietnam and Tim Page who came from my home county of Kent and was wounded on four separate occasions. Their nickname was earned because of their love of loud partying, enjoying drink, food and lots of girls. Shaun had his father's insatiable appetites in this respect and had a yen for Oriental women. I had planned a trip to Laos where Adrian was going to meet me after spending a week in Cambodia. Our intention was to visit the North Vietnam Embassy in Vientiane and I had promised to ask if Larry Burrows and I could enter Hanoi. Very few westerners were allowed into North Vietnam but Verdun Perl and James Cameron had been able to gain access. Before I first came to Vietnam Verdun Perl who was a parliamentary candidate for the Liberals had been pictured with Ho Chi Minh. At a time when Americans were trying to portray him as a monster a photograph of Ho Chi Minh kissing Verdun Perl on the cheek was relayed all over the world.

'I think that you're going to Laos at an interesting time. There's a growing and vocal peace movement back in the States.' Steve was enthusiastic as he drove me to the airport and hoped that I would be able to do an interview with the Prime Minister Savannah Phuma. Phuma was the neutralist in a very strange triple agreement that included a right wing leader sympathetic to the Americans and the leader of Pathet Lao, the Communist leader. The three leaders were all related; two were brothers and one a brother in law. Reaching my destination I thanked Steve for the lift and carried my case and hand luggage towards the Air Vietnam check in. I was one of the first to enter an almost empty aircraft. The airline had suffered two crashes in the last ten days. I tried to reassure myself that procedures might have become more thorough as a result.

Two attractive stewardesses in the airline uniform of pale blue ao-dais greeted me. I sat by the window and was able to stretch my legs and make myself comfortable. The engines began to roar and we climbed into a clear blue sky. Saigon and the mud flaps of the river were soon left behind, replaced by the darker hues of the green jungle. Air Vietnam was always known for its hospitality and passengers were offered an endless supply of food, drink, sweets and hand wipes.

I had just finished eating when the aircraft plummeted like a lift in a tall building. The 'Fasten your Seatbelt' signs flashed on and the stewardesses rushed towards the cockpit. The aircraft steadied itself and then down again it plunged leaving the majority of passengers green and some reaching for their sick bags. I assumed it was the usual thermals but it was an awful feeling dropping so dramatically. People around me were saying a little prayer to their respective Gods but one woman became hysterical. There was no consoling message from the cockpit reassuring them that all was well and no stewardesses in sight. Again the aircraft steadied itself before dropping down again. This was repeated five or six times until the journey became smoother. Everyone was relieved when the intercom came to life to tell us that we were about to land in Phnom Penh. The procedure for leaving the aircraft was quick and easy as the two girls reappeared to open the doors and secure the mobile steps. Passengers were particularly keen to touch terra firma as they passed the stewardesses who on this occasion failed to enquire if they had enjoyed the flight. Indeed they seemed to want to dispose of the grumbling contingent as fast as possible while just managing to smile unconvincingly.

I left the cabin just to get some fresh air, hoping that one day I would return to peaceful Cambodia then climbed back up the steps to continue my journey to Laos. The next leg was far more pleasant and I was soon alighting in Vientiane where customs, visas and health certificates were glanced at before I was waved nonchalantly on by a smiling official who shook my hand. Dr Adrian Pointer appeared from nowhere just as I had concluded the formalities. 'Welcome to sleepyville' he chirped 'what a difference to Saigon; it's as though everyone is working at half of the normal pace here and they are even more laid back in Cambodia.' Adrian had clearly enjoyed his stay in Cambodia and spoke enthusiastically about how Prince Sihanouk had managed to keep his country out of the war, steering a course of neutrality, which made him very popular with his people. 'The war does spill over the Vietnam border,' I replied, 'as the Communists use the jungle corridors to replenish supplies in South Vietnam. With the Ho Chi Minh Trail continually compounded by American bombing the Communists move gradually deeper into the mountainous jungle corridor, often several miles over the border. When Americans bomb and kill Cambodians it becomes an international incident so Cambodian neutrality is under threat even while there is only about a 5% support for the Communists inside the country.'

Catching the bus from the airport we got off at the Grand Hotel which stood just opposite the mighty River Mekong. About thirty American journalists were gathered at the hotel waiting for a wealthy American called Ross Perot. He had flown in with an aircraft full of goods and hoped to continue into

Hanoi and there pay the government to release a number of American POWs. The North Vietnam Embassy had already told him that he should look after his prisoners and they would look after theirs. As a result Perot and the journalists were about to visit a prison camp just eight miles out of Vientiane. 'You should join the silly buggers and look at this prison camp,' suggested Adrian. I agreed and as he took charge of the luggage we agreed to meet later.

Chapter 6

Laos; The Strangest War in the Twentieth Century

Vientiane unlike Saigon was not congested with traffic and our journey took us along almost empty roads once we reached the surrounding rural district. The bus soon arrived after the eight mile journey. The compound looked more like a cattle ranch than a prison camp. It had a high perimeter wall combined with a tall barbed wire barricade. Lookout towers with armed guards strengthened the security. Guards soon opened the tall doors so that we could enter the reinforced security fence. I wasn't sure what to expect but a line of prisoners waited our arrival each squatting in the familiar Vietnamese way. As we walked past them I attempted to say a few words in Vietnamese but I was surprised to see little in communication between the American journalists and the prisoners. I knew only one who was based in South Vietnam and I believe the others were only really interested in the domestic news that related to prisoners' families in the States.

Ross Perot was the first to walk down the row of prisoners followed by a flurry of activity as newsmen recorded the event for posterity. I had no chance to change from the white shorts I was wearing and unfortunately they were too small for me or rather I was too fat for them. I didn't think it mattered but in the preceding years when Perot was standing for the Presidency the recorded television shots always showed him and the newsmen walking through the prison camp. Of course I stood out like a sore thumb and only hoped that no one recognised me!

Most of the prisoners looked Vietnamese rather than Laotian but it was difficult to tell the difference as the races within Indo China mingled quite freely during the French rule. It was difficult to question the prisoners as they were hardly in a position to complain. They appeared to be well fed and I suspect they were much more fortunate than prisoners held in South Vietnam. I even saw a prison guard walking hand in hand with a prisoner. I believe this was possibly a showcase prison camp specially prepared for V.I.P. visitors and perhaps the only one of its kind inside Indo China.

At the outset I was astounded by the assumption that money could buy freedom for American P.O.W.s without consideration for other prisoners and detached from other political nuances. On later reflection I thought it was good that the media in America should be so concerned about the release of its prisoners. At this time Nixon and Kissinger were telling the world that they had won the war and all they had to do was pass over the responsibility to the South Vietnamese Government for finishing the war. Right wing military advisors like Sir Robert Thompson were advising Americans to prepare for a long haul war lasting many more years. The Achilles Heel to this idea was how Americans could ever secure the release of their prisoners without serious negotiations.

After our visit we walked back through the tall gates to alight the waiting bus which took us back to the centre of Vientiane. Ross Perot and his associates looked dejected after being refused access to North Vietnam but planned to stay a few days in Laos before returning to the United States. My reflections at this time were that it was interesting that the delegation should land in Laos before attempting to enter North Vietnam. Of course it was a little closer to Hanoi but if they had landed in South Vietnam and expressed an interest in the plight of all prisoners to this cruel war they could have claimed the high moral ground and at very least possibly secured far more empathy from the Communists.

Then the penny dropped and I realised that Nixon and Kissinger did not welcome this initiative. It brought to the fore one of the insurmountable obstacles. How could they secure the release of American prisoners in the hands of North Vietnam and the Viet Cong? The lies that were being told of military victory were intended for the international community but officers and men recently serving in Vietnam knew that this was a lie as the Communist forces were still embedded within the rural domain.

Adrian met me on my return and was pleased to inform me that he had secured an inexpensive place to stay on the outskirts of Vientiane. It was reasonably clean and provided us with a bed, shower and water closet. Our transient neighbours were hippies who were so stoned that 'Hi man' was the limit of their vocabulary. This was a stark reminder that they were living on the edge of the golden triangle where even a modest income could support a drug habit. A number of addicts mostly from America had settled in Vientiane on a diet of sex, drugs and rock and roll.

Laos was the centre of global espionage and political intrigue. Situated next to North Vietnam the neutrality agreement allowed all the major countries of the world to have an embassy here. Both North and South Vietnam had embassies here together with Russia and China. There was even an administrative centre for the Pathet Lao but it was out of bounds for journalists to visit. The Americans and their various military agencies were the most powerful foreign influence and I saw numerous Air America aircraft at the two airports that I journeyed through. There were also numerous 'pregnant eggs' that were used for reconnaissance flying over North Vietnam.

Adrian and I walked towards the main road where we planned to catch a taxi to the British Embassy. Passing by a small Laotian restaurant we stopped and ordered a poached egg on sweet toast washed down with a glass of iced green tea. Adrian was a great linguist but he found it difficult to order the breakfast but with noises like a chicken laying an egg we managed to have a simple meal. As we sat down in undercover of the morning sun a hill tribesman passed us by. He was dressed like a cave man in a loin cloth but he gave out a squeal of pain. Adrian explained to me that the burn marks on his back were being affected by the sun and had probably been caused by a splash of napalm.

With the aid of a map that Adrian pointed out to the taxi driver exactly where we wished to go and we soon arrived in a sedate part of Vientiane where most of the embassies were located. As we entered the building we were met by the attaché and a woman in her sixties. Both were interested once they knew that we had both worked inside Vietnam for the last year. The woman who was called Peggy Stanley dominated much of the conversation but not in a negative way; indeed she was a font of knowledge about the situation. She was an anaesthetist and she immediately requested that we should join her for a soirée in her flat that evening. 'Just a few of my W.H.O. friends' she wrote down her address and handed it to Adrian. 'You must do an interview with the Prime Minister while you are here; he's a friend of mine so I'll give you the contact through his P.A. La Norrine and he will arrange it for you but you must write down the questions on paper as there are still a few hot head Americans who would like to knock him off his perch.' At this point the attaché gave a knowing smile as he could never say anything like that.

After a fairly relaxing day we looked forward to our evening party. We were to discover what a fascinating woman Peggy Stanley was. She had been a prisoner under the Gestapo, then in the Suez War she was working in Egypt but Nasser allowed her to continue working freely when all other British citizens were arrested. Now here in Laos she often acted as a translator for Souvanna Phoumma as he didn't always trust the embassy one.

As ample food and drink was consumed we met an interesting group of people who were all eager to exchange so many personal stories. I was amused when a Japanese doctor warmly shook me by the hand and said 'We always think of lavatories when we think of the English.' I was taken aback by this but he continued 'Sir Thomas Crapper's invention has saved so many lives throughout the developing world and the battle for sanitation and fresh water is as relevant as ever.'

Amongst the guests was an exceptionally good looking young American couple who were still on their honeymoon and were in transit to working with the Tom Dooley Foundation which was based upstream on the Mekong close to the Chinese border. Dooley had been a young doctor who had created a health centre but sadly died very young but leaving a legacy of good humanitarian work behind. The project was situated in an extremely dangerous position particularly for Americans so I had huge respect for this couple who only had their faith to support them. For me it was a reminder that despite my growing critique of American policy there were so many men and women of goodwill who were guided by altruism. I wished them both well and said that possibly at some future date I would love to visit them.

The bloody conflict in Laos was as strange as the politics. Sometimes there were ferocious and cruel battles driven by the war between Americans and the Vietnamese, but I was also to hear of planned battles between the Pathet Lao and Laotian Government forces in which thousands of rounds of ammunition were fired into the air by both sides to avoid casualties and to please their American masters. Hearing the views of a multinational gathering of doctors provided a balanced view of the insane situation which reinforced the growing belief of Adrian and me that the peace movement was absolutely right. All too soon the time came for our departure after Peggy gave me the details of the Prime Minister's P.A. contact address and an agreement to join her in a few days time for a meal and a trip to the cinema.

The next day I made my way to the government offices with an agreement to meet Adrian at the White Rose Cabin later in the day. As I entered the offices I was greeted by a number of friendly officials who were eager to present their business cards. Their different roles nearly always included the word 'expert' on it; I couldn't help but think this was a humorous way of

114

imitating the Americans and I recall one press release which added to this view. 'The situation is disastrous but not serious.'

I was soon ushered into the office of the Prime Minister's P.A., La Norrine. The name of Peggy Stanley was clearly a popular one who was identified as a sympathetic friend and a few words of banter in her praise started our conversation. My request for an interview with the Prime Minister was immediately approved and when he requested sight of the questions I wanted to ask he was impressed that I had been instructed by Peggy.

'We have to be so very careful of not upsetting the Americans as we don't want to change our position which may be unsatisfactory but much better than being plunged even deeper into the mire. Some American military men are eager to deal with Sihanouk in Cambodia.'

I was surprised by his frank comments but he soon recanted by saying 'Please don't quote me on that; I wouldn't have said that if you hadn't been a friend of Peggy.' I nodded my agreement and added that I believed that the rational solution to the conflict throughout Indo China was a form of neutrality between the super powers. I had a lengthy conversation with the Prime Minister's P.A. and believed that this was a useful way of determining my views which would be relayed to the Prime Minister. I was pleasantly surprised when after he left his office he returned with the news that my interview would take place later in the afternoon.

My first question to the Prime Minister was 'How do you get on with your brother and brother in law?'

'Everyone asks that: when we meet we embrace as brothers but we haven't met recently.'

I thought it was not surprising to ask that as the siblings were leading two different sides in a bloody war but I then tried to ask him about neutrality in general by quoting Thieu who had stated that neutrality was a cowardly position for fellow travellers. He was too experienced to slip up on that question. His reply was 'I can't comment on other sovereign countries but here in Laos neutralists were courageous and retained a strong moral ethos.'

My next question was 'How do you think the war will end?'

He sighed before replying 'We people are just the pawns in a cruel game and the war will end one day when the big global powers decide that it should.'

'When will that be? I responded.

'The sooner the better but when the super powers decide to end the war we Laotians will immediately end the local killing.'

I tried in several ways to get him to say something positive about a form of neutrality playing a positive element in peace negotiations but he continued to play with a straight bat knowing that Nixon had ruled out any kind of neutrality. 'What did you think of President Kennedy?'

'He was responsible for creating the neutrality deal here in Laos so we are grateful for what he did and we are saddened by the assassination of him and his brother Bobby.'

'Do you think he would have secured peace in Vietnam if he had lived?'

'That is speculation; some people think so but I can't possibly comment?'

'Why can't you comment? Is it because you might upset Nixon and Kissinger if you do?'

'As you know I only comment on matters relating directly to

Laos and never on matters relating to other sovereign countries.'

'Do you think that the growing international peace demonstrations will eventually help to bring about meaningful peace negotiations?'

'Americans are human and their casualties keep mounting so I am sure that all of humanity yearns for an end to this cruel war. I think that I've answered all your questions fully so perhaps we should end here.'

'Just one more question I would like to ask; it is your views on the domino theory. That is the idea of many militarists on the far right that any compromise on Vietnam might lead to every country from Australia to India eventually falling to the Communists.'

'That is global politics and I am not able to comment.'

I thanked Souvanna Phouma for his interview and we ended with friendly banter about our mutual friend Peggy Stanley.'

As I left the government offices it was dusk and near to the time that I had agreed to meet Adrian so I made my way towards the White Rose Cabin. When I arrived entering a door the light inside was barely visible but music was playing and I could see that a few young girls were dancing. There were some figures of middle aged western women and I just picked up the sight of Adrian on the other side of the room. A cold pint of beer was placed in my hand and I was ordered to sit down by the girl who had handed me the drink. As I did so another young girl jumped on my lap and placed her breasts in my face. I was anxious not to spill my beer as there was not a table nearby to rest it on. Eventually I managed to take a few gulps and rest my drink on the floor. I could hear Adrian laughing as the two girls were now trying to pull me up some stairs. I resisted and asked Adrian what he was trying to do to me and exactly what this establishment was. Eventually the two girls released their grip upon me and turned their attention to two Americans who had just entered the premises.

Soon Adrian joined me on my side of the room keen to glean any information that my interview might have acquired. Vientiane came to life at night when numerous clubs opened offering food and music. The large number of mostly American civilians associated with the military provided the customers but compared to Saigon it was fairly peaceful.

The next few days were restful and spiritually uplifting. I don't recall hearing one gunshot and though the war was not far away I heard no rustle of bombs in the distance. Drug taking was rampant and clearly visible and I'm told inexpensive for those who wished to partake. One of my favourite places was the cafeteria on the river side where drinks and snacks were served al fresco. I had difficulty quenching my thirst with water alone but the iced lime water that they served did the trick. As we sat in the early evening we could hear communal singing from across the Mekong in Thailand. It was a reminder that village communities could congregate around a fire to eat and sing and enjoy each other's company.

Sometimes there were strange reminders of how poor people could still manage to build six feet rockets, so as to compete with neighbours and fire into the air particularly just before the monsoon. The custom was that this would help to start the rain which was really needed to cool the sticky atmosphere. I had forgotten that explosives were discovered in the east though it was westerners who developed their military use.

Adrian and I visited the North Vietnamese Embassy and

though the diplomats were polite and friendly we were not able to obtain a visa. I later discovered that the very few who did obtain entry only did so after several times of trying. Adrian was disappointed as he was about to return to Kent. but I decided I might try again in a few months time.

As promised we were about to meet up with Peggy Stanley to enjoy a meal at one of the American complexes and then flock into the cinema to watch a Beatles film. One lasting impression was that as the film finished the repeated chorus of 'All You Need Is Love' was enthusiastically sung by the audience of mostly tough gun toting mercenaries. I think John Lennon would have been proud.

Those few days of peace and tranquillity soon passed and Adrian prepared to fly back to England. As an afterthought rather than a planned strategy I called in to the Cambodian Embassy to enquire if I could have a visa with the hope that I might be able to arrange an interview with Prince Sihanouk. The Embassy officials exchanged wistful glances before telling me that there was an embargo on those entering Cambodia, especially reporters with experience inside South Vietnam. They could present my credentials to Phnom Penh but even then it would take a few days for confirmation. I was surprised that there was such a negative response and put it down to bureaucracy following one of the many skirmishes along the border close to the Ho Chi Minh Trail. If I had realised that there was a serious threat to expanding the war in Cambodia I might have waited patiently but I didn't and was soon flying back to Saigon.

When we arrived at Than Son Nhut Airport I placed my case upon the customs table expecting to be waved through straight away. Instead one man turned to speak to his colleague who beckoned an armed police officer to approach me and I was told that I would have to escort him upstairs pending further clarification of my status to re-enter South Vietnam. The police officer was friendly and asked if I would like a chicken salad and a cold beer which I readily accepted.

A couple of hours went by before an official entered and whispered a few words in Vietnamese to the police officer who broke into a broad grin before telling me that I was free to go and that my case was downstairs waiting for me. It was a relief but as I approached the line of taxi drivers waiting for customers a well dressed man brushed them aside and took my case to put into his boot. He was articulate and pleasant asking where I wished to go. I instructed him to drive to the residence of Steve who lived in a large villa with two other American colleagues. The fare for travelling from the airport was far more modest than the usual amount. I had rightly assessed that my driver was a security officer who wished to know where I was staying.

Steve confirmed that I was correct and told me that there had been some trouble when they tried to publish details of the rigged Presidential Election. Duc knew of my arrival and when he arrived he told me not to contact Vinh as he had been put under house arrest for the moment. Now it all added up; they were looking for possible copies of the election malpractices looking at all my papers and scrutinising anything in my case.

Steve was reassuring 'You shouldn't be surprised that the authorities are taking an interest in you. You've spoken to two prime ministers, a former Chief of State of South Vietnam, the

Communists in Vientiane, and tried to publicise information about an election that undermines the authority of the government. My advice is carry on the good work but mix up your contacts with some right wing friends and even write about the bravery of Arvin or the build up of Vietnamese forces.'

It was good advice and I thought I would start with a colonel who was attached to the British Embassy who complained bitterly that the British should provide troops to support the war. I also thought about talking to those working for U.S.A.I.D. about the humanitarian work that they do.

I was interested in hearing what Nhon thought of the latest developments and called on him the next day. There had been some publicity about the house arrest of Vinh and I was very sad to hear that the veteran statesman Pham Khac Suu had been arrested and questioned and though he was quickly released he had died at home just afterwards. Within Vietnamese academic circles the prestige of Vinh had risen and I was pleased to receive a message delivered from one of his family that he did not blame me for the events and despite his arrest he slept sounder in his sleep with the wider world fully aware of why he had been arrested.

Nhon broadly agreed with the advice that I had been given. 'Your position has been strengthened and everyone wants to speak to you across the various neutralists and peace campaigners. As an Englishman you are in a strong position to talk to everyone other than Communists inside South Vietnam whereas we might be in great danger though I think some of your meetings should be clandestine. I would like you to ask one simple question of all those that you meet. Is there a specific idea that you would like to see included in an important peace document? I will coordinate their replies to be able to present a coherent proposal which can eventually be presented to all and sundry including western statesmen.'

I agreed to his proposals and became less concerned about my own safety when I was invited to a dinner party with some members of Thieu's peace delegation home from working in Paris. Before that I was invited to have supper with the wife of the imprisoned Dzu, the Presidential candidate, who stood on a peace ticket. I was greeted by his wife and daughter who was an attractive girl around twenty years old. She was wearing a little pair of white shorts which was unusual in Saigon but she explained that it had been warm and she had been working in the garden. I was not complaining.

Mother and daughter shared the chores of serving the meal and explained some of the details that had led to Dzu's imprisonment. It was the daughter who did most of the talking 'It was the Americans who persuaded him to stand as almost everyone had been eliminated and they would look ridiculous if no one stood against Thieu and Ky. During the election campaign Ky boasted that he would have him caged once the campaign was over.'

'I believe it was an article in the Times by a British reporter that led directly to his arrest and conviction.' They both confirmed that this was the case so I continued 'Have any of the Americans who persuaded him to stand been in touch and tried to use their influence to release him?'

Both wife and daughter shook their head and Mrs Dzu said that they had asked if he could be released so that the family could be exiled but they refused. 'What harm could we do for the world knows exactly what happened and we have nothing to add?'

I expressed sympathy and said 'For what it's worth Dzu has played an honourable role and you can all be proud of his stand. I believe this perpetual war will have to end one day and I hope that you will soon be reunited and free.'

Those were the only words of comfort that I could give so I thanked them warmly for their hospitality wishing to mention me the next time they visited their husband and father in prison and assuring them men and women all over the world were campaigning for an end of the war.

The next day I visited the International School where Nhon had persuaded me to spend one afternoon each week talking about English literature to the older students. He said that it was his practice to invite either American or English diplomats or writers to address the students which was valued by students and their parents. Nhon also said it would defuse any thought of political intrigue at the school. He laughed when he stated this and said that a friend of his, Nhie wished to introduce him to Tri Quang the Buddhist political leader who resided at the An Quang Pagoda. Every reporter visited him so there was no need to be covert but he would ensure that there would be a private conversation.

Nhie arrived on his scooter and invited me to join him on the passenger seat. I was to discover he was a devout Buddhist who cared passionately about the hopes for a peaceful future for his wife and four daughters. It was quite an experience riding through heavy traffic sometimes hurtling on both sides of us until we arrived outside the pagoda. I was happy to follow Nhie to this shrine where Tri Quang appeared wearing his familiar saffron robes giving a familiar Buddhist greeting bowing deeply as I approached him. Nhie began the introductions as another monk presented iced tea for us as we started to explore the reason for my visit.

The usual global view of Buddhists was that they were the power for peace and reconciliation that had led the rebellion against the unpopular Catholic regime of Diem and were associated with mass demonstrations of monks protesting against the war and the dreadful sight on a few occasions of monks pouring petrol over themselves before setting themselves alight.

My prepared question of exactly what he could contribute to a possible peace proposal must have been familiar to him over many years. However he patiently answered my question by saying that even if the super powers agreed an end of the war he had serious concerns of events immediately following a ceasefire. He reminded me of reprisals following the Indian partition. He feared the same could happen in Vietnam. He hoped that religious groups would work locally for arbitration.

He then drew three circles upon the ground; the larger one representing his hopes that an international conference should be held similar to the 1954 Geneva Conference. The super powers should underpin the future independence of the three countries inside Indo China. Inside the larger circle he believed that the next circle should represent the two Vietnams and concentrate on how they could develop a future federal structure working for the eventual unification of Vietnam. This was very close to the aspirations of the 1954 Conference. Tri Quang's third circle inside the other two he explained would need to deal with the massive demilitarising of the country, even village to village and would need a powerful role of the religious groups backed by a much strengthened International

Control Commission. This comprised of support by the three countries of India, Canada and Poland.

There was a great deal of logic behind what he said though at the moment there was little sign of Nixon and Kissinger agreeing to such a plan, yet he had prepared a pragmatic blueprint in preparation for his hoped for end of the bloody conflict. Our conversation continued with me asking probing questions of how a future election inside South Vietnam could overcome the numerous obstacles. After a long and exhaustive interview we exchanged pleasantries and parted with the usual goodwill gesture. Soon I would be speeding back to the Saigon centre where I would present the nuances of Tri Quang's views to both Nhon and to Nhie who had listened patiently to our conversation.

Once Nhie departed, Nhon was excited to tell me that he had been approached by a leading group of Vietnamese lawyers who wished to meet me as soon as possible. They wanted to speak to me together rather than in their usual daytime offices. Nhon explained that to do so the meeting would take place in the evening after dark but would need to be covert and in the most discreet way. Nhon explained that such a meeting was extremely dangerous for them for though they could conduct individual business in their offices during the day; but at night they would sleep in different places to avoid the secret police and possible assassination. These are Vietnam's leading lawyers including Lieng who would have been the running mate of Big Minh as his Vice President. Nhon looked straight at me before declaring 'this is serious politics and could be dangerous even for you: are you up for it?'

Chapter 7

The Third Force for Peace

I hesitated before answering Nhon. 'I have heard some rumours about a possible coup. I'm not a military man so I have no wish to be involved with something like that; in any case I don't think that anything not agreed by Kissinger or Nixon would stand a cat in hells chance of succeeding.'

Nhon shook his head 'No this is not a military plan: I do agree with you that it would be suicide to try anything not approved by the Americans. These lawyers have a great deal of credibility and contacts all over the world even in the States. They simply wish to exchange ideas and explore if there are things that they can help with.'

'In that case I will go ahead with the meeting but South Vietnam is such a leaky sieve that everyone knows what's going on. I doubt if the authorities will not find out about the meeting: after all I'm being followed everywhere that I go.'

'We must trust our colleagues about their plans but you will be picked up and dropped off at the appropriate place and no one knows how to shake off a tail more than they do. Leave it to me and I will let you know where to be picked up.'

The next day I was told that this clandestine meeting was arranged in three days time and the location where I was to be picked up. The weekend was coming and I looked forward to spending it with my girlfriend though I would try to attend a Sunday lunch time service in the Protestant Church where Michael Counsel would conduct the service.

It was some time since I had attended a church service and I always enjoyed services conducted in this church. The sermons were never too long and there was always a cool drink waiting afterwards and on this occasion an invitation to lunch. 'We always enjoy our after lunch debates when you attend as you have an alternative view to our American Republican friends.'

Indeed I was soon to find that there were around fifteen earnest pro-war young Americans anxious to cross swords with me on the merits of the war. I did feel though that their cock-sure attitude had waned since our last encounter and some of them were beginning to doubt if the war could be won in the time left for them to do so. The clamour of the peace movement in the United States grew ever stronger each day with seasoned officers and men joining in the debate.

I upset some of the lunch guests by suggesting that their principles of freedom and democracy did not extend to other races either here or in the Southern States where Afro-Americans were still being denied the right to vote. The Reverend Michael stepped in to cool the atmosphere and attempt to find common ground. Sadly there wasn't much common ground and I couldn't resist giving a parting shot by saying their legacy when they left Vietnam was misery and bloodshed and little that was compatible with the Christian ethos.

Before parting, a neutral lunch guest quietly congratulated me on my debating skills which she described as rapier sharp. My ego was given a boost but I did have doubts about what I had been asked to do. Those doubts would remain mine alone but in prayer I did ask why I should be in such a position.

Surely someone more erudite and academically gifted should be in a much stronger position to play the role of peacemaker. The whole world cried out for peace so if there was to be some sort of miracle it would be appropriate if someone more virtuous than me should play such a role; perhaps a prelate or man of the cloth and definitely not a man sleeping with a girl outside of marriage.

Yet something drove me on: I could never forget the child who died in my arms or zigzagging on the pavement to avoid treading on a starving amputee man, woman or child. Or even the young American waking up blind. I was out of my depth but somehow when speaking to statesmen now or in the future I found the words that simply were beyond my own. One young woman friend was to describe it as the Holy Spirit. I did not feel in any way holy! My ultimate hope and ambition was that I might be able to pass on my experiences and aspirations to someone more suitable for the task of peace making.

The time soon emerged when it was time for me to be taken to the covert meeting place with lawyers. I stood just outside a shop close to the International School. A young man riding a scooter speedily drew close to me and beckoned me to jump on the back and I was whisked away in seconds. I looked back to see if anyone was following us but there was just the flurry of traffic all around. Weaving in and out we were now in an unfamiliar part of Saigon. Very soon the scooter came to a sudden halt and I was ordered off where a middle aged woman beckoned me to enter her residence. Her door was quickly opened and shut once we were inside, I was told to walk to the back of the house where a girl aged about fourteen opened the back door and beckoned me to follow. I was led through a backyard into a narrow alleyway.

It was dark and foreboding and the alleyway led to a labyrinth of several adjoining ones leading to either the left or right. The girl pointed for me to take the right one and then quickly disappeared. An old man was waiting who guided me to follow until it led to a tall fence where a door was opened and as I entered a back yard I saw a few figures inside a dimly lit room. As I approached the back door it opened and a smartly dressed man in a suit and tie greeted me and led me to meet his colleagues.

He introduced himself as Tran Ngoc Lieng the leader of the most powerful political movement aiming at peace and reconciliation in South Vietnam. I knew that he had bravely defended a number of dissidents and opponents of the Saigon regime and lives in constant fear of the secret police. A middle aged woman was the first person that I was introduced to; she was Madam Ngo Ba Thanh. As we shook hands I mentioned that I had heard of her verbal encounter with General Westmoreland.

'You mean the time when he summoned us to a big meeting and lectured us on how he was here to build freedom and democracy?'

'Yes and your reply that if you can ask a question you boldly asked when are you going to stop killing my people and go home. I bet he was a bit numb struck when you asked that. How did he reply?

'Oh he answered with the usual paranoia about stopping the spread of communism.'

There were about fifteen lawyers in the room including one Senator who told me that there was a time when he was a

129

friend of Thieu but he said that he is now beyond the pale with no idea of how to end the war but just does as Kissinger and Nixon tells him day by day. Conversations ebbed and flowed with most of the group adding their views.

Lieng summed up a lengthy discussion by saying 'the strategy of the Americans of trying to create a similar situation to Korea would take all of a decade to complete and then only be possible by defoliating the whole country. The terrain, the politics and the military situation is quite different to Korea. The carnage and repression of the people would not only be unacceptable here but would tarnish the reputation of America all over the world; indeed all that they are doing here is an affront to the principles of the Founding Fathers.'

He continued 'We believe that Britain could do so much to resolve the situation. As co chairman of the Geneva Conference with Russia and as you co-exist alongside China in Hong Kong and are the best friends of America surely your influence could be so beneficial.'

I agreed and asked if they had any conversations with those working in the British Embassy?

They exchanged looks with each other and stated that they were so disappointed with the attitude of most of the diplomats in the Embassy. Lieng replied 'I believe they are ruled by a group of elderly military men who take the opinion that if only the British were in charge they could have had an outcome similar to that of Malaya.'

Madam Ngo Ba Thanh continued 'They have no understanding or sympathy with our people: I think they spend all their time with the cocktail set conversing exclusively with Americans and Australians and not even with the French. If they at least listened to us they might begin to think of us as human beings who simply wish to live in peace.'

'I have a friend who is a doctor and he describes them as the Somerset Maugham set, living in another bygone age. The problem is that they are in a position to influence the views of those in government back in Westminster.'

Before the meeting was concluded, a full record of what was intended to be said in peace proposals was in general agreement with their aspirations. When they mentioned strategy, I could only answer that we have to pick the brains of friends back in Britain before deciding exactly how we can proceed.

Lieng's parting words were 'We have contacts in the universities in the States, even Yale and Harvard and we will support and try to strengthen what you're doing. Thank you for your friendship and support; we will always appreciate what you're trying to do.'

A young man on a scooter appeared outside in the street to whisk me back to my home just before curfew time.

Two days later I was to attend a dinner with several members of Thieu's peace delegation together with Nhon. I never quite understood how some meetings would be considered safe whilst others were considered dangerous. I was guided to sit alongside Van Bong the man suggested by U Thant as a possible arbitrator and prime minister of a civilian government.

As the food was devoured I could converse with him and my first question was 'How did Thieu respond to the U.N. Secretary General's suggestion?'

His reply was a rather disappointing one, 'I'm afraid Thieu was rather angry with both me and U Thant. I enjoyed the prestige but I was given the cold shoulder by several of my colleagues and downright hostility from a partner in my own party, Wei.'

'And what of the Americans? Was there any support or encouragement from any of them?'

'I'm afraid not; the whole thing was very disappointing.'

'Is there any indication from the Americans that there could be any reaction to the growing peace demonstrations in the States?'

'I wish that I could be more helpful but we are just going round in circles and here in Vietnam the social position of our people continues to deteriorate. A growing number of families are now suffering from malnutrition and I have heard of several cases of where rat poison has been taken to end their misery. We spend more on one day's munitions than a whole year's budget for healthcare.'

The conversation was depressing but at least Van Bong was a man appointed by Thieu who was concerned at the depreciation and suffering of his people. We shook hands at the end of the evening and I wished him every success in Paris.

A couple of days later as I was finishing talking to a class at the International School an ebullient Duc entered the room. 'Have you heard the news? General Don has made a speech stating that South Vietnam should now seek a position of non alignment.'

Other than Thieu and Ky, General Don was probably the most famous military man inside South Vietnam. Not only was he the Chairman of the Senate Defence Committee but he retained cordial relations with both Thieu and Big Minh. Historically he was a key ally to Big Minh when he organised the coup against Diem. Now he socialised with both Thieu and

Big Minh and his sociable personality enabled him to talk freely with senior American military men. Yet to talk of non align-ment would be a major breakthrough of policy quite different to the long held policy of his American masters. Vietnamese politicians would see this as a radical change of direction which would inevitably lead to an American withdrawal.

Soon we were joined by an excited Nhon who claimed that he could work with Don and wished to engage with him at the earliest opportunity. This triggered several meetings with General Don, either in his restaurant or in the Senate and also in the home of Big Minh. On the first occasion that I met him he declared that he liked Nhon and what he stood for and would be prepared to work with him. Nhon was more posi-tive and suggested that the two of them should visit London together with the hope of persuading Wilson to play his role as Co-chairman of the Geneva Conference.

Nhon said 'If the two of us work together; you representing the military and I representing the civilian side of Vietnam we will be an almost unstoppable force for peace.'

Don answered 'We still have to persuade both Nixon and the Communists that there was merit in our proposals. It won't be easy, though Kissinger and Nixon are sinking into a deeper hole every day with wholesale insurrection inside America.'

I said 'I will try to organise some meetings before you visit London but we really do need a well prepared document stating exactly what we are striving to achieve. Only then will we be able to reach world statesmen but I'm sure that we will have a growing number of supporters including U Thant.'

The three of us agreed on a strategy that I would first fly back to London in the early spring of 1970 and make contact with known politicians. Nhon would then follow and start work on the peace document before General Don would join us to attend various meetings.

I wished to see some old friends before returning to England including Doug Grey who was pioneering a project for polio children living in the various orphanages. I promised to start a small charity that would support his work but of course my priority had to be political. Two interesting characters approached me before I left: one was the uncle of the last Emperor of Vietnam who now resided in Bavaria. Ung An pleaded with me to speak to Prince Buu Loc on my way through in Paris. I agreed to do so believing the more support from where ever it came could be beneficial.

The second man was General Tat who represented the Cao Dai religion. They were a religion similar to the Bah Hoi believing in a humanist faith and they had their own Pope and were guided by spiritual séances.

He was eager to tell me that they knew what we were doing and wished to tell me that through a spiritual circle that included Victor Hugo and Winston Churchill that they supported us in our mission for peace. I thanked him for his blessing and thought what an unusual team of saints we had to support us!

I was invited to parties and dinners before parting for England. One memorable occasion was the river side al fresco restaurant where many of the teachers from the International School gathered for a really joyous get together. Duc made it into a musical evening by breaking into his out of tune rendition of a Vietnamese song. This film producer had no inhibitions and as usual was surrounded by young would-be starlets. There were those of a more serious disposition but the atmosphere was of genuine friendship and human warmth. Knowing of the tasks ahead I only hoped that somehow my work could help to provide a more stable and happy environment for them that they so richly deserved.

As the time for curfew came and gradually everyone began to disperse Duc spotted someone at an adjoining table and his hilarity changed into a deep gloomy one.

He whispered to me 'Don't let him see you looking but the man on our left two tables down is a political assassin; he has killed several people and works for the Vietnamese equivalent of the C.I.A.'

I glanced around to see a good looking man in his early thirties. I hoped that he didn't notice me but he certainly recognised Duc and came over to chat to him and introduce himself to me. He was smartly dressed and spoke excellent English displaying a sociable disposition. I hoped that he had his eye on one of the beautiful actresses sitting amongst us, but we exchanged pleasantries and expressed what a pleasant evening we all had.

My old friend Xuan invited me to join his wife and daughters for an evening at Maxim's Night Club which was one of the most up-market places providing first class food and cabaret. Beautiful hostesses and possible dance partners mingled with customers later in the evening. The meal was followed by a variety of entertainers including acrobats, magicians, singers and dancers. A beautiful exotic dancer called Thu Thuy took centre stage and began a combination of stripping and erotic movements in time to the music. As she stripped down to a G string she looked in my direction and drew closer.

Maybe I had a sympathetic face but it was a familiar event that on the few occasions that I was witnessing sexy dancers they invariably approached me to jump on to my lap. Still, I never complained.

A couple of days later walking through the centre of Saigon looking for nostalgic presents a friendly voice shouted me to join him for a coffee. It was from our sociable assassin that I had met with Duc. Of course, I walked over and sat beside him.

'It was a great evening the other day: I love dining next to the river; it just adds a tranquil touch to the occasion.' I began our conversation.

'You've been enjoying yourself in the last few days' he laughed as he added 'I saw you at Maxim's with Thu Tuey cavorting on your lap.'

'You were there too? I never noticed you.'

'I know that you love beautiful girls. We have plenty of those; you should come and work for us. Just give us the word and I can arrange for Thu Thuy to be with you tonight. You can have as many different girls as you can cope with each and every night and you will never need to worry about a tight budget ever again.' It appeared that I was being propositioned by the C.I.A. or at least by the Vietnamese version.

'That sounds great but why would you want me to work for you? I'm flying back to England in a few days time.'

'You can still work for us in London, Paris, here or possibly in the States.'

Repeating the question of "Why Me?" his response was 'You have an influence with leading Vietnamese whom we are unable to reach. We would like to widen our government and indeed Nhon once stated that we should build a coalition of non communists to counter the threat of the Viet Cong and North Vietnamese.'

'There was some logic in what Nhon said but for the two Vietnams to live side by side in peace and perhaps some kind of federal structure must allow for communists to have a form of accommodation within South Vietnam. Nixon has ruled out coalition and neutrality and that remains the obstacle, but America is in ferment and his policy does not enable P.O.W.s to be freed. Huge human and financial resources are being poured into the Vietnam War and something has to change in the next few years. The Senate and Congress are threatening to seriously cut back on funding.'

'You've summed up why we want you to work with us. We have a million men in the Armed Forces and the Vietnam Air force is the third biggest in the world but it still isn't enough.'

'Its global politics and the big powers must want the situation to change. The only reason that I might be able to help is that I believe Winston Churchill was right in 1954 and Jack Kennedy was right in 1963; I'm afraid Kissinger and Nixon still have not grasped the nettle.' I hoped that I had not gone too far so after a pause I continued, 'I hope my country can help but it will be far more than my personal contribution. I could only ever work for my country but I will promise to be open and transparent and hope for an end of this cruel war and a solution that your people richly deserve.'

He seemed satisfied with my reply and we parted on good terms. I now completed my goodbyes with friends and colleagues and prepared for parting. Nhon offered to drive me to the airport and I promised that I would arrange for him to have somewhere to stay in London and begin to prepare for some meetings.

I climbed aboard the Singapore Aircraft and during the journey would eat an endless supply of sweetmeats, washed down by a constant flow of drinks. The attractive hostesses were attentive and charming, thus ensuring a pleasant flight. Singapore was always a favourite location of mine and during my two night stay I made my way towards the Perfumed Garden Hotel which had an adjoining patio surrounded with an eight foot wall of fuchsias. Each table was topped with a Chinese lantern and gentle melodic music was played in the background. Polite and pleasant waiters served excellent food. This was a place that I would definitely hope to visit on a future occasion.

The A474 aircraft took me on the long journey to Paris and when I embarked, there was a chilly night air that contrasted with the tropical temperature of Singapore. Once in the hotel I phoned my parents to tell them that I would see them in a couple of days time. I slept soundly but woke with a jolt; it was so quiet. I was so used to sleeping with the rumble of bombing in the distance that it felt strange to sense normality.

I did call on Prince Buu Loc who was the last prime minister to serve under the French. It was historically interesting and understandably the old Emperor Bao Dai was keen to return to Vietnam where his elderly mother still lived in the Hue Palace. As both Laos and Cambodia still had titular Royal Families some Vietnamese believed there could be a similar role for the Vietnamese one. I'm afraid there was little consensus for this but it was right to collect opinions from all and sundry particularly those who had once played a leading part.

Returning to Heathrow I was numb with cold and keen to catch a bus back to the city centre. I looked at my change that the conductor gave me and found a strange shaped coin that had replaced the old ten shilling note. Another passenger noticed my stare and told me that it was legal tender recently introduced. It felt so strange to be back in England. I had heard many Americans talking about going 'back to the world' now I knew what they meant. It was as though everything was in slow motion. In a war zone there was always an adrenaline rush; a kind of constant preparedness for any eventuality: such as shooting in the street or an explosive device going off nearby. The survival instinct meant that each person had to construct a cocoon of a selfish defence structure regardless of what horrors surrounded us. The only thing that mattered was survival for we simply couldn't think too much about others.

Those who have a political or religious gene often neglect those they love without intending to do so. They are driven by obsessions that they believe will benefit humanity and hope that those nearest and dearest will understand and one day benefit. As I travelled to visit my parents I realised the distress and trauma that I must have caused them to travel to the most dangerous country in the world, where killing was being filmed and then shown in living rooms on television. It must have been an anxious time when I was reported missing in a Vietnamese jungle. My return was a joyous occasion and I learned that my younger sister was to be married in June so I hoped to be present then and of course exchange news with friends and family alike.

Ted and Helen Harrison were old friends that I first met when they were both first year students at Canterbury University and now Ted was fast building a career for himself in journalism, first in radio and then on television. As soon as I arrived in England he wrote an article in one of the newspapers and arranged for me to broadcast about what I was doing. I was keen to arrange a few meetings before Nhon and General Don arrived as preliminary introductions before a comprehensive brochure had been published. I attended a meeting of the Peace in Vietnam Committee which was chaired by Lord Fenner Brockway but on this occasion in Parliament the meeting was chaired by the Vice Chairman Frank Allaun who also happened to be the Chairman of the Labour Party.

I arrived a little late so crept into the back of the room and listened to the proceedings. Discussions centred on vile weapons that were being used in Vietnam. Frank Allaun spoke about the use of gas when a hostile journalist interjected to ask if he had any confirmation of this. At this point I just had to intervene and say 'Yes I can; I experienced it on two occasions'. I then mentioned the occasions and how it felt which led to a number of reporters moving in my direction to ask if they could speak to me after the meeting which of course I did. A B.B.C. broadcaster recorded an interview inside Parliament and needless to say this triggered off in depth conversations with Frank Allaun and supporters of the Peace in Vietnam Committee.

I contacted Jeremy Thorpe to arrange a meeting with Nhon as soon as he arrived. As a Liberal activist before entering Vietnam I had been elected to the policy making body for the Liberal Party and on the last meeting Jeremy Thorpe sat beside me for both the morning and afternoon sessions. I was flattered to be able to converse with the new party leader who had taken over from the great Jo Grimond. He had married a beautiful and likeable young woman and I assumed that he was very happy. I knew nothing of his previous private life and was oblivious to the threatening dark shadow that would eventually overtake him. I only knew that he had a good working relationship with the Prime Minister Harold Wilson.

Nhon arrived on a bitterly cold February day but was relieved that the National Liberal Club was always warm; he loved the history of the building and immediately made friends with some of the elderly members and he beat several of them at chess. Also he had an uncanny knack of winning the prize money at the cash machines.

Jeremy Thorpe soon contacted me, saying 'Brian, I'll love to hear what you've been up to and meet Nhon. I have a really full agenda at the moment but would a half hour slot suit you to start with? That will give you and Nhon a chance to present your proposals and we can then discuss the issues more fully later.'

We accepted Jeremy Thorpe's invitation and at the subscribed hour we were ushered into his room in the House of Commons. He greeted Nhon in French to which he eloquently replied that for my sake it would be better to converse in English. I believe Thorpe had never spoken to a Vietnamese except in French. Nhon made use of the half hour to present his policy brief but stressed how dangerous it was for many neutralists to present their opinion in public and this was why it was necessary to present a peace initiative from within Europe. Nhon asked Thorpe to arrange a meeting with Wilson to which he responded 'Let's see a well prepared brochure presenting your views and we can go from there.'

There was a good rapport between Nhon and Thorpe and when the half hour was up both Nhon and I were pleased with the meeting. Whilst in Parliament I put in a green card for David Crouch to thank him for offering to help my parents when I had been reported missing. He was very interested in what we were doing and immediately offered to arrange for a meeting to brief the Conservative Party Foreign Affairs Committee which we were pleased to accept. We also arranged for meetings with Eric Lubbock who was the Chief Whip of the Liberal Party and with a woman who was linked with several international organisations.

We heard that General Don was to land at Heathrow. So at his time of arrival we waited and were told that he would arrive through the VIP lounge which had been arranged by Julian Thompson but that he had now left for his suite in a Kensington Hotel. He contacted us and apologised for the mix-up and asked if we could call on him at his hotel. When we did so it was luxurious and his manner was completely changed from when he was in Saigon.

He recanted on what he had said about the need for South Vietnam to become nonaligned and he told Nhon that they knew what he was doing and that he should return immediately to his wife and family. Someone had put the frighteners on him and for Nhon it was a terrible betrayal. The two men representing both military and civilian non Communists were in a powerful position to present an alternative strategy for peace and reconciliation and had huge potential for global support. Nhon was now stranded in exile, for to return he knew that others had been killed and tortured for doing less than him for trying to change the war policy.

Chapter 8

The Peace Initiative

I controlled my emotions of anger at Don for I would have understood if he had declined Nhon's offer to join him in England, but to simply wait for him to become fully committed and then retract from working together created an extra burden and possible danger for him. It was Nhon who was in the hot seat and was for him to decide what next he should do. Sadly if he continued his work in England it could mean he could be separated from his wife and children for a long period of time. It didn't take long for him to reply to Don.

'I came to launch the ideas of many of our leading citizens to at least present an alternative to perpetual bloodshed and misery. It was not for personal ambition but I am driven by conscience and faith. My wife is a devout and active Christian who is dedicated to social and charity work. In this she has the respect and friendship of the President's wife so I'm sorry to be apart from her but I believe she will be safe keeping a wide birth from politics.'

I think General Don was shamed by this and quietly spoke of how he had flown over the Cambodian border and saw Viet Cong bunkers built several miles inside Cambodia alongside local villages. I was surprised that he should bring this subject up as the position in neutral Cambodia had not changed for years as it was difficult for them to do anything to prevent the powerful Communist and American conflict to spew over the Ho Chi Minh Trail.

Two meetings had been arranged for the following day and I suggested that we should honour them. The first was with Eric Lubbock who was the Chief Whip of the Liberal Party which we attended in Parliament. Eric began by welcoming us all and saying that he believed that we were planning a new peace initiative but General Don said that it was not really much that was new and praised the armed forces of South Vietnam. Both Nhon and I were fairly mute but at least Don confirmed that he dissented from his views expressed in Saigon. Nhon and I left this meeting in a fairly sullen mood but we drove in Don's limousine the short distance to the National Liberal Club.

Out of earshot of Don I whispered to Nhon that the next meeting was with a woman who would record what was said and relay it in the public domain to all those participating within negotiations in Paris. At least it would be known that Don had changed his political position and that Nhon was now abandoned in exile. After this meeting we parted with Don in the knowledge that friends back in Vietnam would know what had happened. Don would soon prepare to become Thieu's last prime minister but would never again be associated with peacemaking.

Nhon and I would prepare to brief the Conservative Party Foreign Policy Committee with the agreed proposals agreed with colleagues back in Saigon and I contacted James Cameron for some practical help in polishing up our brochure and preparing for media presentation.

We entered the prescribed committee room to be greeted by Richard Wood who was the son of Lord Halifax and was destined to become the Minister of Overseas Development within a few weeks. He introduced us to his colleagues including John Biggs Davidson and Eldon Griffiths plus three other men. Nhon made a reasonable presentation of his position and both he and I praised the role that Britain had played as co-Chairman of the Geneva Conference in 1954. As the discussion progressed, Eldon Griffiths was the most hostile, questioning the criticism of the Presidential Election; Biggs Davidson had the reputation of being a right wing Catholic and began in a confrontational way but as Nhon replied by stating what he had done to create a government party which Thieu was to take over, he gradually warmed to Nhon and his position. At a later date we were to learn from the feedback of a mutual friend Phyllis Bowman that he had been most impressed by Nhon.

Richard Wood who had lost both his legs during the Second World War was by far the most sympathetic. He had scrutinised everything that was said and as the meeting neared its end he said 'You are providing the Americans with a way out without losing too much face. Surely they must listen to you.' He then concluded by saying 'Let me know if there is anything that I can do for you.'

As Nhon and I left Parliament we were delighted at the reception as we feared that Conservatives could be the most critical of what we were doing. A telephone message came from James Cameron stating that he had managed to arrange a television programme on BBC 2 to promote our peace proposals. Though Nhon and I believed that this was a little premature before our brochure had gone to the printers and we were a little disappointed that neither Nhon or I had been invited to participate in this programme I had appeared however doing a four minute lead story on ITV news and Nhon had spoken many times on the religious radio programmes broadcast on Sunday mornings. James said "if I can launch your ideas you will be in great demand from the media immediately following the show."

James made a reasonable presentation at the start of the programme but he was followed by a journalist who had spent two months in South Vietnam. He expressed the opinion that the Americans had won the war and with a million men under arms and the third biggest air force in the world, Thieu was firmly in charge. An academic who had once worked with Diem, the hated dictator who had persecuted the Buddhists was the next to appear. He clearly hated those who had replaced Diem and made a vile attack on Nhon.

'I don't know him; I can't even find his name in the Saigon telephone directory.'

Sadly James Cameron tried to answer his volatile opponent but simply didn't at that stage know of the background of Nhon and the positions he held in Vietnam. If Nhon or I had been on the programme we could have provided the details of his background. He was once the Secretary General of the Freedom Democratic Party now the established government party of President Thieu; he was nominated to stand as President and until he came to Britain he was Principal of the International School in which both the President and Vice President sent their children and as Protestant Pasteur he had regularly broadcast as the Voice of Christianity.

The weakness of our position was known very well; we couldn't reveal all the names of those who supported the peace proposals without endangering their lives.

After the broadcast several messages of protest went to the

146

BBC, including, from a few of the doctors who knew Nhon in Vietnam. I wrote insisting on a right of reply to rectify the character assassination of Nhon. The two hostile broadcasters were completely out of date in their description of the military situation which I had first heard from Philip Noel Baker who told me that the Americans had told him that they had won the war. Events in the next few months would totally undermine this lie.

Medical Aid for Vietnam invited representatives of the North Vietnam Government to visit London. Dr Adrian Pointer and I were invited to a reception held in the Lancaster Hotel. This gave us an opportunity to officially meet Madam Binh and Le Van Sao and several other leading Communists. There were several diplomats from the Chinese Embassy wearing pale blue boiler suits and all looking exactly the same. I spotted Vanessa Redgrave at the other side of the room and began to make my way towards her. Before reaching her, a dapper Russian diplomat introduced himself and was most keen to hear of what I was doing. His name was Gennady followed by a complicated Russian name beginning with a Z. He told me to call him Genner as that was what most of his friends called him. He had spent seven years based in Bangkok and now had a special brief to deal with Vietnam. Handing me his card he insisted on continuing our conversation, offering to pay for dinner. We agreed on a date and at my suggestion we would meet at the National Liberal Club.

Circulating with an interesting group of doctors and political activists, I was soon engrossed in conversation with Le Van Sao who was one of the leaders of the Viet Cong Government. We both had full pint glasses of beer and exchanging views and stories when we were joined by Adrian. To my embarrassment

Adrian told of how one of his rockets had blown me out of bed. In satirical style he stated that it was more effective than an alarm clock. My new Viet Cong friend looked concerned and put a consoling hand on my arm: 'It was nothing personal you know.' His words would always be with me and only drew us closer in our mutual distain of war. I never did meet Vanessa Redgrave, for every time I attempted to approach her someone interesting stepped into the way.

Sihanouk was out of Cambodia when a coup took place to replace him as head of State. The response to peace initiatives was countered by Kissinger and Nixon starting yet another war. Neutral Cambodia had struggled to stay out of the war and its inhabitants were grateful to Prince Sihanouk for avoiding the bloodshed, though they knew the Ho Chi Minh Trail extended about fifteen miles inside the border. American and South Vietnamese forces advanced into Cambodia and a massive blitz began on that country. By kicking out the popular Royal Family, Americans managed to unite the Royalists, the Democrats and the Communists. During the Indo China conflict the Americans were in the process of dropping more weight of bombs than by both sides in the Second World War. In Cambodia they had managed to transform a peaceful, kindly indolent people into a nation of psychopaths.

Nixon had shown a callous disregard for human life and also clearly indicated that the war was far from finished. There was uproar throughout America with students protesting and four of them were shot dead. Pol Pot who according to official sources had less than five percent support amongst the people was now, presented with the ultimate power of his country. There was a debate in Parliament with Michael Foot proposing a censure vote against American policy. I briefed him just before the debate and his oratory was superb. To my disgust Jeremy Thorpe and the Liberals abstained from the vote. I could not understand how a man could say one thing in private and do another in a public debate. A few years later I would understand that he was completely under the thumb of the C.I.A. due to the problems in his private life.

Britain was soon to be engrossed in a General Election and on the 18th of June to the surprise of most pundits, Ted Heath and the Conservatives won and formed their government. Nhon, James Cameron and me, discussed how we should deliver our brochure. We had all been numbed by recent experiences but decided that we put diplomacy and politics first and then back it up with media presentation. For protocol we agreed to send directly to President Nixon first and foremost. After all it was aimed at his government in the hope of a change of policy. Two weeks later we prepared individual letters to Senator Fulbright, Chairman of the Senate Defence Committee, U Thant, Secretary General of the United Nations, Ted Kennedy, George McGovern, and Eugene McCarthy.

To our pleasant surprise our peace proposals were printed in a Saigon newspaper, but just afterwards the paper was closed down. Of course the government controlled papers renounced the peace plan and insisted that the war must continue.

Everyone replied promptly though the reply from the White House was signed by Nixon's assistant and was little more than an acknowledgment. U Thant wrote a positive reply but added that he would never again name anyone as a mediator. The news had just broken that Van Bong had been blown to pieces and his wife loudly proclaimed that those responsible were not the Communists. Ted Kennedy wrote that he agreed that there has to be accommodation for the Communists within South Vietnam: his reply was positive and friendly as was that of George McGovern. After this we presented to other various sources, including the Vietnamese ones and Genner with whom I met quite regularly, nearly always for dinner at the National Liberal Club. Since the American invasion Philip Noel Baker had changed his mind on the military status of Vietnam. Writing to a mutual friend Pax Perl, who was one of the first westerners to visit North Vietnam and was kissed on the cheek by Ho Chi Minh; a photograph that was relayed all over the world, she sent me a copy of a letter originating from the Nobel Peace Prize Winner.

In it, he said that our brochure was the most constructive that he had ever read for ending the war in Vietnam. Praise indeed from a Nobel Peace Prize Winner and Chairman of the Labour Party Foreign Affairs Committee. Nhon was making many friends in England including M.P.s and various Christian groups including the Quakers and he spent some time in the Friend's Meeting House in Holborn. The widow of Gerald Bowman the writer, Phyllis Bowman, became a particularly good friend. She was an active Catholic and became sympathetic of Nhon's plight, his suffering and being separated from wife and family for the cause of peace.

Dr Adrian Pointer and I planned to take a trip to Paris and attend the Vietnam Peace Talks. There were always numerous talks in private between the different factions and regular press conferences in which government spokesmen gave the latest interpretation of events. A big burly American read his statement and then waited for questions. I soon put my hand up and was allowed to speak which I did clearly and loudly and then asking Adrian to interpret in Vietnamese and French.

'Now that institutions and constitutions are being discussed, will the United States agree to the neutralists' proposals for calling for a proper internationally controlled election for the South Vietnamese people in which all sides would be able to participate?'

He clearly didn't like the insinuation that the word 'proper' was used and replied that he thought elections in Vietnam were no more corrupt than they are in Chicago. After the press conference ended several journalists clambered around to ask about the nuances. Particularly pleased was the spokesman for Hanoi, Le Phu Hao, and we adjoined to a back room where I showed him some of my correspondence. He asked if we could meet the following morning which we did in his lavish apartment.

'This is very bourgeois' said Adrian as we entered the palatial room. He had a knack of breaking through an atmosphere with a dry wit and his words were met with laughter.

The North Vietnam spokesman asked if he could photostat my correspondence and send it to Hanoi?' In the atmosphere of goodwill that existed both yesterday and now I said that I have an idea that could move things along.

'While Nixon is blitzing your country I realise that you cannot appear to weaken, but if you were to release the names of American P.O.W.s in your possession inside North Vietnam to Ted Kennedy, it would show that you would be prepared to seriously negotiate if the U.S. was to be represented by an honest broker. The emphasis on the human factor would add pressure from families and friends on Nixon to deliver a meaningful end to the war.'

My words were well received and Hao stated that he would put my idea to Hanoi. Three weeks later the list of names of P.O.W.s was given to Ted Kennedy, who duly passed them to the State Department for distribution to the relevant families. It was the first time that the families knew that their loved ones were alive.

Our brochure boldly called 'The Solution For Vietnam' may not have ended the war but it did provide an agenda for negotiations in Paris and for debate around the world. It presented an alternative strategy for Americans and provided gravitas to the peace movement. We built contacts and friends on both sides of the conflict and established relationships first with Russia and eventually with Mark Pratt, Kissinger's top man in charge of the Indo China desk in Paris.

Immediately following the American invasion of Cambodia there were some articles from elderly military men in the Daily Telegraph expressing support for the invasion. I recall saying to Nhon that I thought their expertise belonged in the Second World War and one in particular appeared to believe that they would find a nerve centre for the Viet Cong similar to a Whitehall Department.

Sadly the war in Vietnam ground inexorably on and had now spread throughout Indo China. The Paris talks were again moribund. The armies in the field were deadlocked. The shedding of Asian and American blood could have gone on for years. And still the conflicting ideologies were no nearer conciliation. It was a depressing time for all concerned.

Nhon and I had been elated late in 1970 but during 1971 war continued, though with little comfort for the Saigon regime and Nixon. In Cambodia the Khmer Rouge captured numerous villages and small towns leaving the larger cities and towns cut off by road. A similar situation existed in South Vietnam so government structures were increasingly expensive to maintain. Democrats in the States were gradually putting financial restraints on the continuing war.

A Presidential Election was due for South Vietnam in the autumn. Peacemakers believed that if Nixon was serious about ending the war this was an easy way to do so without losing face. If it was assured that the election was not to be rigged and Big Minh was allowed to stand against Thieu, he would be elected by a landslide. Then Big Minh with the support of the American military and the forces of South Vietnam, would be able to deal with the Communists from a position of strength. He could offer the prospect of neutrality within a federal structure, with unification elections internationally organised and the steady withdrawal of American forces. At some point the release of all P.O.W.s could be negotiated and even a possible aid plan agreed.

Such hopes of peace were dashed with news that some of Big Minh's supporters had been killed and Nhie who was now working in the Vietnam Embassy in Kensington reported an unusual incident to Nhon. When I heard it I arranged a meeting in the Commons with Frank Allaun, and three journalists, Peter Snow ITV, Ted Harrison BBC and Arnold Wilson. Nhie, Nhon and I would also be present.

Nhie began to tell his story, that an unusual package arrived at the Embassy addressed to the private armoury of President Thieu which was to be despatched through diplomatic security. On further inspection of the large package he discovered that it contained guns with telescopic sights. In view of the forthcoming election and the killing of Big Minh's supporters he was profoundly concerned.

Peter Snow dismissed what Nhie had said 'You don't want to be involved with this Oriental intrigue.'

Frank Allaun was thoughtful before speaking 'I believe everything that you have said but I'm not sure I can do anything.'

Nhie had risked his life and job by repeating what he had seen but what kinds of powers were we subjected to? I believe all of us present were concerned at the situation.

After a few days of reflection, Nhie reported the incident to colleagues in Saigon and Big Minh announced that he would not be standing for the Presidency. The Election Day passed with no one standing against Thieu and the one who did so four years ago, was still in prison. Thieu would hold on to power for a while but his democratic credentials were nonexistent, something that Kissinger recognised which would make his regime dispensable in discussions with the Communists in the next year or so.

President Nixon would have to face an election in November 1972 and he knew that if he did not change his policy on Vietnam he would face the wrath of the American people. For the first time, serious and direct top secret talks began between Hanoi and Washington. The prime objectives of Kissinger and Nixon were to be able to withdraw all American troops from Vietnam together with the release of P.O.W.s, regardless of the bloody carnage left behind. Maps were exchanged between the military leaders of the United States and North Vietnam, in which provided a patch work quilt of territory claimed by both sides in South Vietnam. The Communists claimed to control large rural areas whilst the Saigon regime claimed much of the urban areas. Understandably there were many contested areas, some of which crossed over the main road networks between major cities.

With such a map eventually agreed it was obvious that it would be impossible for South Vietnam to exist without mediation and accommodation between the two sides. Otherwise military conflict was certain to continue. The Communists were keen to stop the bloodshed and they knew the withdrawal of American troops would mean eventual victory.

An important part of our peace brochure was the creation of a National Reconciliation Council that would represent the three elements within South Vietnam and be responsible for the future development of South Vietnam. Thieu and the Americans would not agree to this but information of all the other aspects of the plan were made public. The fact that an agreement was so close, that would at least see the end of the war for Americans and the release of P.O.W.s, was enough to persuade the American people to re-elect Richard Nixon as President. Representatives of the Viet Cong Government visited London in the hope that Britain as the co-chairman of the Geneva Conference would support this policy, that would bring about mediation and neutrality. They addressed a meeting of over a hundred M.P.s chaired by Fenner Brockway in Parliament. Sadly there was no indication that Britain would risk upsetting Kissinger and Nixon and a major bombing campaign would take place until the Communists signed what was known as the Kissinger Tho Agreement.

After the meeting in Parliament, James Cameron, Nhon and I joined the Vietnamese delegation and chatted until taxis arrived to transport them to their hotel. I looked round to see that just one unarmed police officer stood by the door of Parliament whilst nearly all the Vietnamese group waited on the pavement. In future years I would recall that other conflicts would require much greater security around Parliament.

From the text of the agreement in November 1972 to the signing in late January 1973 only three words were changed: 'the Government Structure' was deleted from the Reconciliation Council. Thus the Americans had bombed away the prospect of a negotiated settlement which would have brought about a form of neutrality.

Still the agreement was a massive historical event and at least showed light at the end of the tunnel. Nhon wrote a personal letter to President Thieu appealing for him to respond and be prepared to work together for the sake of the country. Sadly there was no response. If there had been even the slightest chance that Thieu would have been prepared to talk about the future mediations, Nhon would have returned to Saigon but as he said, there was no point on returning just to go to prison or worse. I told him that within a couple of months when the dust had settled, I would fly to Saigon to see for myself what was happening.

On the day that the Kissinger Tho Agreement was announced I was invited to join Ted Harrison in the B.B.C. newsroom. Both before and afterwards I have made numerous broadcasts on TV and radio but on this occasion I just froze. I was not sufficiently briefed on what was happening in Vietnam and I was very conscious that my words would be heard in Vietnam and I believed that I would soon be meeting members of Thieu's Government if not the President himself. The questions that were thrown at me in the broadcasting room included 'Was it the right time for the large aid and charities to become involved? Would the bloodshed continue when the Americans left?' These were questions that I did not know the answers. When I returned from Vietnam in 1970 I was familiar with the military and political situation. Now there were conflicting thoughts in my mind. I was elated that the Americans were leaving but anxious and profoundly concerned of what would happen in the future. I was told that dissidents were still being assassinated by the secret police and the Reconciliation Council was ignored by Thieu. I was to later hear that a Frenchman playing a similar role to myself, was shot in Saigon. Perhaps after all I had a guiding angel!

Television screens were filled with departing American service-men and P.O.W.s being returned to their loved ones. Sadly there were also scenes of carnage including a man being killed in An Thanh, close to where I stayed back in 1968 with Steve.

In April 1973 I flew to Saigon and was met by my old friend Doug Grey and Mrs Nhon. The two had been united in their charity work. Doug had scraped enough together to pay for a villa which he had turned into a polio centre for children, from the orphanages in and around Saigon. He had also built a little team of young women who had learnt how to look after the children. They were a credit to him for the children were washed and clothed immaculately and every child had its own programme for treatment. Crutches and equipment had been begged and for those children who required surgery, regular visits from visiting American doctors who either operated locally or in a few cases were transported abroad.

Mrs Nhon bravely continued the work of Principal of the International School, brought up her four children and worked tirelessly on numerous projects in cooperation with the Protestant Church. She and the work that her husband was doing for peace, won huge admiration from all who knew her, not least from the staff of the school and political colleagues. Doug and I dined with Mrs Nhon before I found a reasonable priced hotel just on the road to Cholon.

Saigon was much quieter without the ever present rumble of bombing from the American Air Force. There was an eerie feeling of expectation as everyone hoped for something positive yet feared for something worse. Mrs Nhon stressed that the people were poorer than ever without the economic boost that American presence had brought. As soon as the news of my arrival spread, many of Nhon's friends and colleagues invited me to dinners and meetings.

Immediately following the Kissinger Tho agreement, Jim Callaghan, Ian Mikado and Tom McNally flew to Saigon and met some of the Deputies and Senators who supported the neutralist cause, but sadly they failed to persuade Thieu to recognise the role of the Conciliation Council. Vinh was one of my first visitors and he was confident that I would be able to succeed if I was able to talk to him. A car arrived at Mrs Nhon's residence late in the afternoon just as we were about to leave for a dinner appointment. Four of Thieu's top advisers who were known to Mrs Nhon entered her residence. They were keen to hear my views on the practicalities of activating the Conciliation Council and what security would ensure their personal safety once the Viet Cong were allowed to participate within the democratic society.

I was pleasantly surprised that a Senator who had been a personal friend of Thieu was very keen to support the neutralist cause. When he learnt that I was dependant on others and sometimes even taxis to transport me to various meetings he made a very generous offer of supplying a car, chauffeur and a bodyguard during my stay in Saigon. I met the Government Spokesman at the Press Centre and prepared a solicitous request to meet President Thieu for a confidential meeting. In my presentation I stressed a gradual evolution with religious leaders, meeting and helping to guide charity workers who wished to be involved. In some ways my proposal was similar to the one made by U Thant which sadly ended in the killing of Van Bong.

After asking for an interview with the President the Government spokesman confided in me and said that he and his family had applied to settle in New Zealand. He pessimistically forecast that Thieu and the ruling Generals would prolong the war long enough for them to build a nest egg for them to live in exile. He stressed his belief that only when South Vietnam faced total defeat would they then fly out to leave others to their fate.

I would wait for the reply from Thieu but I was disappointed that the International Community was not putting pressure on Thieu, to at least start to talk with the Conciliation Council rather than arranging for the rotten establishment to plunder resources and retreat to a safe bolt hole. When I conferred with Mrs Nhon, she claimed that the establishment were plundering everything with the currency racket and that exit visas being a remunerative form of corruption. She told of Province Chiefs selling fuel on the black market and then holding their hands out to Uncle Sam for more.

Chapter 9

Killing Fields and the Boat People

Big Minh was in a key position to speak and inspire others to put pressure on Thieu but as Madam Binh once said, his brain was controlled by General Don and he had sold his soul. When the Americans were involved, Big Minh believed that power would be handed over to him as a part of a negotiated deal with both the Communists and Thieu. Now he just made a few public statements such as 'I am ready to serve if it is the will of the people' and 'Thieu was a loyal and respectful colleague when he was under my command and I believe the same may be true today'. What was missing was a public declaration that peace and reconciliation could become a wonderful reality if we grasped the nettle. Alas, his intentions were good but he simply believed that one day he could play a role similar to that of General de Gaulle. If he had been given power at this stage he would have appointed a civilian administration to unite the people and deal from a position of strength with the Communists, while he still had control of an army of a million men. His one quirky stipulation would have been that any government official would have to have been born in the South of Vietnam and not have originated from the North.

In 1973 General Tat the Cao Dai leader asked me to join him in confidence and alone for supper. We were joined by a Colonel who had been trained for intelligence by the French.

It soon became apparent why he wanted our conversation to be discreet. He was impatient with Thieu and had lost confidence with Big Minh. I listened impassively as the two men talked of possible means of a coup, to change the situation. I immediately stated that I was not a military man and would not be involved with military action. One idea that did interest me, was that they claimed that in the most southern provinces of South Vietnam, several Chiefs of Police and Province Chiefs were prepared to declare U.D.I. in favour of the Conciliation Council becoming the government structure.

I hesitated before answering this proposal. 'However admirable the intentions of your colleagues, I know the proud boast of the military, that air power can bring troops anywhere in South Vietnam within ten minutes and I fear that Ky and Thieu would quickly smash any insurrection and call it a Communist conspiracy. However if they were able to organise a large religious gathering for peace it could lead to a momentum as it did in the United States. The right of being able to organise a mass rally or even the freedom to hold a moderate political gathering is still denied so if religious leaders were able to start such a movement it might be difficult to stop.'

I was sorry to dampen their enthusiasm but I felt it was right to express my cautious views. Sadly the regime had a great deal of experience of crushing any kind of revolts even when the Buddhists had played a big role.

I visited the British Embassy curious to know what messages the diplomats were sending back to Britain. The first man that I spoke to expressed the view that it was a pity that the coup in Cambodia had not taken place while Sihanouk was in the country, so that he could have been killed. I listened impassively as he then told me, that now the Americans were no longer there, the South Vietnamese Army would soon invade the North. I was about to leave such loony tunes behind and leave the Embassy, when a younger man who was new to me introduced himself. He was the first diplomat from the British Embassy who impressed me with his knowledge of the situation and I was very surprised that he had been briefed on my activity.

In a visit to the Anglican Church I was sorry to learn that the Counsels had departed and a new Pasteur presided over the service. There were several diplomats' wives in the congregation and I overheard their conversation about the various charities and my ears pricked up when I heard Doug Grey's name brought up.

'He's gone native; I don't think he can be doing much good when he spends so little time with his own kind.' This was a similar charge that had sometimes been made of my old friend Dr Adrian Pointer, even though he won the friendship of many of the countries academics.

On a following Sunday I accompanied Doug with a few of his patients to attend a church service. The children were smartly attired and were proud of how fast they could walk with their crutches; clip clop they went and sat silently through the entire service. They eagerly drank the cool drink that was offered at the end of the service and as they left to go to the ice cream parlour, I heard one woman say 'Well perhaps he's doing some good after all.' Sadly it didn't prevent the Embassy giving away their Land Rovers to new and richer charities and not giving Doug a sausage.

I was invited to a gathering of Senators and Deputies who had joined together as Social Democrats. This was a real attempt to bring most of the religious and political groups together under one banner. Deputy Ham was the prime mover; his district was the northernmost part of South Vietnam, which was now occupied by the Communists. I was surprised how many were in attendance and was delighted to join a representative of Sweden's Social Democrat Government as guest speaker. I was told that many of them had met Jim Callaghan and his group and they had now signed a manifesto that each Senator and Deputy had signed. It was ceremoniously handed to me, to hand deliver when I returned to England. Their manifesto was an appeal to put pressure on Thieu for the right to free assembly and to activate the Reconciliation Council.

Though I attended a host of meetings during my stay, I did make time to relax with a Tom Collins in the popular bar of the Continental Hotel. I purchased an English language newspaper and glancing through the pages, I found an article written by an American. In it he said that at some time in the distant future, the United States would have to build military bases throughout the oil producing Middle East, to ensure the supply and price of oil. At the time I thought that his views were crazy as it would inevitably lead to bloodshed in Muslim countries. Surely after Vietnam the United States would seek a friendly and diplomatic business relationship with the oil producing region: in hindsight how wrong can one be? I was reminded by a friendly American civilian that on this very day the American troops were leaving Vietnam for the final time.

News from Cambodia was fast deteriorating for the American backed regime and there was a flood of stories reflecting a brutal slaughter of prisoners. The early American casualties of the Cambodian war had been Sean Flynn, the son of Errol Flynn and Larry Burrows the photographer that I had hoped to work with. Tim Page was not with his friends due to recovering from a wound.

Since I had last been in Vietnam I learned that Madam Ngo Ba Thanh had been in and out of prison on several occasions. The little charity that I had helped to set up in England had succeeded in transporting medical equipment to Doug Grey together with toys for the orphans free of charge through Air France. Nhon had passed on the details to friends of his in France and under the auspices of the World Christian Peace Movement, goods were sent for Viet Cong prisoners held in South Vietnam; It was Madam Ngo Ba Thanh who was organising things at the other end which resulted in her being arrested and imprisoned.

Saigon was a very strange place in 1973: the river was peaceful and it was so quiet without the rumble of bombs but a steady number of funerals still carried recent casualties of war. It was soon time for me to return to England though I would return four months later for the third time. As I flew out of Saigon I was astounded that all the bomb craters that had reminded me of Emmental cheese, had now been covered with green foliage.

Once I returned to England I made contact with Jim Callaghan's department and handed over the communiqué from the Senators and Congressmen directly to Tom McNally, Callaghan's assistant. I had two or three lunches with Tom where I sensed empathy but little indication of anyone putting any kind of pressure on Thieu, to allow the Conciliation Council to function. Alas, still worse, I heard that brave Deputy Ham had become seriously injured from a grenade attack. To add more depressing news, a rumour had spread that Thieu was to be made welcome in Britain if and when there was a collapse of South Vietnam. Apparently the Americans told him that they couldn't guarantee his safety if he came to America.

I was invited to have lunch with Vernon Dawson at the Commonwealth Club; he was the General Secretary of Liberal International. When we did so, he said that he had heard from Sir Robert Thompson that if the Americans pulled out of Vietnam the Communists would soon take over Thailand followed by everywhere from Australia to India: this was the old Nixon paranoia. He wanted to know my alternative view as he was concerned at the loss of tin supplies from Thailand which were in short supply and necessary for ball bearings. I despaired of such military thinking and stressed that even Communists were human and if we really were concerned at the ideology, we should create a superior one.

I would return once more to Vietnam in the autumn of 1973 but must tell the supporters of a third way that Britain was not the same as Britain of 1954 when Winston Churchill was prime minister and co chaired the Geneva Conference. There was no one of his ilk in the present generation of British politicians and even though three cabinet ministers had said they supported our position when asked to say so publicly, each declined. British foreign policy was created in every nuance by Kissinger and Nixon and even a tin pot dictator like Thieu was allowed to ride rough shod over us.

There was an air of impending doom in South Vietnam and increasingly, small businesses such as fishery and forestry hoped that they would be able to work with the Communists. I was invited to dinner in my honour in the centre of the Chinese centre in Cholon. It was a delicious meal which started with a suckling pig with crackling that melted in the mouth. Everyone hoped that the Communists would be kind masters as the hope of mediation melted away.

Thieu and Ky boasted that they would be the last ones to leave; as someone commented, they are boasting that each will be prepared to fight to the last drop of someone else's blood before flying out.

Mrs Nhon was now despairing of the immediate future as she said, being associated with an English language school, so many people are looking for vengeance and may be in ignorance of what her husband was trying to do. For the first time she was afraid and wished that she could leave before a possible blood bath in Saigon. I was still taken to some of the orphanages that were running short of funds and perhaps the most despairing sight of all was a centre for teenage amputees. Some had legs or arms missing and one poor girl just had one limb out of four. Doug Grey was still functioning and had found a home for a youth who had lost both his arms just above the elbow but he still managed to grasp a paint brush between his two stumps to redecorate the walls.

As I departed for the third time, I hoped that I would return again and tried to arrange a television crew to visit some of the horrific scenes. Sadly a union dispute prevented this from happening.

Early in 1974 Britain was to have a surprise snap General Election. There had been a strike by miners and following electricity stoppages, the winter had been wretched and many workers were only able to work four day weeks. The Conservatives believed that a General Election would increase their majority and strengthen their hand. A new and larger than life Liberal M.P. Cyril Smith, phoned up Joe Gormley the miner's leader and asked if he would deal with the collective of the three party leaders in order to negotiate an end of the strike. His positive reply took away the idea that only the Conservatives could end the strike and it took the lead out of Ted Heath's pencil.

Several friends of mine were standing as Liberals and my friend John Holmes, who was the Home Counties Regional Organiser in charge of ninety four seats, asked me to act as Kent Coordinator for the duration of the General Election. This brought me back into micro politics and briefly away from macro arguments. I had the good luck to recruit a wealthy sponsor, Lew Cartier, who was prepared to spend several thousands on our campaign. He was keen to pay for an aircraft trip for Thorpe to fly around the country, which he declined for reasons I was later to discover but Cyril Smith was keen to take up the offer. The intriguing story of working with Cyril Smith and Jeremy Thorpe after the war will be revealed later but it has to be mentioned that there was a change of government with the return of Harold Wilson, though without an overall majority.

Nhon has some hope that the new government would have a new impetus for a negotiated peace but such hopes were short lived and he decided to live in Paris where the three groups were mingling as never before. Peter Williams was keen to take a television team to Saigon to film the despair and squalor of the orphanages and the street scene. To precipitate this he hired an aircraft to take us to Paris where Nhon organised meetings with all three groups.

Ted Harrison accompanied us; he had polled the highest vote ever for a Liberal in Kent but was compelled to give up his parliamentary aspirations in order to pursue his career as a broadcaster, where he was to soon become the BBC Religious Affairs Correspondent. On the morning of our departure from a small airport in Lympne, Kent, we arrived when rain was pouring down and a vicious wind was blowing. We were met by the pilot who was just as I had imagined the pilots in the RAF were at the time of the Battle of Britain. His name was Julian Soddy and he said on greeting us 'the conditions are absolutely impossible, do you want to give it a go?' I stayed silent but Peter replied 'Yes let's give it a go!'

We piled into the single engine aircraft where the four of us were seated in line - myself at the rear. We bounced up and down as we attempted to fly and when we were over the Channel it felt as though we were flying backwards. Once we were over France it was no surprise that we were told we should make an emergency landing at Le Touquet Airport. We were forced to continue our journey by bus. Peter had a little grumble about the extra Weekend Television costs which he was responsible for but we were safe and the pilot assured us that on the return flight the wind would be with us.

Nhon was waiting to join us in Paris and despite our late arrival we were able to visit the leaders of the three groups. First of all we met the North Vietnamese and Viet Cong Delegation, then Thieu's Delegation followed by some of Nhon's group. Ted recorded numerous interviews for various BBC programmes whereas Peter built up his background knowledge in preparation to make a presentation to the money men in ITV. In the evening several members of the three groups assembled for a very special dinner debate at a Vietnamese restaurant. About twenty five of us attended the meal and it was chaired by Nhon and as well as the three groups, we were joined by French Government representatives. The television cameras recorded the event and I was told that it would be relayed all over the world.

Before the meal was finished Nhon started the debate. He controversially said that it was a pity that negotiations for peace didn't take place in the middle of the battle field where he believed a more speedy resolution would be reached. It was difficult for me to follow all that was being said as the discussion was relayed in Vietnamese, French and sometimes English. I was soon asked to speak but kept it brief as there is nothing more tedious than repetition. Television cameras moved around the table as the debate continued. I would continue to eat my prawn balls and other Vietnamese delicacies as a lengthy debate was conducted.

When at last coffee was served I found that sitting on my right hand side was Le Phu Hao the spokesman for Hanoi and on the other side a member of Thieu's delegation. I had a fleeting thought that if these two were to meet inside Vietnam they might try and kill each other. I found it much easier to talk to the North Vietnamese spokesman than it was with Thieu's man. I was asked if I thought Nixon would be impeached and I said that it was becoming increasingly desperate for him to carry on as the evidence against him grew by the day.

There was a great deal of goodwill between various groups and an overwhelming desire for peace and reconciliation. Nhon's Social Democrats or as many journalists had called them the Third Force, had growing support. The younger brother of Diem, the first American backed ruler, offered to make a contribution to the cost of the dinner. The Vietnamese Royal family backed the movement and I received a good will telephone conversation with General Khan who ruled South Vietnam after Big Minh. It appeared that the Vietnamese across the political spectrum were anxious to avoid the bloodbath that was beginning to take place in Cambodia, as now only the large cities were still in government hands and they were surrounded.

Peter and Ted would soon depart to catch the aircraft back to Kent but Nhon and his friends asked me to stay a few more days in Paris to discuss future strategy. He wrote a diplomatic and solicitous letter to President Thieu offering to fly back to Saigon and work with him to build a safe environment for the Reconciliation Council to function. Alas there was no response from him and as Nhon said, "there was no point in returning to Saigon to be imprisoned or stifled like Big Minh unless there was some indication that Thieu was at least prepared to listen."

During 1974 I came to and fro to Paris and on one occasion Nhon and his colleagues asked me to phone Wilf Burchett and his wife to join us for supper at a Vietnamese restaurant. When I did so it was Mrs Burchett who answered. 'You will never guess where Wilf is' and answering her question continued 'He's in America with a Chinese table tennis team on a Cuban passport.'

That was amazing, for Wilf Burchett was an English born International Communist who had written numerous books and had bravely travelled with the Viet Cong on many occasions. At this time the Americans didn't recognise China, or Cuba and certainly not Wilf Burchett. This was the embryo of an historical event as it was preparation for Nixon's visit to meet Mao in China. Within a few weeks the world would be shocked by this news. Mrs Burchett did join us for supper and filled us in with the nuances. Like her husband she was a professional writer with Paris Match.

On another trip to Paris, Nhon and I had an appointment with Mark Pratt, Kissinger's top man in charge of the Indo China desk in Paris. As we entered the Embassy, Nhon flirted outrageously with two or three American girls who were amused at his boldness. We were to have a long and useful conversation which was blunt but sociable. Of course I mentioned that it was a pity that more pressure was not put on Thieu to accept the Conciliation Council. At this point Mark Pratt stressed that it was now up to the Vietnamese to sort out their differences. He then turned to a huge global map on the wall and pointed to Vietnam and Cambodia which was painted red as was China and Russia.

'Our priorities are now oil and salt: Strategic Arms Limitation Talks.'

It was revealing information for while Cambodia and Vietnam were still being supplied with arms and the military were still enthusiastically perusing a policy of war, the American government was admitting that the war was lost.

My response to this was 'Surely if only for the sake of the second tier of the military who fought with you, pressure should be put on the Saigon regime to compromise and mediate, for they will not all be able to fly out like their senior officers. There are hawks and doves on each side so a negotiated end would strengthen the role of the doves but if the war ends in a bloodbath the role of the hawks will be strengthened.'

To my surprise Mark Pratt made a sympathetic reply 'If the

names of Don and yourself Nhon, were offered to both sides you would have the first two names of the Third Force within the Conciliation Council.'

Though I doubted if the Communists would now consider Don as a neutralist for he had become Thieu's prime minister and many of Nhon's colleagues no longer trusted him, but he was once the human link between Big Minh and Thieu and had spoken publicly about South Vietnam becoming a non aligned state. At the moment Thieu was not considering or speaking to Nhon or anyone associated with him. Any concession had to start with Thieu at least speaking about free assembly and the future role of the Conciliation Council.

I couldn't resist asking a barbed question in the most solicitous way that I could. 'Why was the United States so supportive of military led regimes when more altruistic and democratic activists could become friends and allies if they were treated fairly?'

The reply of this senior Republican diplomat was interesting 'Many countries in the developing world are held together by the military so we have to deal with them and influence them as best we can.'

The thought flashed through my head that George Washington was a military man who had enabled the Founding Fathers to build their infrastructure. Alas many of the jack boot dictators that Americans supported, had no interest in developing democratic government. Our conversation did touch on what had happened in the British General Election and just how hard it was for a third party to break through a two block system. The clash of ideas between some kind of socialism and western free enterprise was dividing the world causing bloodshed and misery and yet Nixon and Mao were talking to each other.

Nhon and I left the American Embassy in Paris in a pleasantly optimistic mood. I believe Mark Pratt was genuinely concerned at what would happen to so many of those he must have known in South Vietnam, if the Communists took over. The news from Cambodia was that Pol Pot was ruthlessly slaughtering supporters of the American backed side and only beleaguered cities resisted the advance of his forces.

Back in Britain, a group of Vietnamese had visited with a young girl who had survived the My Lai Massacre. She told her story of how she hid under the bodies of her family until the American soldiers' ceased firing. No one could fail to be moved by her emotional testimony. When I attempted to speak in Vietnamese to her she put a consoling hand on my arm and said 'You're hopeless.'

Following the resignation of Nixon the military situation for the South Vietnamese regime deteriorated faster than expected. The Province Chief of Pleiku had sold the fuel on the black market and held his hand out for more. This time it was not forthcoming and thirty aircraft were captured on the ground because of the lack of fuel. Thus began the erosion of an armed force of a million men and an air force numerically larger than the RAF.

By a coincidence I was in the South Vietnamese Embassy in Kensington where I told one of the diplomats there, that I had just heard on the BBC that Da Nang had been captured by the Communists. He replied 'No, surely you mean Hue.' He eagerly strode to his teleprompter that he had not seen that morning. His face was white as he returned saying 'you must excuse me but I must speak to my family.' His reaction was understandable for there had been such a cruel war regardless of politics. His concern was for his direct family and the many associated with the government who desired to take their loved ones out of the country.

Thieu ordered a retreat from the northern provinces of South Vietnam turning a defeat into a rout of the country. From a situation in the fifties when Eisenhower had said, 'If there was to be an election in South Vietnam four out of five would vote for Ho Chi Minh'. There was a situation created after the killing of Kennedy that included drafting all those of military age into the armed forces. In an Orwellian way each man had a little gun in his hand and a larger one in his back. He may have hated the government he served but he feared those who he had fought against; the survival instinct prevailed. That was what held South Vietnam together.

Now South Vietnam was to fall like a rotten plum from a tree. Officers, province chiefs, government officials, police officers all saw and heard what was happening in Cambodia, with bloody and cruel reprisals as Pol Pot forces advanced through villages and were now fighting in the outskirts of the larger cities. They feared for themselves and their families and most of them simply wanted to leave the sinking ship. Even the bar girls who had befriended Americans were becoming desperate to find a way out.

Mrs Nhon was fearful for her family and children and sensed that those who stayed behind in South Vietnam would suffer hideous austerity if there was a Communist takeover without any kind of international aid. Her brother was a pilot in the Vietnamese Air Force so covert plans were made to smuggle the whole family onto an aircraft and fly out of the country. When they did so Thieu ordered it to be shot down but his order was countermanded by Khan who knew that Thieu and Ky were planning to do the same and soon depart. The aircraft carrying the Nhon family was to land safely in Singapore.

Nhon was pleased that his family were safe but still offered both the Communists and the South Vietnamese government, to return if he could play a useful part in bringing the bloodshed to a halt. Doug Grey had been granted money to leave Vietnam but instead spent the money on buying rice and chicken soup for the children. Eventually American friends persuaded him to leave Saigon. I had several long conversations with Mark Pratt who told me that Don was presently in Africa. I didn't question what he was doing there but I guessed that it might be to secure some fuel. The pace of the Communist advance must have alarmed Americans as the hue and cry around the Embassy was turning into a great panic and so many files of collaborators had still not been shredded.

On the seventeenth of April Cambodia fell to the Communists and film of soldiers threatening the residents in Phnom Penh were shown all over the world. Thieu and Ky flew out of Vietnam handing power to the elderly Vice President Houng. Thieu was seen taking large gold bars out of the country by Big Minh who persuaded him to leave some behind.

What was to be the last weekend before the war ended, I spent time with Nhon and a group of triumphant representatives of North Vietnam and the Viet Cong. Their troops were now advancing from Xuan Loc and some had severed the road from Bien Hoa to Saigon. The Communists were keen to minimise casualties and waited patiently for American employees and collaborators to leave, though more and more anxious families turned up in the hope of joining the exodus.

The war was effectively over when after a few days power was passed to Big Minh. Saigon and the Mekong Delta were still controlled by the South Vietnamese Government and it was possible in theory to continue the bloodshed a little longer. The Communists had a date in mind when they would like to enter Saigon; May the 1st. If that date was passed Ho Chi Minh's birthday would be celebrated later in the month.

Nhon's friends were keen for me to travel to Saigon but there was little to achieve except to advise Big Minh to announce an end of the war and begin a stand still cease fire. The only bargaining point would be to stop the slaughter and possibly enable the huge international aid which was promised, to be made available. Big Minh had a brother who was a General in the North Vietnam Army and after consultation he decided to surrender so the Communists won an outright victory.

Cambodia became a killing field until the Vietnamese invaded a few years later and numerous Vietnamese families attempted to leave the dire poverty in boats. South Vietnamese ex-military were consigned to serve in rural areas to increase food production.

The aftermath of the war left a huge legacy of disabled people and casualties continued for many years from unexploded weapons and the affects of the chemicals such as Agent Orange, which produced several generations of malformed babies. It is estimated that around ten million were killed in the American War in Vietnam, Cambodia and Laos. Alongside the sixty thousand Americans killed in combat one hundred thousand suicides have been recorded.

Yet over the years Vietnam has become a popular holiday destination for Australians and Americans and tourists often proclaim what lovely people the Vietnamese are.

Brian in his twenties; the photo was taken in Vietnam.
All photos are the author's own, unless otherwise specified

Viet Cong bunker being bombed.

Refugee camp in Vietnam.

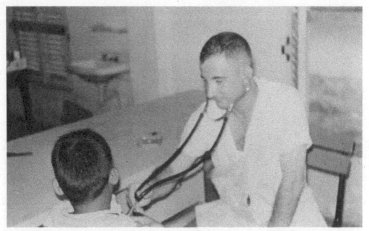

Dr Adrian Pointer: member of the British Medical Team and colleague in the Paris Peace Talks.

Protesters to end the Vietnam War which became a global campaign.

Photo courtesy of the SEARCH Foundation, from the collections of the State Library of New South Wales

Sky raider before dive bombing raid.

Bombing Viet Cong bunker; photo taken from inside
aircraft. In a secluded corner of the Tan Son Nhut Airport
many hundreds of wrecked aircraft and helicopters were
collected covered with beetroot red blood.

Some of the teachers of the International School in
Saigon together with Brian.

Two Vietnamese orphans being treated for polio.

In a land of orphanages many died of malnutrition and some with napalm burns and some to this day are still being born with physical defects from Agent Orange.

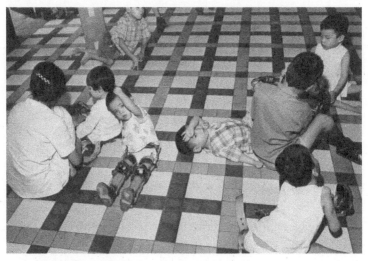

Doug Grey's polio project saved numerous lives.

Artillery fire could be heard every night throughout
Vietnam together with the rumble of bombing.

Photo courtesy by The New York Public Library on Unsplash

Sixty thousand American combatants were killed during
the war and double that number have committed
suicide since the war ended.

*Photo courtesy of the National Archives and its Education Team and
published in the Public Domain*

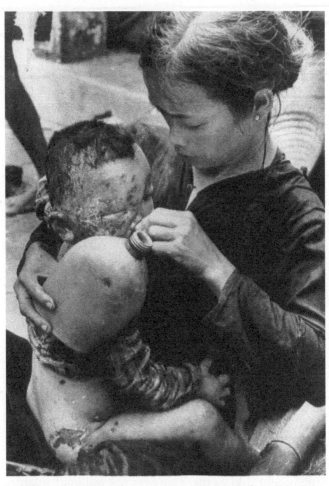

Women and children were the biggest casualties of the Vietnam War. Fatalites since the war ended from chemicals and unexploded munitions now exceed three million. Amputees and seriously injured victims are three times that number.

Photo courtesy of Alamo and printed under license

Brian in 2019 handing a cheque of £2500 for Agent
Orange victims to the Vietnam Ambassador. The
Ambassador told us there are over five million casualties
including three million fatalities mostly after the War.
Agent Orange is the chemical used by the
Americans to provide a clearer firing line.

Photo courtesy of the Vietnam Embassy

Jeremy Thorpe the leader of the Liberal Party and the first
party leader to be charged with conspiracy to murder.
Photo Keystone Press printed under license from Alamy Stock

Brian and Martin Vye at the start of election campaign
for election to the Kent County Council.

This girl walked for two days and nights just to meet us and plead for us to support her in education.

The blind school in Dharan which was one more project that the Gurkha Peace Foundation has supported.

Brian in Nepal at one of the Gurkha Peace Foundation projects.

Photos courtesy of the Gurkha Peace Foundation

Gurkha protesters in military uniform.

A triumphant Joanna Lumley outside the Old Bailey.

Two Victoria Cross holders at first denied access to Britain for medical treatment even though they had saved numerous British lives.

Brian with Joanna Lumley and leaders of the Campaign for Gurkha Justice outside the Old Bailey.

Photos courtesy of Martin Howe and Company

Chapter 10

National and Local Politics

Throughout, I have attempted to record historical events and conversations as objectively and clearly as memory allows. I have tried to concentrate on political memoirs and minimise personal details.

In an age when most of us have valued friends together with much loved members of our families across the political spectrum, I believe it is right to establish my heritage that has built my philosophy, faith and core values before entering the murky world of party politics. I was born into a working class family and my father was a Christian Socialist. He practiced what he preached and worked hard all his life: he installed in me a strong work ethos. Though he was active in the Labour Party he chose as my godfather a son of the local Tory alderman, who was sadly killed in the RAF. Politics never came between his friends and he installed in me the idea that it was right to vigorously campaign for what one believed but to always avoid personal malevolence.

Curiosity and a desire to improve life for those around me was also a driving force. As a child of five I remember being carried into a cinema to see a full length film of the concentration camps as they were being liberated. My parents couldn't find a baby sitter and on entering the cinema the commissioner said I shouldn't see this film. My father's reply was 'He'll fall asleep as soon as we go inside.' Needless to say that was a reason for staying awake and afterwards my first political question was 'Why do they (Germans) hate the Jews?

Though born in Deal I was transported to a village in Yorkshire in 1940 where I spent my earliest memories and was a happy and spoilt child of five before travelling back to Kent early in 1945 just before the war ended. My father had managed to hold on to a Ford Prefect car and enough fuel to drive back with. It was a long tiring journey taking ten or twelve hours. There were no motorways; sign posts had been removed to confuse the Germans if they had invaded but certainly they then confused the British.

To add to the confusion city and town centres had been devastated by bombing. The most vivid memories of that journey were the sight of half demolished houses with a bath or bed hanging out over a gaping hole; a stark reminder that someone had once lived there. I recalled my own grandparents being blitzed out of their London home and sharing our small terraced house in Yorkshire for a few weeks until they were able to return to another dwelling.

Just after moving into our new home in Deal, I recall great outbursts of joy when the war in Europe came to an end. Everyone came onto the streets to greet each other and street parties were organised for children. Many families must have emptied their larders of a packet of jelly or cake mixture in order to treat the children.

In July a General Election was held and our little Ford car was plastered with Labour Party posters. Of course I knew little of this but I overheard conversations of my Father's colleagues talking of personal experiences. Their generation had experienced the depression of the thirties and the hopelessness of unemployment. Living within a mining community there was bitterness of their treatment, such as a lack of pit props that led to disasters and the exposure to silicosis, from stone dust, that stayed in the chest and lungs.

During my childhood I was heavily influenced by what I heard and particularly family experiences. One of my uncles on holiday from Yorkshire, woke the whole household up as he dashed to an open window and stuck his head out. The story emerged the next morning that his father had been entombed alive and his mother went insane thinking about his fate. My own father was to suffer from silicosis and a military doctor ordered him to not go down the mine again. Three times he went before a board to claim compensation and was twice turned down, though on the third attempt he was awarded full compensation. Determined to continue work he received less than £900 settlement to help him become self employed.

From the age of eight I worked under the direction of my father. There was a plague of rabbits from the coastal mined strip once it had been cleared. My father working with a couple of friends culled as many as thirty in one night. Once they were skinned and cleaned my job was to carry six at a time and knock on the doors to sell them. There was such a lack of meat that almost every door that I knocked on was eager to buy a rabbit. From this small enterprise my father began a greengrocery round using his car and trailer and eventually a van until he could afford to rent a shop.

During these formative years I shared many of my father's beliefs in social justice and his disappointment at union leaders. Responsible unionists had visited Germany to advise them to just have one union per industry and to elect an employee on to the management team of large industries. Such policies provided Germany with a successful economic structure. However British unions continued to exist as a federal structure. When the coal industry was nationalised the management board asked the union to cooperate electing employees onto the National Coal Board: they refused and wanted to keep fighting against management. An admiral was then appointed as the head of the Kent coalfield and in his first speech he said 'I've never been down a mine but it sounds like fun.'

I always had an empathy with the left of politics from an historical perspective. From the Levellers, the Chartists, the Suffragettes, the campaigners to abolish slavery and introduce electoral reformers, to the first old age pensions and universal healthcare. However I had a growing love of community politics and economics based upon human need. These ideas were expressed by Schumacher when he wrote 'Small is beautiful' stressing the need for medium term technology and that balance between macro and micro structures was expressed by Jo Grimond who called for a realignment of the left.

After completing a three year agricultural course my father offered me a partnership which led to several years of hard work for my parents and me, creating a small company which eventually led to the creation of a small fruit farm and wholesale distribution business throughout east Kent.

Only those with a DNA for either religion or politics will understand the motivation and obsession to pursue moving away from commercial success and working intensively for a cause that was thwart with risks. After studying a night course of sociology by the W.E.A. which provided Oxford

University lecturers, I took an active interest in politics and soon found myself the Parliamentary Agent for the Canterbury Constituency in the first General Election, that I was old enough to vote in, for the Liberal Party. This was followed by another General Election eighteen months later in which we registered the ninth best result in Britain.

Still in my twenties I was elected to the national policy making group of the Liberal Party. This gave me an opportunity to exchange views with many of those with ambitions to enter Parliament and several who were to take up a career in law. We younger Liberals were described as Jo Grimond's Red Guard by the Tory press, as we dared to campaign against apartheid, criticise American carnage in Vietnam and propose a pension system similar to that in the Scandinavian countries. As a contrast, the Young Conservatives were openly encouraging the South African regime to execute Nelson Mandela.

At this time in the sixties Labour policy was dictated by unions that had a block vote, so an individual member had little chance to determine policy. They planned to extend still further the number of nationalised industries with little change of status for employees. I believed the two major parties were similar and were too centralised and elitist. Many years later I would recall the words of Jo Grimond who said 'that there were conservatives in every political party.' At this time I didn't think that this would one day apply to liberals who too would be throttled by the embrace of the establishment.

Until the sixties the Conservative and Labour Parties operated almost as a duopoly, with smaller parties including the Liberals squeezed out. Three former members of the Liberal Party joined the other parties and became Prime Ministers:

Winston Churchill, Clem Atlee and Harold Wilson. When the charismatic Jo Grimond became leader of the Liberal Party it was close to being dissolved. In the last days of Winston Churchill's premiership, he had offered the leader of the Liberal Party, Clem Davies, to join him within the Conservative Party. Though this had been refused, in the 1955 General Election less than a million votes were cast for the Liberals and of the five seats retained it was only a result of Conservatives not standing against them that this number was elected.

As soon as Grimond became leader he said we either have to fight back or get out of the system. Speaking about basic policies he struck a chord with many of the electors and debate within the Universities and success in by-elections resulted in two remarkable victories in Torrington and later in Orpington, which raised an interest in a possible Liberal future. Even political opponents admitted that if Jo Grimond was to join either of the other political parties he would immediately become a contender for the top job.

Jo Grimond was very much a believer in the European Community and expressed the view that if we were in it at the start we would be in a stronger position to influence it. His belief in the role of small businesses and community values meant his vision was for a community that would be beneficial for the people and participating democracy, operating from the bottom up rather than a remote centralised and elitist bureaucracy. One policy of the Liberals at that time was, that there should be a minister to represent small business at the highest cabinet level. This long discarded policy could have made all the difference to how the European Community was developed and over the years perceived.

In those days there was a clear dichotomy between the party of labour and the party of capital. More often than not it was identified by class distinctions. In the pre Thatcher days the Conservatives were a status quo party and Labour was dominated by union leaders who were more concerned with industrial conflict than any kind of wealth creation. The result was a stagnant economy that lost the competitive edge, that began a long and steady decline including the loss of the British car industry. There were some extraordinary strikes including one where wood and metal workers went on strike because they could not agree which of them should weld together in the ship building industry.

As a teenager I came across an electricity worker who boasted that his idea of economics was to do as little as possible for as much as he could get and he was brazenly practising what he preached. A contrast to this was in agriculture where the farmers, smallholders and farm workers worked long and hard. Kent was then called the Garden of England and there were numerous smallholdings that were highly productive. The freehold land and dwellings belonged to the state and gave farm workers a chance to become tenant farmers. At this time the revenue from agriculture was six times greater than our biggest export which was cars. In Kent, Wye Agricultural College worked in tandem with farmers and smallholders, with advice and support with research and development, such as soil analysis and cold storage facilities. Lecturers enjoyed the practical work of market development and the interaction with producers.

Of course the smallholders could be more efficient with support and investment but the beady eyes of financiers were focused on the value of dwellings and land. Responsibility of overseeing the smallholdings was in the hands of the County Councils and so despite the demand for farm workers to become tenant farmers which was greater than ever, the financiers wanted to boost their budgets by selling both the land and the dwellings. This meant that land was sold for less intensive farming and dwellings were sold off to satisfy eager housing demands. This was perhaps the beginning of the flog everything mentality, even before Thatcher.

Where economics and technology demanded larger units Liberals believed in the profit sharing principle of co-ownership. Schumacher believed that medium term technology often related to building economics based upon human need and community values. Units that were very large often created a soulless atmosphere with remote bosses and power becoming centralist and elitist. In simplest jargon the needs of sleazy money lenders, arms dealers and oil barons hijacked localism and eroded any sense of purpose but the greed of a minority to accumulate wealth: brazen wealth alongside dismal poverty, does not in my mind equate with a healthy democracy but demoralises the large majority.

Holland is currently the second highest exporting country of agricultural products; only the United States exports more. In recent years marked or small apples have been exported to Holland where they have been made into juice or apple pies and sold back to Britain. The Dutch produce chipped and peeled potatoes ready for sale to chip shops while British growers have barns full of potatoes unsold. I am told that lorry drivers delivering to Holland are made welcome and invited to have breakfast as the vehicles are being unloaded. Their counterparts in Britain are told to go away if they are too early or arrive during a lunch break.

Though today it is still a minority idea, the policy of the Liberal Party was that Britain should share a comprehensive nuclear deterrent but should not duplicate what we already had by retaining a so called independent weapon. In other words our policy was exactly the same as Australia, Canada and Germany and numerous other countries, that we should rely upon the United States for the deterrent factor and transfer resources into strengthened strategic forces. This was the policy of Grimond, and was continued by Thorpe and Steel until David Owen took over. To this day, all three parties continue with the same policy even though Mrs Thatcher's defence minister and many senior military men believe that Grimond was right, as our real threat is not from Russia but suicidal terrorists.

Returning to my personal experiences, I believed that the Liberal Party was fairly sound on policy but needed to concentrate on building resources and organisational structure. In hindsight I still believe that if Liberals had continued where Grimond left off, there would be a Liberal Government today similar to that of Canada. I had spoken at a fringe meeting at the Liberal Party Assembly about opportunities and mentioned what a wonderful institution the National Liberal Club was and yet they still didn't allow women members. As soon as I finished speaking Jeremy Thorpe spoke up and clearly didn't like my suggestion that there should be women members of the National Liberal Club.

At the last meeting of the Liberal Policy forum before I went to Vietnam, the new party leader, Jeremy Thorpe, sat next to me at both the morning and afternoon session. I had a good impression of him and was sympathetic, when he was savagely attacked by all and sundry at this time. Taking over from Jo Grimond was a hard act to follow and I believed he needed more time especially as he had recently married and had understandably spent a great deal of time with his new wife.

On returning to Britain in 1970, one of the first leaders I introduced Professor Nhon to was Jeremy Thorpe. I believe that Nhon was the first Vietnamese that Thorpe had spoken to who spoke impeccable English and he began to speak in French, but for my sake the conversation continued in English. After an intensive discussion, Thorpe was excited that he should be asked to introduce Nhon to the Prime Minister Harold Wilson and said "let me have a brief written outline and I will do everything that I can to help." Eric Lubbock too was enthusiastic about what Nhon was doing, though of course General Don doused cold water on us all by reversing what he had previously stated back in Vietnam.

Conversing in Liberal circles the name of Peter Bessell was often mentioned. He had been a Liberal M.P. who was now living in America. He had a good reputation on transport but he was always very right wing on foreign policy, but this had never been his brief, so I didn't take much notice of him especially after he was considered a somewhat corrupt individual from the past. He had made a brief trip to Vietnam I believe long before I did but what I did not know was that he was a C.I.A. agent and a close friend of Thorpe. His influence on Thorpe was close and personal but certainly not known to me and the general public at the time.

As previously stated, much of my time was spent dealing with negotiations relating to Vietnam. The first General Election of 1974 was held early in the year. It was cold and miserable, made worse by electricity black outs and four day weeks. There was a clash of wills between Ted Heath's government and the miners. He and the Conservatives believed that even though they still had until June 1975 before the need to call a General Election, that this was an opportunity to win a massive majority. Cyril Smith a newly elected Liberal M.P. phoned up Joe Gormley the miners' leader and asked if he would be prepared to speak directly to the representatives of the three political parties in order to settle the strike. His positive reply was made public and it did take the wind out of the Conservatives sail, as it showed that the strike could be settled without a General Election.

Several friends of mine were standing as Liberal candidates so when John Holmes asked me to work for the party as Kent Coordinator for the period of the General Election I was happy to accept. The first task was to ensure that all the Kent constituencies had a suitable candidate in place. I felt a positive vibe at this time and John Holmes worked hard to fill all ninety seats in the Home Counties region. We knew that in the West Country they intended to fight every seat so we believed that if we could do the same it would send out a positive message to Liberals throughout the country. This would be the first time that Liberals were standing in almost all seats, since the disastrous General Elections in the early fifties. The very last seat to commit was Chatham and Rochester in Kent: fortunately we found a young barrister who qualified as a candidate and we were able to provide the constituency executive with assurances of backup.

I believed the first task was to strengthen the links between all the constituencies by providing names and phone numbers of key activists together with a comprehensive list of media links. The campaign was going well and there was a buzz of excitement in the committee rooms. On one particular evening I arrived home late and had just changed into my pyjamas when the phone rang. It was the candidate for Canterbury, Sarah Goulden. A man had arrived claiming that he and his company wished to pay for newspaper advertisements throughout Kent. Sarah asked if it was too late to send him round as she said that she believed that he was genuine.

It was almost midnight when, wearing my pyjamas and dressing gown, I received a ring ot the door and greeted Lou Cartier. He reminded me of Colombo the television character. Speaking softly he introduced himself as a managing director of a freezer food business with retail stores throughout Kent. All his directors were alarmed at the number of electricity cuts and were critical of Ted Heath's handling of the miners' strike. His firm spent a huge amount of money on newspaper advertising and wished to donate space to the Liberal Party in Kent. I explained the legality of dealing with each parliamentary agent and the registering of expenses. He agreed to this and most parliamentary candidates and agents agreed to working with Lou.

During the rest of the election campaign I worked closely with Lou who spent a great deal of money on the advertisements. Within a week or two he approached me by saying 'Get your leader off his arse.' He then volunteered to pay for an aircraft to fly Jeremy Thorpe around the country. I discussed his proposal with John Holmes and Tim Beaumont who was a senior activist and personal friend of Thorpe. He explained that Jeremy Thorpe had no intention of leaving North Devon for the duration of the election and a television link had been established in his constituency. A few years later I discovered that Thorpe was afraid that Norman Scott, a former gay lover was about to release love letters to the press, so he wished to stay local in order to deal with the threat.

The offer that Lou Cartier made was too good to dismiss so my thoughts first went to Jo Grimond, but he had retired and his constituency was in the far north; Orkney and Shetland. I then thought of Cyril Smith. He was a new M.P. but had made quite an impression in the media. Appearing on television with Jimmy Saville he described how his mother earned a living scrubbing the steps of the Mayor's Parlour in Rochdale. When he was made the Mayor of Rochdale he made his mother the Mayoress, so one day she scrubbed the floor and the next she became the Mayoress. This endearing story was reinforced by the fact that together, with his brother Norman, Cyril had created a company employing a hundred employees and gave 25% of the profits back to the workers on top of their salary. His self deprecating humour made him popular, with the story of when he addressed the Ginger Bread Club which campaigned for single parent families, he declared that he had been born out of wedlock. He declared 'that makes me the biggest bastard that you have ever known!'

Contact with Cyril Smith was made and direct contact with Lou helped to ensure that he agreed to fly to Kent and do a walk about in several Kent towns. I sat next to Lou in his Rochester office and discussed what would be required to make this event a success. Lou was prepared to bankroll the whole enterprise so we planned for Cyril to fly to Manston airport in Thanet where a group of supporters would be waiting. As we spoke, Lou rang up and ordered a small aircraft that would be available for the day starting early in the morning, by flying Cyril from Lancashire to Manston and departing from Rochester airport later in the afternoon. He then ordered a coach for the day to carry supporters and journalists first to a factory near Whitstable, a part of the Canterbury constituency, then to Faversham, Sittingbourne, Gillingham, Chatham and finally to Maidstone, before he would depart from Rochester. Including the Thanet constituency where we planned for him to land, six constituencies would participate in the day's activity. Cyril would then fly back to attend a rally in Lancashire. Lou asked one of his staff to arrange for six girls to wear orange mini-skirts for the event as they would hand out leaflets for the walkabouts. Lou and I drove to London to pick up election material and posters and we had cooperation on reaching the media. Never forgetting detail, Lou even provided wine and refreshments for the journalists as they travelled on the coach.

On the morning of the event my phone was hot; as soon as I put it down there was another call from a journalist asking for more details and location of the airport. As I eventually arrived at Manston a crowd of supporters and journalists had gathered just on the perimeter of the small airport. Around thirty journalists were present together with three separate television crews. Every national newspaper was present together with local ones. Until this time I don't think the Liberals had ever enjoyed such attention from the media.

As I entered the throng I was told that a bolshie official had ordered all the rosettes to be removed before Liberals could enter the reception area to greet Cyril. I was about to protest to the official when one parliamentary candidate quietly whispered to me, 'Let it go Brian, the cameras have picked it up and even showed babies being deprived of their rosette; he will look a fool and it will do us no harm at all.'

There was no time to argue as everyone was allowed in and the little aircraft was just about to land. When it did so out came thirty stone Cyril wearing the biggest rosette that I've ever seen in my life.

'Careful Cyril, wearing that rosette' shouted one Liberal supporter.

'Why is it the wrong colour?' Cyril responded.

'No, they wouldn't let us in without covering our rosettes up,' I shouted back.

'Oh tell them to get stuffed' came the loud reply from Cyril.

We all greeted Cyril as we departed from the airport and began to reveal our rosettes. The television cameras looked at the cheerful throng and also had a casting look back at the stone faced official. Cyril's response was broadcast on BBC and ITV news programmes and relayed all over the world. According to one opinion poll, his remark won the Liberals a million votes because people were fed up with soulless officials ordering them about.

After the fall of Saigon in 1975, I wished to play a part in British politics in a professional capacity. John Holmes had been promoted to be Chief Agent and encouraged me to apply for his old position as Home Counties Organiser. I did so and had a fair hearing but there were two men who had made a bigger contribution to the party than I, who also applied. One had stood as the parliamentary candidate in a by-election and the other one was destined to soon become the head of Liberal Party Organisation. Nevertheless, I did work in a number of different ways for the Liberal Party which introduced me to the Marginal Seats Sector and the Celebrity Committee. During this time I had an active part in organising a by-election which was different from other elections and I gained useful experience.

As in life, it is often the little things that make a difference. I was responsible for organising about a third of the Carshalton constituency which was furthest from the High Street HQ. I recall a bitterly cold March when this by-election was held and it was at a time when the first whiff of scandal reached the media. There was mention of a bank that had charged extortionate interest rates which Jeremy Thorpe had a financial interest in and for the first time there was a mention of Norman Scott and a homosexual relationship with Thorpe. It was important for the Liberal Party that this by-election was not a complete disaster.

One supporter handed me a £5 donation which instead of handing over immediately, I asked a kindly and willing supporter to start a soup kitchen with it. This meant that every volunteer canvasser or leaflet distributer was offered a bowl of soup and a roll and a cup of tea before or after they had spent time delivering on the streets. Volunteers had come after work in the city and appreciated the gesture and contributed for the soup. Those who had intended to work for the party once a week returned three times in a week and soon this part of the constituency was the most advanced, both in canvassing and distributing leaflets and the original £5 contribution was increased considerably. Soon this more remote part of the constituency displayed more posters and I believe delivered the most votes for the party. It was not a great result but it was certainly not a disaster that some had predicted.

Unlike the two major parties, the Liberal Party lacked financial support from big business or the unions but so many good people at the grass roots of the party desired healthy community values together with social justice. They resembled a non league football side playing against a premier league club. I was astounded when John Spiller who was one of the party's most respected campaigners told me that the National Liberal Club was about to close. I had been a member for several years since Tommy Nudds, the candidates' secretary had introduced me and had expressed my views that this was a wasted asset.

On hearing the news I immediately travelled to London and spoke with the club secretary Coss Bilson, who confirmed the news and assured me that there was nothing that anyone could do. He said that only a wealthy benefactor could save the club. I didn't argue but I believed that what it did need was some- one with imagination and a modicum of business ability. He handed me a copy of accounts and told me that Jeremy Thorpe had passed a copy of them to George de Chabris but there had been no response and now the club was to close within a few days. When I studied the accounts it confirmed my belief that the National Liberal Club was a great asset that was about to be thrown away. Indeed, I was astounded that with so little rent for the lease and a hundred and forty bedrooms on the equivalent of the top three floors on a ten story building on the Thames Embankment it was almost impossible not to make money from the Club.

I made my way to the home of George de Chabris who lived close to my home in Canterbury. After a discussion with him, we were soon driving towards the Club in his new Rolls Royce car. As we entered what resembled a mausoleum, I was full of enthusiasm and promised that if George was to take it on, I would be prepared to work alongside him.

In hindsight if I had known what would happen both in the Club and Liberal Party in the next few months, I would not have been so keen to be involved. Events would lead to a murder conspiracy trial of Jeremy Thorpe and a former treasurer; a personal clash with a powerfully built paedophile; a reign of fear and terror for many of the staff in the Club and the growing knowledge that honest senior police officers and journalists were prevented from doing their job.

Chapter 11

The National 'Buggerall' Club

George de Chabris and I wandered around the National Liberal Club and I knew that every minute he became more keen to see the huge asset that was being offered to him. A few hapless souls were gathered in the bar but the bedroom roster showed that most of them were unoccupied. Gladstone's tatty old but famous bag was encased in a glass display cabinet. A large portrait of a young Winston Churchill was placed in the large foyer and a portrait of Gladstone's first Cabinet hung on the wall. I had previously been told the space between government ministers was where Sir Charles Dilke had once stood, but after his scandal of sleeping with two women at the same time he had been painted over.

We walked up the wide marble stairway then passed into the large smoking room, where further portraits of Lloyd George, Campbell Bannerman and Asquith hung on the wall. I was once told that in the 1905 General Election as results were coming through they were flashed onto a magic lantern where all four future prime ministers were watching. It was hard to imagine that at that time Britain had an empire of a quarter of the world's population and was possibly the most powerful country in the world. The National Liberal Club was called the focus for radical reform. Now it was reduced to this squalid dilapidated empty building.

George de Chabris and I then walked past the Lady Bonham Carter room which was for the ladies only. As Griff Evans once said "we have made a concession to allow ladies into the club as long as they don't sleep with their husbands." On the Thames side of the building was the palatial dining room with a statue of Gladstone standing at the entrance. This backed onto a wide esplanade that looked out over the Embankment and the River Thames. George and I both envisioned Paris like parasols under which drinks and light refreshments could be served throughout the summer. The empty dining room and balcony space emphasised the hideous neglect of the building and when we strolled into the kitchen we discovered a thick layer of grease over work benches and ovens. We both agreed that if a health inspector was to see this sight it would be immediately closed down.

We walked up to the next floors and discovered the wonderful library in which every election address from the birth of democracy was held. I hoped that I would one day have an opportunity to browse through these brochures. The top three floors of the building contained 140 bedrooms. The top floor was used by waiters and servants but it left almost a hundred bedrooms available either for members or hired out to other groups. Everywhere there were signs of dilapidation and neglect but the elderly Irish servants kept the rooms clean and usable.

We strode down to the ground floor past the row of offices and Victorian loos and then descended to the large snooker room that contained three tables. This was where the television programme 'Pot Black' was held and which developed into a more lucrative game when coloured television became universal. George commented that there was room down here for a sauna, gymnasium and even a squash court. We passed the small balcony which Gladstone would talk to the multitude, ten or twelve feet below. In an age before microphones sound travelled better from a higher altitude. We then inspected the wine cellar which had seen better and fuller days.

After glancing both outside and inside the building, we came to the conclusion that the building though neglected was structurally sound but that the heating system needed attention and the kitchen needed cleaning up. There was need to create a long term plan where bedrooms would become en suite. The immediate situation would be to reassure existing members that the club had a future and start to build the membership and fill the bedrooms.

My original idea was to contact a few wealthy Liberal Party benefactors to build a syndicate but there was little time to do this and pound signs were flashing in George's eyes, so he was eager to take on the responsibility himself. I agreed to work with George in a week or two once I had honoured my responsibility with the Party but with one important proviso, that we lower the annual membership fee and do away with the introduction fee. I also insisted that we would welcome women members immediately. That meant we would have to build a few more loos as the lack of plumbing was the usual excuse for not allowing women members. George agreed to my conditions and I looked forward to the challenge.

In the next few days George de Chabris wasted no time in completing the formalities with the trustees to take over the club; I understand they were relieved to pass on the responsibility, as they feared there might be financial penalties claimed by the landlords, the Crown Commissioners. With the help of Jeremy Thorpe, the national newspapers were told that a wealthy benefactor had been found to save the National Liberal Club. A dinner had been held in which Jeremy Thorpe told the guests that the de Chabris family would be remembered alongside other great Liberal families such as the Asquith's, the Lloyd George's and the Gladstone's. George had responded to such lavish praise by claiming that he saw no reason why, with financial backing Britain should not have a Liberal Government just like his native Canada.

About ten days after my initial visit to the club with George, I arrived on a Monday morning to start work with him. He greeted me by saying, "we all have to muck in to keep the place ticking." The middle aged and elderly women who dealt with reception and bedroom booking had been kept on, and the Irish women were still seeing to the bedrooms but several key staff had left, including those working in the bar. George asked me to help him carry several tins of paint back to the club, as he had apparently started one man painting. I thought this was a bit strange but cooperated and when I returned with him he introduced me to Mike Wood whom he had appointed as manager.

'Can you help Mike in the bar just until we are able to hire staff as a few old members are arriving and there is no one to serve them?'

I did try to help and found myself serving some of the senior officers of the party including our President Elect Basil Goldstone. I was quite hopeless as a waiter but at least thirsts were eventually quenched after a long wait, and I had some light hearted banter with Basil. Mike Wood was strutting about shouting at staff who were trying to provide an improvised salad bar and lunch. His manner resembled an overzealous sergeant major. He then started to shout at me until I reminded him that I was not a bar man and was simply helping out; at least I had kept a few key members supplied with drinks.

At the first opportunity when lunch time drinkers were leaving and George de Chabris had returned, I spoke to him and we agreed on terms of reference for what Wood and I would do. George agreed, that I could offer each member who gathered in the early evening a free drink. I accepted that a general manager was needed for the hiring and firing of staff and the place was desperate for a complete shake up, though my first impressions of Wood were not favourable. My separate responsibilities were the retention and expansion of members, filling up the bedrooms and media. In the club's heyday there were flourishing circles such as golf, snooker, dinner debates etc, which I wished to restore. There was also work to be done on rebuilding cooperation with other clubs with reciprocal arrangements all round the world. Using my political links I would try to bring Liberal Party Organisation and similar elements into the club. This would mean more people would eat and drink within the premises.

My long term aspirations were to create an advisory group of leading Liberals such as David Penhaligon, John Holmes, Basil Goldstone and Cyril Smith, to strengthen the links between party activists and the club. I was not convinced that the reactionary clique that almost ran the club into the ground, were liberals and given the chance I believed it would like to return to an elitist and exclusive club. I was enthusiastic with the energy and innovation of George de Chabris but was somewhat concerned that the profit motive was uppermost in his mind, rather than any altruistic purpose. My vision was to create a Mecca for progressive debate where men and women would fully participate. I always believed in breaking down the barriers of class, creed and race, so the elitist element disgusted me.

Despite his loud voice and constant request to advance yet another task without giving time to complete an existing one, I came to like George and his family. As time passed I discovered that there were two sides to him, the one that I liked and another one that was prepared to be devious and dishonest. Even before I started work in the club I discovered that the Gladstone Library had been transferred to Bristol University and that some of the 'I Spy' caricatures had disappeared together with a few portraits.

Worse still, just as I was trying to reassure members of a more positive future, one of the snooker tables had been taken away in the middle of the night and the removal was seen by one of the members. The next morning Wood had a smirk on his face after completing this task. He encouraged George in his unsavoury if not dishonest behaviour. There was no excuse for this asset stripping as within days we were transforming the cash flow situation. I expressed my displeasure when George turned up and told him that this was undermining my position. I emphasised that the sooner we build up the membership the more support we would have with diners and drinkers and the money would flow in.

On a positive note George acquired a secretary; Carol was a tall and beautiful Texan girl from Dallas who had previously worked with Robin Cook and also with two Liberal M.P.s. Her temperament matched that of George; when he shouted at her she shouted right back. I also acquired an excellent P.A. Vivien

Gay. She was an erudite and well educated girl but despite her upper crust background was easy to work with and became a huge help to me. Not only did she keep an up to date diary but her diplomatic skills guided me on who I should prioritise with time and meetings.

I would begin each day by glancing through all the newspapers that were delivered to the smoking room. Media coverage was reasonably good for the Club to start with but George sometimes put his foot in it and one paper discovered that he was American rather than Canadian and that he had previously used several different names. The most memorable one was 'His Serene Highness'. There were also unfavourable mentions of Jeremy Thorpe who was no longer the leader of the Liberal Party but was still the spokesman for foreign affairs.

Every week we advertised the Club in Liberal News together with regular articles. I was handed a list of officers in each of the constituencies so we sent them all brochures and an invitation to join the Club. I would follow this, by phoning them up so this would result in a regular number of new members.

Either through the Tourist Board or one of the hoteliers that George and I spoke to, we met a remarkable man called Eddie Eleazer. He spoke Arabic and Mandarin as well as the principle West European languages. Based in Éire he constantly travelled across the world filling aircraft with passengers and hotels with guests. He applied to the Guinness Book of Records to be the most travelled man other than astronauts but a Turkish man was able to show that he was slightly in front.

Eddie soon found a group that were looking for accommodation in London. We were soon able to fill the majority of bedrooms with groups of mostly young Swedish tourists. They wanted inexpensive bed and breakfast facilities in London. They loved shopping, sightseeing and visiting the theatres. George was compelled to spend a great deal of time abroad which meant that Eddie would phone me from some foreign country, often that I hadn't even heard of and inform me of how many tourists would be arriving and at what time and for how many days. I would then pass this on as soon as possible, so that the bedrooms would be available and full English breakfasts accommodated.

Within days rather than months the cash flow deficit was transformed into a healthy trading balance. The mostly young Swedish women enjoyed the facilities of the Club but some traditional old members were not very pleased.

'There are Swedish girls everywhere and some of them are inappropriately dressed, wearing tight jeans. Gladstone would not have approved' complained one elderly member.

'No but Lloyd George would', I replied facetiously.

Of course I explained it was an important part of the rescue plan which of course he should have known. Amongst the new recruits were the first three lady members. They were Margaret Wingfield, Penny Jessell and Susan Clark. I thought it was appropriate that poor Margaret was amongst the first lady members after hearing the story of how when she was canvassing in the Manchester Exchange by-election, it started to rain. Standing outside the entrance of a high rise block of flats she had stood contemplating with colleagues how to canvass the flats but when she felt it start to rain suggested that they move inside. One of her colleagues realised that it was only raining on them and looking up saw several youths urinating from a great height.

There were a number of amusing incidents and conversations during this time as we all had renewed confidence in our mission. The gay waiters who politely and efficiently served the meals would relax once the members had departed. One late evening they hadn't noticed that I was sat quietly in a corner reading some documentation and their frivolities began. They displayed a self deprecating humour with calls of 'I'm free' and 'What a gay day' were heard and then they playfully grasped each other's balls and wildly gesticulated with their hands. Not having had the privilege of a public school education I hadn't experienced anything quite like this before. As I emerged they were apologetic for their behaviour but as long as it wasn't in front of members I was not concerned, though on another occasion they had placed a cucumber between Gladstone's legs and forgot to retrieve it, so the next morning it was still visible for members and guests to see. Fortunately most members and guests saw the amusing side but a few members complained. The cucumber was soon removed and I did remind the member that Gladstone was popularly known as the 'peoples' willy.'

Three successful by-elections meant that Clement Freud, Cyril Smith and a Yorkshire lay preacher all shared the same room. Each was quite different to the other.

'He's a right bugger' began Cyril repeating what Freud had said to him. 'Do you know what he said to me? However many seats we win in the next election I'll still be able to get my leg over all of your secretaries.'

Though he was the grandson of Sigmund Freud this was a typical wind up as most of the secretaries were no more promiscuous than other girls, even if a few may have succumbed to his invitation to join him to see around Parliament or the

Playboy Club. Such an invitation would inevitably lead them to enjoy a very special meal that he would cook for them in his flat. At this time Freud regularly appeared alongside a dog with an expression similar to his own on television adverts. When he was seen in the street the kids would shout 'bow wow' but afterwards he would say 'I hate bloody dogs.' He would often arrive for meetings with a beautiful girl younger than his daughter. He would introduce them as his niece and everyone commented that he seemed to have a lot of nieces.

Negotiations between George and the former trustees of the Club were entirely dealt with by George but he wished me to deal with the representatives of the Crown Commissioners. Understandably they had been concerned when it appeared that the Club would close and also that the publicity George was having in the media was not always favourable. They were pleased that the Club was springing back to life and I reassured them that as the cash flow was improving, we would begin a long term business plan to improve the building inside and out.

George and I made contact with the representatives of the Westminster Chamber of Trade. We wished to fill the empty office space and offer corporate membership to small local businesses. We soon managed to let one floor to the Liberal Party Organisation, and accommodated the European move-ment, Liberal International, a French language school, a small publisher, the Liberal Electoral Reform Society and even one office to the Dalai Lama. I had lunch with the head of Liberal Publications to offer facilities which I believed would eventually be accepted once their existing agreements had been met.

George loved the ego boosting prestige of media publicity and agreed to appear for an interview with Jeremy Paxman. A few members including George's family crowded into the television room to watch. Paxman fired a few hostile questions about his other names and the fact that he was American rather than Canadian. Some of the allegations printed in The Times were mentioned to which George de Chabris coolly answered by saying "that he had instructed his lawyers to sue The Times for a million pounds." After this comment Paxman quickly closed the interview.

If a wealthy man issues a legal threat it would lead to a cautious approach by investigative journalists and editors alike but if such threats were not forthcoming eventually news hounds would become even more tenacious. George de Chabris had an enormous ego and enjoyed the favourable publicity that he received but he would eventually experience a more destructive force. He made the most incredible promises including an offer to hold a party inviting every member of the Liberal Party to attend. It could be done with forward planning but the Club had already experienced a small explosion in the entrance, which had scared a night porter who had originated from Londonderry. George had handed me a letter which he had received which was anonymous. Like the best film dramas it comprised of words cut out of newspapers and stuck on to a piece of paper. It stated 'Let us know when you are going to have your party so that we can plan to blow you up including that pervert Cyril Smith.'

At this time there was a constant drip of information emerging about the past life of Jeremy Thorpe and an inference that there was a strong link between de Chabris and Thorpe. Under these circumstances I advised George that we should postpone any plans for a party and if challenged, state that there were security problems that we did not wish to discuss.

The eccentricity of George was of increasing concern to me. He wished to start a campaign called 'Axe the Tax' which he wished me to be involved with. I refused to cooperate with this though I appreciated that there was a need to hypothecate tax and that most of us would like to pay less, however it should not be at the cost of diminishing healthcare and already inadequate pensions. For some reason he had booked a small aircraft to fly to the Isle of Skye but then cancelled it. Carol told me that he had asked her to arrange to hire a television studio but again she had to cancel it; and he told her that Jeremy Thorpe had arranged for him to practise interviewing techniques with the tutoring of Robin Day. I have no idea if this was true but if it helped him to be far more circumspect with the media it would be most welcome. Letters were arriving in the mail box of Liberal M.P.s and they would inevitably be passed on to me to answer.

Members of the Club were keen to hold a parliamentary presentation and reception to give them a chance to chat with the M.P.s. About a hundred and sixty guests turned up for this function. As each one entered the smoking room before meeting the line up of David Steel and his team, one competent waiter quickly wrote the name on a piece of paper and passed it to me and I would loudly proclaim the name of each guest. I had never experienced such a large number of titled guests. There were Lords and Ladies, Honourables, doctors, professors and councillors. An attractive woman in her late twenties arrived on the arm of an elderly lawyer. I read out her name as the Countess Veronica and thought no more about it until later in the evening. After spending the evening circulating with guests and friends, I eventually approached the Countess and after speaking to her declared that she spoke perfect English with no Italian accent.

'Oh Countess Veronica was the name that I used when I did my strip tease act.'

On a more sorrowful note Jeremy Thorpe attended with his second wife Marion. He was drawn and painfully aware that his position would become worse before it improved. I had more insight of what might develop from information from various investigative journalists, but despite his wrong doing I hated to see him so dreadfully miserable.

One weekend spent at home in Canterbury I received a phone call from a house master at King's School. I was told that de Chabris' son had been expelled and he had been unable to speak to his parents who were abroad. He had been expelled for distributing drugs to his fellow pupils. I was asked to visit him at his home in Charlton Park which I did, and found him happily in the company of his girlfriend. When George came back into the country he treated it as a big joke and I soon discovered that it was Mike Wood who had given him the drugs. A few days later sat in the smoking room, I heard Wood boasting to one of his friends that it would be easy to kill de Chabris junior and put his body through a large drain under the wine cellar that led to the River Thames. Apparently the boy had named Wood as the supplier of drugs.

Someone stuck a large picture of Hitler on the office door of Mike Wood. His reaction to this was to leave it up as he declared that it 'showed I'm doing a good job.' There was a constant stream of stories concerning Wood but they were simply hearsay and I had more than enough to do without prying too much. The relationship between Wood and Philip Watkins and de Chabris deteriorated after he caught them together in an obscure upstairs loo. Though I thought little of it at the time I happened to be passing as Wood emerged from his bedroom with two children of about eleven years old. He sheepishly said that they were his sons but didn't introduce them and was eager to part. At the time I was dreadfully naive but later I was to realise what may well have been happening.

One day near the foyer, Wood and de Chabris had a loud row that could be heard throughout the ground floor of the Club. 'You can keep your fucking job' Wood shouted at the top of his voice. I thought that would be the last I would see of Wood but when he had quietened down he changed his mind and said 'I will show him that he can't sack me; I'm bringing in some powerful business friends to talk to him.' Needless to say I had no idea what he was talking about but I listened without speaking.

A few days' later four men in suits waited in the reception area to see Wood. I heard him being beckoned on the calling service from my office, so popped my head round the corner to see who they were. They didn't look like usual business men and I soon learned that they were a night club owner with three of his bouncers who had travelled from South Wales to speak with Mike Wood and George de Chabris. I would later learn who they were but what was curious was that George was far more quiet and subdued with Wood being his usual cocky self after this meeting.

Carol was to approach me trembling like a leaf not long after this. She had left the office for an errand for George and Philip Watkins had joined him in his office and was deep in conversation. Hearing my name she hesitated before returning to George's office and listened in to their conversation. Philip prophetically said that he thought I was linked to Scotland Yard and he should try to get rid of me. George said he didn't think that was the case but the conversation continued with the mention of Norman Scott and the rumours circulating about Jeremy Thorpe.

At the time Peter Hain who was chairman of the Young Liberals wrote in his news sheet questioning who exactly George de Chabris was; the article headline asked 'Who is the God Father.' Talk of a hit man and a shot dog was increasingly mentioned in the press which made Carol frightened of what was going on particularly following a number of violent incidents involving Wood, which members of staff had spoken to her about.

I did my best to pacify Carol and she spoke of going back to America but I advised her to stay calm with her eyes and ears open but her mouth shut. In addition I said, if she heard any more conversations or events, to write them down and then pass to me and I would discuss matters with friends such as John Holmes and Basil Goldstone.

One more incident was just too much for me to bear. A sixteen year old boy approached me by asking me to take him to hospital as he had been beaten up and buggered. This I did and after hearing his story the next morning I confided in Basil; he had often said that as the Liberal Party President he was the conscience of the party. After listening to me he was shocked though not particularly surprised by these revelations. I said bluntly that I was not prepared to live with this situation now that I have been brought directly into the incidents. Either Wood would go or I would. Basil pleaded with me to write all these incidents down but stay calm as he shook his head saying 'What kind of people have we been working with?'

I had a great deal of respect for Basil and was guided by him but in the next few weeks either through Carol or Rory, the night porter, a great deal more information was accumulated. Rory knew that I was not a favourite of Wood and Watkins, who had given him a verbal warning and would like to be rid of him as they believed that he had heard too much.

Out of sight of Wood and his clique, Rory beckoned me to whisper 'Be careful Brian these people are violent; the other evening I was walking on the pavement just outside of the Club when a car pulled alongside me without stopping and two men stared at me menacingly without speaking. They continued at the same pace that I was walking so I increased my pace to draw closer to other pedestrians and the car eventually drew away.'

Rory was no shrinking violet but a tough Irish man who had come from Londonderry and had continued in his job even after experiencing an explosion in the entrance to the Club. He was a frightened man who knew of several violent incidents with Wood and had recognised seeing George Deakin named and photographed in the papers as the man who had hired the hit man for Jeremy Thorpe. My advice to him was to stay calm and carry on but let me know of any other incidents that he may experience.

When I prepared my statement for Basil Goldstone he looked at me wistfully and said 'Brian I daren't even look at it.

All my life I have worked for a party and cause that I believed in, yet even after receiving a great accolade and honour of becoming President I am confronted by criminal behaviour; I'm heartbroken, trying to concentrate on the altruistic heart of liberalism, is like farting against wind.'

Roger Courtier one of the investigative journalists building a mosaic of incidents surrounding Norman Scott and the shot dog incident, wished to bring two Welshmen into the Club to possibly look at the carpets which de Chabris had bought for the Club. John Le Mesurier was the Welsh carpet dealer who had been photographed handing over money to the hit man. I was relieved for the de Chabris family that the carpet link was not confirmed but in conversation over lunch next door in the Royal Horse Guards Hotel, one employee of Le Mesurier told of a conversation that he had had which he would be prepared to repeat in court. The second man who was present with his wife was a pools winner who had been advised on investments by David Holmes and Jeremy Thorpe. These two men were prepared to become prosecution witnesses if there was to be a criminal trial.

Within a few days I received a polite phone call from a police officer. 'Detective Chief Superintendent Challes would like to speak to you. Would it be convenient if he visited you in your home in Canterbury next Monday?'

Chapter 12

The Establishment Cover-Up

Two policemen came exactly at the agreed time, introduced themselves and sat down to coffee and biscuits. I had prepared a rough draft statement from which I believed they could extract a copy of the details that they may believe relevant. Both Detective Chief Superintendent Challes and his assistant carefully read my copy before asking questions. My knowledge was mostly hearsay and peripheral to the basic facts that their inquiry demanded. Whatever I said was in sorrow rather than anger, for I was still a Liberal and had once held Jeremy Thorpe in respect and empathy.

Our meeting was diplomatic and I signed a much abbreviated version of the original statement. I don't think even the most ambitious police officer envied them their task for the facts that were emerging were shocking and almost unbelievable, based upon a highly popular public figure who had friends in high places. Yet facts were being unearthed by investigative journalists that couldn't be ignored. How I wished that this scandal belonged to one of the other two political parties!

Harold Wilson the Prime Minister believed that B.O.S.S. the South African Intelligence Agency, had deliberately set Jeremy Thorpe up. Strong opposition to apartheid was led by Liberals and the Young Liberal leader Peter Hain was demonstrating this at sports grounds and on one occasion an over enthusiastic supporter even dug up a cricket pitch. Anything that hurt the Liberal Party would be welcomed by the racist regime in South Africa. Roger Courtier and Barrie Penrose, two B.B.C. journalists who had been approached by Wilson to investigate events soon returned to say that they believed the culprits responsible for the shooting incident was closer to home than South Africa.

Media frenzy followed the investigative police officers around but I was pleased that my meeting with them was unknown to almost all of them. I continued to work in the National Liberal Club but my great enthusiasm was beginning to wane. At an earlier stage I had described to a friend that working in the National Liberal Club was like making love to a beautiful woman in a mine field. It was exciting and pleasurable but you never knew when it was going to end in a big bang.

Brendon Alimo, the architect, spent many hours inspecting the heating system to ensure that no serious breakdown would occur during the next winter. He began to cost a phased conversion of bedrooms so that they would all eventually become en suite. I thought a three to five year plan would be appropriate which would enable us to introduce other features which were promised to the members. When Alimo claimed some expenses for his consultation and cost estimates, de Chabris refused to pay him and said that I should have ensured that only when work started would he be paid. This was despite the fact that some urgent repair work was already undertaken for work on the heating system.

More revelations were made, some from across the Atlantic and evidence was piling up against Jeremy Thorpe. Private Eye had revealed that Mike Wood was a paedophile convicted of offences against ten and twelve year old boys. Philip Watkins was a magistrate at the time and introduced him to de Chabris, with a recommendation that he should have the job as manager, hiring vulnerable teenage boys who would be living in as a part of their duties.

The Club continued to flourish and there were happy moments such as when David Steel and some of his M.P.s dined together with a few of the professional agents that worked for the party. Afterwards the M.P.s met and I joined the agents in a pub just outside the Club called 'The Ship and Shovel'. They included Peter Bray, one of Jeremy Thorpe's agents based in North Devon and David Steel's agent with an unpronounceable name who I called 'Rumble Dumble'. It was good to converse in politics rather than criminology and I refrained mentioning some of the unpalatable incidents. I returned a little before the others and found David Steel waiting and he asked 'Where's my man?' It was difficult to say 'Ship and Shovel' when you have had a few drinks but I returned to the pub to bring back the Scotsman.

In all the problems I deliberately refrained from unburdening myself on David Steel. I knew from journalists that they had confronted him with information that they had accumulated but his position was terrible. He had worked with a friend and colleague only to discover on replacing him, that dreadful and murky events were arising in the media. As the party leader he was functioning as best he could and attempting to play a Statesmanlike role in the newly formed Lib Lab pact. Wilson had resigned passing a poisoned challis to Callaghan who faced militant unions who were creating hyper inflation. David Steel and the Liberals were trying to bring down inflation and they were partially successful in doing so.

I had a great deal of respect for David Steel but he was never a barn storming orator but a quiet and sincere man, doing his best in an almost impossible position. Cyril was a little unfair when he said 'David couldn't make a bang if you stuck a firework up his arse.' I thought a quiet yet tenacious approach was all that could be achieved in such circumstances.

Felicia de Chabris, the daughter of George, was a beautiful and sweet natured girl of twenty years. She mixed freely with the young Liberals and argued with her father if she thought he was being unfair to the staff. Having viewed the television series called 'Roots' which described the hideous treatment of slaves, I heard her confronting George on some of his right wing views. My last vestige of hope was that the influence of Felicia and her brother and sister, would have a positive influence on her father which together with the increase of active Liberals within the Club would make him realise that he had a vested long term interest in looking after the Liberals.

The annual Party Assembly was usually a pleasurable occasion and I looked forward to a few days by the seaside at Scarborough. The Club would have a desk in which I hoped to recruit a few more members and I hoped to hear a few debates and attend the social events. Carol and George would be there and I intended to take Carol to the Assembly dance. I would arrive a day later than George and Carol after attending some duties at the Club. When I arrived George hurriedly handed the Club stall over to me and said he had to hurry back to London taking Carol with him. I soon discovered that George had attended the press briefing and interrupted David Steel when he was addressing journalists. Not surprisingly he put

George in his place and they had a row in public before George withdrew in a huff.

Late one evening after attending one of the fringe meetings I was walking back to my hotel alongside the promenade when a familiar voice rang out. 'Brian come here I want to talk to you'. It was Cyril Smith who was sat next to his mother on a bench facing the sea. 'Put your plates of meat here.'

I sat next to him with his mother on his other side. 'This is confidential and has come directly from the Home Secretary. George de Chabris is a crook with a shady past. He started a building society in the Cayman Islands and managed to collect several hundred thousand in investments. He emptied the bank accounts and cleared off and his creditors are now in hot pursuit. I would get out if I were you before the shit hits the fan.'

Nothing shocked me any more, so I listened impassively and decided that I would confide in him in the future but that this was not the occasion to discuss paedophiles and violence in the presence of his mother. I thanked him for confiding in me and told him "that a great deal was happening in and around the Club that would shock him. I would continue the conversation after the conference."

I had first met Cyril in the first General election campaign of 1974 when I organised his aircraft trip to Kent. I had a rapport with him and appreciated his open and straight forward manner. When I collected him to go to a rally in Chatham he attempted to shake hands with almost everyone and when a little old lady had been forgotten in the corner he strode up to her and introduced himself putting a big smile on her face.

Attending a marginal seats conference in the West Country I

recall a heavy snow storm and we were lucky to reach the hotel. We were stranded in a warm and comfortable hotel for a few days surrounded by heavy snow. We couldn't leave if we wanted to, so we spent the first evening propping up the bar with Larry Lamb the editor of the Sun. As the night wore on the conversation drifted to the Australian Prime Minister Gough Whitlam. Cyril and I were interested when Larry Lamb stated that 'We put him in and we kicked him out.' This reflected just how much power the Murdoch press believed they had and in future years explained why both Thatcher and Blair spent more time with the Murdoch team than with their own cabinet.

Cyril had resigned as the Liberal Chief Whip following a torrent of questions from media men wanting to know about Jeremy Thorpe and the shot dog incident. Cyril was under sedation in hospital when a reporter calling himself a nephew managed to gather a newspaper headline stating 'Someone's telling bloody lies.' Cyril also repeated what Thorpe had said to him, that he had the support of the Prime Minister, the Monarch and M.I.5.

Before the scandal began to break Cyril would openly talk of how boys would run away from a remand home and knock on his door sometimes as late as ten o clock at night and that he would always make them a cup of tea and listen to them before returning them to the home. Therefore when Thorpe had mentioned that a twelve year old boy had been caught in his hotel room, for many years I believed that this was just an attempt to shut Cyril up by Jeremy and his clique.

When Liberals were free of scandal Cyril had invited me to serve on a Celebrity Group and we hoped to organise a fund raising concert with Rod Stewart and Bernard Braden.

Wishing to promote the Club I met the manager of the Whitehall Theatre with a view to promoting a joint venture of parties having a meal at the Club then watching a show and then staying the night at the National Liberal Club. Within a couple of days Cyril had visited the theatre where Warren Mitchell was doing a nightly show called 'The thoughts of chairman Alf'. Once Cyril was sighted he was invited onto the stage and the whole evening of entertainment comprised Cyril and Alf Garnet drinking whisky and producing a hysterically funny show.

Long after the assembly, I chose a quiet moment to confide in Cyril about the incidents involving Wood. His response was to explode with expletives but not long after this, I found it strange that he no longer stayed at the Club but in a nearby hotel.

There had been some peculiar traditions at the Club; for example the bedroom doors were unlocked which enabled the elderly Irish maids to present members with a cup of tea when they were awoken. If shoes were kept outside of the door they would be cleaned over night and as a reflection of bygone days chamber pots were provided. One day a happily married member had fallen asleep but was aroused to find a naked girl wrapped around him. She had arrived very late and found his bedroom number on the reception register. The next day the member quietly asked if he could have a lock on his door.

George de Chabris publicly declared that he would throw out the Liberals from the Club if they didn't work more closely with him. He was spending more time abroad leaving me to answer any queries. I was shocked when I received a phone call from Christie's and when I explained George was abroad and then told him that I was the Membership Director, he said 'I have found a buyer for your Club.' I said that George would be returning next week and he should speak directly to him. Within a few days a Frenchman visited the Club and inspected the premises.

I felt betrayed by George. I had always been loyal to him even when it would have been easy to depart. I respected his innovation and business ability to take on a near bankrupt business and transform it into a lucrative concern. I heard from Leonard Smith who was still technically the chairman of the Club that within a few days time the original trustees would surrender the lease to George and his holding company of Charlton Park. He had presented me with one of the hundred shares and I heard that he would sell the lease for half a million pounds, so my share would be worth £5000 but I wanted no part of it so handed it back to him. All I ever collected was a meagre wage for I believed that what we were doing was of historical significance for the growth of the Liberal Party.

I would be compelled to do a great deal of soul searching in the next few days as George was loudly boasting in the press that he planned to kick the Liberals out of the Club. This would lead to a great deal of egg on the face of David Steel and the whole party. My own position would also be tarnished as I had recruited 600 new members promising them that there would soon be a new gymnasium, sauna, solarium and squash court together with steady improvements to the bedrooms and dining facilities.

Brendon Alimo the architect called to see me to see if there was any chance of being paid for the work that he had done. I confided in him by telling him that if the change of ownership took place there was no guarantee of what might happen to the premises. He and I knew that the Club did not need investment as the cash flow was quite capable of paying for improvements but that the original trustees had told the membership that only a wealthy benefactor could save the Club. Alimo said, "that in that case why don't they approach Anthony Dobson to over ride any difficulties in moving things forward." I learned that Dobson and Associates had an excellent record on the stock market and for rescuing thousands of jobs.

Anthony Dobson and his chief accountant David Britain were Sheffield men who enjoyed a remarkable record of rescuing several near bankrupt companies. Alimo was to explain to them the situation as he was familiar with the condition and problems that needed attention in the Club. When I met them they emphasised the key to their success was financial analysis and they were to soon understand the key factors of the Club and were keen to be involved. I spoke first of all to the party President Basil Goldstone who urged me to speak to the Club Chairman Leonard Smith.

When I spoke to Leonard Smith I emphasised that I believed de Chabris should be treated fairly as he had taken on the responsibility just before the Club was to close and that under his leadership it had been transformed into a vibrant and profitable business. Like any executive who had achieved such success he should be entitled to a fair settlement but not half a million. If a change was made I wished that the pledges that I had made to members to introduce the improvements to the Club would be honoured. Unlike several of his colleagues serving as trustees and members of the management committee I believed that Leonard was a Liberal even though his support for a reactionary clique was not compatible to my own belief of building a party of the people.

From this point onwards matters were out of my hands. Dobson and Britain had met several times with the trustees and management committee and with their legal backup had scrutinised the agreements made to George de Chabris and Charlton Park Holdings and offered to take over from de Chabris and run the Club. They offered to soon bring about the increased facilities and to create a new company in which all members would be offered shares. To strengthen the links with the Liberal Party they offered the Liberal Party Organisation to stay in perpetuity free of paying any rent. Further more they offered to make a prominent M.P. David Penhaligon, the President Basil Goldstone and the Chief Agent John Holmes a directorship of the proposed holding company.

On the two days before the planned takeover George de Chabris had made an outburst that he was about to throw the Liberals out of the Club. The transfer of ownership of the lease to Anthony Dobson & Associates was less amicable towards George de Chabris than I had hoped, but there was little sympathy for him as news filtered through that he had started to accrue a considerable sum from the Club and that investors in his project in the Cayman Islands were now in hot pursuit of their monies.

The new owners of the Club lease confronted Mike Wood and told him that they didn't believe that a convicted paedophile should be in a position to control teenagers but gave him a fair settlement on leaving. A new manager was appointed and employment contracts were soon implemented for key members of staff. Though planning and negotiations were ongoing my sixth sense told me that all was not well. Basil Goldstone told me that Jeremy Thorpe had told him not to have anything to do with Dobson. When asked why and asked if he had anything against them, Thorpe did not reply. What I feared would happen, did, when the agreement with Anthony Dobson was terminated without explanation.

I was told by Leonard Smith and a triumphant Philip Watkins that they had found a new benefactor, Lawrence Robson. He had a good reputation amongst Liberals and his wife had been recommended for a peerage by Jeremy Thorpe. The original reactionary clique that had almost bankrupted the Club was now back in control; all that the stewardship of de Chabris and Dobson had achieved was to show them what a profitable business the Club was. I was told that I should answer to Philip Watkins in the immediate future. I asked if the new ownership would honour the promises made to new members. I was told that would be up to Lawrence Robson.

Lawrence Robson made no attempt to speak to me and I soon learned that Wood was now seen back in the Club. The staff was demoralised and my P.A. and secretary resigned. If I had any doubts about my future when I discovered my private papers in my office had been tampered with, then I decided that I should resign. Watkins was delighted at the news and I packed up my personal belongings and left. I had been a member of the Club for several years before becoming an employee so though I had lost my personal quest, I would seriously consider speaking at the pending annual meeting when the official transfer of power would take place.

After my resignation I was pleased that I had been offered the chance of acting as parliamentary agent and campaign manager of a pending by-election. Understandably I refused the offer and planned to give up any ambition of a professional political career. Peter Hain had joined the Labour Party and some friends wondered if I might do the same but Labour still had the block vote and was dominated by reactionary union leaders who were stifling the economic growth of the nation. I still had a passion for small businesses, co-ownership and community values.

I conferred with several journalists, who were appalled that even with enormous evidence no one was charged with anything. Police officers were only able to investigate what journalists had uncovered and I knew of nothing that had been discovered independently of reporters. Attempts had been made to interfere with editors and media proprietors to stop the continual revelations surrounding the shooting incident but the establishment was still trying to cover up events and prevent a possible prosecution.

Why was there such determination to cover up an alleged murder conspiracy? This was far more than a Liberal cover-up. I understand that Special Branch did try and still does today to protect the reputation of around thirty M.P.s to prevent them being blackmailed or manipulated by foreign powers. I recalled the story of Reds in the bed which told of a Conservative M.P. who was seduced by a beautiful Russian girl and who then later discovered it had been recorded on film, when attempts were made to pressure him to spy for them. At this particular time the threat to Thorpe had come from revelations of a possible homosexual affair. Until the sixties it was illegal even for consenting adults to have a homosexual relationship. When Scott first claimed to have sex with Thorpe he was under twenty one which was still a criminal offence.

If embarrassing details of a former lover had been revealed and had come from a girl friend, I'm sure Thorpe or anyone else in such a position would have repeated what Wellington had once said: 'publish and be damned.' The mood at this time was still hostile to homosexuals but over the years has greatly changed. It's possible that if Thorpe had been content to just be an M.P. and not a party leader or foreign affairs spokesman he might have just ignored the love letters that Scott was showing to all those who were interested. I believe the establishment cover-up began long before the plot to kill Scott and was a result of the law being such an ass. The belief was probably that they were just covering up an indiscretion. When it developed into a full blown murder conspiracy the establishment was already compromised. Another factor was that before taking Scott home on the first night of seduction, he called upon a famous and influential friend simply to impress him with his important friends. This entirely innocent friend would need to be protected by Special Branch in case there was guilt by association within the media.

It was with incredulity that Thorpe had persuaded so many friends to be involved with a plot to kill someone. Besides himself and a former treasurer of the party David Holmes, there was the man who hired the two possible hit men and the man who was photographed passing £5000 to the would be killer; the man who refused to do it and the man who had attempted to kill Scott. It was possible, together with these six that at least two or three more men were involved. What kind of low life were these men? Certainly they were a far cry from the high principled and consciencous men and women who are generally motivated by altruistic public service. Surely the reaction of most normal men would be to tell Thorpe to rid himself of such thoughts of murder.

On the evening before the big meeting in the Club I had two long telephone conversations; first with Emlyn Hooson in Wales and then one with George Mackie in Scotland. They were two senior Liberals; Hooson had stood against Thorpe for the leadership of the party and Mackie had insisted that Thorpe should resign as the leader of the party. I told them of some of the events within the Club, to which Hooson responded by saying that, "nothing would surprise me about Thorpe," Both of them said that I should follow my conscience and neither attempted to dissuade me from spilling the beans at the next day's meeting.

Around lunch time the next day I met Roger Courtier and Barrie Penrose at the Charing Cross Hotel and afterwards we walked towards the Club and together with other journalists they had asked me to join them in the Royal Horse Guards Hotel next door to the Club immediately after the meeting. I strode into the meeting alongside Susan Clark. The smoking room was packed with approximately a hundred and sixty members. I recognised several of Thorpe's close friends together with judges, magistrates and lawyers. Alan Beith the Chief Whip came alongside David Penhaligon, together with officers of the party including Basil Goldstone the party President.

I waited for the right moment before putting my hand up to speak. Leonard Smith conducted a quiet meeting and probably dreaded the moment when I started to speak as much as I did. I knew that as soon as I opened my mouth it would mark the end of any ambition to ever stand as a

Parliamentary Liberal candidate. I had looked around at the portraits of great Liberals from the illustrious past and said a little prayer for inspiration.

I started by quoting the 'remarkably low rent that was paid for the premises together with the rates and the largest building expenditure for heating.' Compared to the income from membership and the hire of bedrooms there was no need for the Club to have become so close to bankruptcy. Both de Chabris and Dobson had clearly shown that the Club could be a highly profitable enterprise and that improved facilities, promotion of membership and filling vacant bedrooms could easily pay for steady improvements in the building out of cash flow. All that was necessary was a modicum of business ability and the ability to communicate with fellow Liberals.

I then continued to the highly contentious issues of violent incidents that had occurred in the recent past. I stated that such activity was not compatible with Liberal principles and highlighted a few events, such as taking a boy to hospital after being beaten up and buggered and the conversation of an intention to kill de Chabris junior. My speech was described later in Private Eye as a furious tirade but it was a controlled outpouring of emotions. As an employee of first de Chabris then Dobson and for a few days until my resignation, the original reactionary clique, I had been unable to speak publicly about the controversial events of the Club. I expected that the chairman would intervene, but I was able to say about three quarters of what I wanted to say before he did. I had decided not to argue against the chairman but simply said in parting 'does the truth offend you?' If I had continued my speech by arguing with the chairman I would have been portrayed as a rebel rouser for there is a convention in politics that chairmen have the ultimate control of political meetings, whether it is the Speaker in Parliament or Mayors and chairmen of councils.

I had achieved all that I believed possible and with the background of expectation the newspapers were calling for an end of the cover-up concerning our former leader. There were many profoundly concerned members who would abstain when the motion was passed to make the member's club into a proprietor's club with many of those who had previously been responsible for nearly closing it now back in control albeit on the coat tails of Lawrence Robson.

I understand that several elderly members had become incontinent during my speech. Sadly I was told that Basil Goldstone was almost in tears and I understood that what I had revealed was not welcome from many genuine Liberals, who may have spent a life time working for a cause that they believed in. Yet at least I had opened the eyes of many who had previously hoped that all the present unpleasantness would go away. I believed then and now that evil exists when good men do nothing.

The die was cast and I walked out of the room as quickly as possible, though one or two members wanted to ask me questions and one was 'Did the chairman have anything to do with the shooting? I replied that I didn't think so but as a friend of Thorpe he was keen to cover up for him.'

Susan Clark arrived at our planned rendezvous' with the journalists' eager to say what had happened, a little before me. I did a brief television interview with Gavin Hewitt but I was content to minimise my own role in the proceedings as the whole business made me sick in the stomach.

It was not many days later that four men were summoned to attend a police station in the West Country, charged with conspiracy to murder. They were Jeremy Thorpe, David Holmes, George Deakin and John Le Mesurier. They were then released subject to bail conditions, to wait for the remand proceedings. Though this was no surprise to those who had followed the case, it still came as a great shock to the whole nation when a leader of a major political party was charged with murder.

I had always enjoyed the creative side of politics but events had become so awful that I was pleased to be free of it. Two B.B.C. journalists called unannounced at my home in Canterbury and told me that they were going to do a Panorama programme based upon the recent events at the National Liberal Club. I found it all a bit of an anti climax but gave them some information that they wanted. When they broadcast the programme Lawrence Robson asked Philip Watkins to resign following financial irregularities.

A great deal of my speech was printed in Private Eye and soon afterwards I received a phone call from Scotland Yard. 'Detective Chief Superintendant Ray Small and Detective Chief Inspector Frank Rushworth from the Serious Crimes Sector of Scotland Yard would like to speak to you. Can we visit you in your home in Canterbury?' An agreed time and date was agreed.

Chapter 13

The Lost Liberal Revolution

A Jaguar car similar to that shown in the Morse television series drew up on the drive and the two officers alighted, strode up the pathway and introduced themselves. As we sat in the lounge a number of questions were put to me in a brisk and businesslike manner. As the questions proceeded some were for cross referencing so if anyone had deviated from the truth they would soon be discovered. Questioning continued for about three hours when we adjourned for a ham salad lunch and a glass of beer at the village pub.

During the morning session I believe the officers had established my position and the afternoon session proceeded in a slightly more relaxed atmosphere. I passed them a draft statement and suggested that they should see several key members of the Club. Journalists such as Roger Courtier and Barrie Penrose would have a great deal of information that they had collated particularly as they tried to trace the donation that was used to pay off the hit man. I believed that they had also traced monies that were meant to help Liberal party funds that found its way into personal back pockets.

I believe the Scotland Yard inquiry terms of reference were not directly concerned with the murder conspiracy but rather concentrated on matters within the National Liberal Club. First there were the incidents relating to Wood; I only hoped that the victims of assaults would have the courage to say what had happened. The other matters were concerned with financial irregularities in the Club or elsewhere. My motivation for my speech was simply to stop the violence and possible sexual abuse and to establish a semblance of truth for all those who had become involved including investigative journalists and police officers at various ranks. I did not seek retribution even though I was saddened at my dashed hopes for the re-establishment of the National Liberal Club as a centre for radical and social reform.

After a full day of questioning the Scotland Yard officers were to proceed with their inquiries during a time when the media was concentrating on the coming events surrounding the committal proceeds of Thorpe and his three fellow defendants. At this time I had a lunch with a Mirror journalist called Barbara Drillsma. She came from Blackpool and told me that there were stories circulating in Lancashire about Cyril Smith. I had reached saturation point on hearing about wrong doings of political colleagues and believed that he had been smeared by the Thorpe clique to shut him up from talking about the shooting incident.

I first met Cyril when I had organised his aeroplane trip into Kent but during the next few years came to regard him as a friend. He was proud of his working class background and would speak up for the underdog particularly single parent families. He championed small businesses, community values and when economy of scale dictated, the principle of profit sharing co ownership. When Richard Marsh resigned as the leader of British Rail there were those in both management and unions who wanted Cyril Smith to apply for the position. The reason for this was his view that there should be far more participation by both employees and rail users in the management of British Rail. In hindsight it's a pity that he didn't apply for the job but I confess that I was one of those who urged him not to apply as he was such an important cog in the Liberal machine.

In the few years that I knew him in the seventies I never detected any irregular tendencies. He had been shocked by the revelations of a murder conspiracy and had grown apart from Jeremy Thorpe. In the spring of 1978, I confided in him about the paedophile activity from which he reacted with several expletives. I subsequently thought it strange that he started to stay in a nearby hotel rather than the National Liberal Club after our conversation, but only in hindsight did I notice that I saw very little of him from this point on.

The committal proceedings for Jeremy Thorpe and his three co defendants began at Minehead on November 20th 1978 and would take three weeks to complete. The press was eagerly looking forward to the event with a frenzy of excitement. For me and most Liberals there was no joy but only inevitability about the revelations first read in the newspapers that would now be presented in court proceedings? The four defendants exercised their rights to make the prosecution lay out its evidence and to be able to cross examine the witnesses speaking against them. At the request of Deakin and the delight of the media, the defendants exercised their right to lift reporting restrictions.

Clement Freud M.P. entered the court with Jeremy Thorpe and sat beside him during the first day's deliberations. Peter Taylor Q.C. the Crown counsel began to present the prosecution case. 'Jeremy Thorpe was elected a Liberal M.P. in1959. In the early 1960's he had a homosexual relationship with

Norman Scott. Scott was a danger to his reputation and career, a danger of which he was constantly reminded. Scott was pestering him for help and telling others about it. Mr Thorpe's anxiety became obsessive.'

Some nuances were presented to the Court about this relationship which began when Scott had visited Thorpe in the Commons to seek advice and help. Later that same day Thorpe took Scott to his mother's home in Oxted where they started a homosexual relationship which would continue on and off until 1963. Lurid details of the intimate homosexual relationship were related to the Court to the delight of the media but induced a feeling of sickness to many of us who had once known another positive side of Thorpe.

Jeremy Thorpe confided in Peter Bessell who was also a Liberal M.P. He helped Thorpe acquire a lost suitcase belonging to Scott which contained a number of affectionate letters written by Thorpe. He also started to give Scott money and assistance. The persistent threat had a depressing effect upon Thorpe, who convened a meeting in Parliament with Bessell and David Holmes (who had been his best man at his first wedding). He had also once been a deputy treasurer of the Liberal Party.

The meeting held in 1967 was to mention details of possibly killing Norman Scott. Thorpe had said 'It's no worse than shooting a sick dog.' Those words repeated by Peter Taylor Q.C. in open Court were to make the headlines across the world's media the next morning.

Jeremy Thorpe became the leader of the Liberal Party in 1967 so the threat of his past homosexual life being exposed became an ever greater threat. His relationship with Scott in the early sixties was illegal and he had to lie to his fellow Liberal M.P.s when they had responded to a complaint by a woman friend of Scott in the early seventies. He would always be trapped by that lie and would never admit that he had a sexual relationship with Scott despite the obvious evidence that he had. It must be hard for the younger generation to imagine that even homosexual relationships between consenting adults were illegal in those days. Today, both the big political parties have gays amongst their Cabinet members and the leader of the Scotland Conservatives is an openly gay woman; which does not appear to have harmed her career at all. A whole new attitude of live and let live philosophy has emerged.

The prosecution case continued to state that a temporary rescue of Scott resulted when he married. But Thorpe still favoured the ultimate solution. The prosecution now focussed on Devon in 1974. Scott was depressed once more and began to talk to a South African reporter called Gordon Winter. The first 1974 General Election campaign was proceeding, in which Liberals were playing a greater part than for several decades. Scott was paid £2500 in exchange for more intimate letters. The money was paid by Holmes indirectly through Scott's doctor. The doctor passed the letters to Holmes who burnt them. Holmes was repaid when Thorpe asked a wealthy bene-factor, Jack Hayward, to deposit £10,000 into a bank account in the Channel Isles from where the monies were transferred to Holmes.

Liberals fared extremely well in the General Election, advancing from two and a half million votes in 1966 to over six million in February 1974. This resulted in neither Labour or the Conservatives having an overall majority. Ted Heath the incumbent Conservative Prime Minister stayed in Downing Street for a further three days after the election result and entered talks with Jeremy Thorpe, with a view to forming a coalition government. Heath offered a Royal Commission on Electoral Reform which would be heavily weighted in favour of a form of proportional representation. The obstacles for this were that grass roots Liberals who had just fought a good campaign against the Conservatives did not approve, nor was there any guarantee that Conservative M.P.s would support a change in the electoral system. The rumour mill also stated that Harold Wilson phoned Heath to remind him that the reason that he could not make the Liberals an offer of shared government was that Special Branch had three files on leading Liberals that comprised a security threat due to their personal lives. Heath moved out of Downing Street and Harold Wilson formed a minority government.

Throughout 1974 Scott remained a threat to Thorpe. The Sunday Mirror acquired a copy of the letter that Scott had sent to Thorpe's mother. It had been left behind in an old office once occupied by Bessell. The newspaper handed the original copy back to Thorpe but kept photocopies. Thorpe knew damaging material was in the offing. Later that year Holmes agreed that Scott would have to be killed.

Holmes knew a man called John LeMesurier who owned a discount carpet business in South Wales. He introduced Holmes to George Deakin who was a night club owner in Port Talbot. The three met and Deakin was told that a friend of Holmes was being blackmailed. Did he know anyone to frighten the man off? Deakin had a conversation with an airline pilot called Andrew Newton. He had remarked 'I hear you want someone bumped off? Who wants him bumped off?' 'A friend who is powerful and influential' came the reply from Deakin. Holmes said later he would get £10,000 for the job. A few days later Thorpe wrote to the millionaire, Jack Hayward, and asked for another £10,000.

Newton started his work, eventually tracing Scott to Barnstaple. He tried to pacify him by telling him that he was there to protect him. He persuaded Scott to travel with him in his car, together with his Great Dane dog, Rinka. Newton drove along a coastal road to a secluded spot where he stopped the car and produced a gun which he used to shoot the large dog through the head. Newton then told Scott that it was his turn next, and pointed the gun at the startled Scott, but the gun then jammed. Evidence was presented to confirm that the type of gun had a record of jamming. Newton was eventually convicted of shooting the dog and jailed for two years. Clearly the trial of Newton gave Scott an opportunity to make his allegations in court and was fraught with danger to those who had conspired against Scott.

David Holmes was to visit Peter Bessell who had now settled to live in California. Bessell was persuaded to write a false letter claiming that Scott was a blackmailer which was Newton's own bogus account at his trial. It was Thorpe's idea to hire Newton to kill Scott, Holmes told Bessell. Scott made his homosexual story a public allegation. Thorpe was to phone Bessell admitting that he had instigated the attempt to kill Scott. The prosecution counsel stated 'Thorpe was showing himself fully privy to what was going on in the conspiracy.'

Newton came out of jail and agreed to accept a half payment of £5,000 for the bodged attempt to kill Scott. At a secluded rural setting on St Brides Common in South Wales, John Le Mesurier handed Newton a bundle of notes to the value of £5,000. The handover was secretly photographed by private detectives and printed in a newspaper. Peter Taylor Q.C. stated 'A number of characters had started taping conversations. Experts will confirm their authenticity. They are powerful support for the prosecution case.'

Jeremy Thorpe handed a prepared statement to investigating police; when questions were put to him he refused to answer. He emphatically denied a homosexual relationship with Scott or any part of a conspiracy, or making payments to Newton or Scott. He claimed that the £20,000 given to him by Hayward was a personal gift to him and not to be paid into Liberal Party funds. 'The prosecution states this is untrue. It was expressly arranged to be passed to Mr Holmes.' Taylor said; we submit that Mr Thorpe instigated and was a party to a conspiracy to kill Mr Scott.'

Peter Bessell realised that with growing allegations he had become liable after sending the bogus blackmail letter and making several payments to Scott. Indeed he could be seen as the prime instigator of the conspiracy with the denials of Thorpe. At last he decided to tell the truth.

Thorpe saw Hayward again before charges were laid. He tried to get Hayward to put pressure on Bessell not to come to England. Bessell owed Hayward money. The idea was that Hayward should threaten to serve a writ on Bessell if he came to England. Taylor claimed that the prosecution was a very long and bazaar story. Hayward would have nothing to do with the scheme.

'Despite this attempt to keep Mr Bessell away and threats made in open court of what would face him, Mr Bessell is here and I propose to call him,' thus concluded the opening prosecution case.

Peter Bessell was the first and prime witness for the prosecution. In the early seventies many of Thorpe's close allies mentioned the pro war views of Bessell who had spent a few weeks in Vietnam in the mid sixties. It came as no surprise to me when he later admitted being in the pay of the C.I.A. He was a devious character who had retreated to America leaving behind financial irregularities and later was to attempt to defraud Hayward. Admitting that he had lied to cover up Thorpe's affair with Scott, Bessell's credibility was low, though one police officer told me that it was common for a former member of a criminal conspiracy to give evidence against his former conspirators in order to save himself.

Bessell was cross examined for three days by Thorpe's and Holmes' lawyers. He told the Court that Thorpe had confided in him in 1965 about the troublesome relationship that he had in the early sixties with Scott. Homosexual relationships were illegal and Scott was blabbing about it and showing letters of affection from Thorpe to all who were interested in the events. Bessell tried to alleviate the illegal and indiscreet outpourings from Scott but the emotional and neurotic behaviour continued long after their physical relationship had ended.

In 1967 Jeremy Thorpe was elected the leader of the Liberal Party and he was to meet and marry his first wife Caroline Allpass in May 1968. She was an attractive young woman who would soon become the mother of his son. Jeremy Thorpe was enjoying increased support and publicity in the media but following the leadership of the charismatic Jo Grimond, being the new leader was no easy task. In the summer of

1968 I attended the Liberal Party Council in Birmingham and for both morning and afternoon sessions found myself sitting next to Jeremy Thorpe our new leader. Most of those who had been elected to this quarterly session were young parliamentary candidates and lawyers who were ambitious, both for themselves and the Liberal Party. As neither leader of the two major parties, Harold Wilson or Ted Heath, were particularly popular, it was felt that Liberals should be making more progress and many of those attending this meeting were hostile to Thorpe. They expressed their feelings quite strongly and perhaps unfairly as he had spent time out wooing his new wife. It must have been just after this time when I had flown to Vietnam for the first time, that Thorpe had suggested to Bessell that Scott should be killed.

Once the verbal battering of Bessell had been completed it was the turn of Jack Hayward to give evidence. His credibility was unquestioned but the prosecution case stated that monies donated by him had been used to pay for the shooting incident. Bessell had given evidence of Thorpe's intention to plot murder. Hayward had testified about the means to pay for the crime and then Newton described the method to kill. Norman Scott testified about the motive. He described in lurid details his homosexual relationship with Thorpe and his constant pestering for help which was a real threat to the political career of the leader of the Liberal Party.

Evidence was given by David Miller who was a friend of Newton the 'hit man'. He described how after the night of the dog shooting he came upon Newton trying to release the firing pin of his gun. He said that he saw Newton pull a bullet out from under the firing pin. Newton had then reassembled his gun and fired a shot into the wall. Miller told how he heard Newton phone Deakin to tell him that everything had gone wrong. He had shot the dog and was prodded to add that the gun had jammed. Recorded conversations implicated Le Mesurier who had been photographed handing over £5,000 to Newton.

The Crown introduced Colin Lambert who would reinforce the evidence against Le Mesurier. He was a former employee of Le Mesurier who had been present at our lunch at the Royal Horse Guards Hotel next to the National Liberal Club, together with Roger Courtier. What he told us then, was passed onto the police by Courtier and would later become a vital part of the prosecution case. Terry Gibbs a football pools winner who was also at the lunch became another prosecution witness. I recall him mentioning how he had met Thorpe and Holmes who were to persuade him to first of all lend Le Mesurier a £10,000 interest free loan and later, to invest some of his winnings in the carpet firm.

In all there were ten prosecution witnesses who would face questioning, plus twenty eight who gave written evidence that was uncontested. As the case was completed in the fourth week of the hearings the chairman of the magistrates declared 'We find there is a prima facie case in each of the four of you. There is also a prima facie in respect of you Thorpe, of inciting Holmes to murder Norman Scott. You will all be committed to stand trial.' Each of the defendants was released on bail of £5,000 pending the trial at the Old Bailey.

There would be a General Election before what the media described as the 'trial of the century.' Most Liberals had hoped that Thorpe would not stand for re-election but his lawyers advised him not to step down as it might be construed that it would indicate that he was guilty. Meanwhile the Scotland Yard inquiry continued, though Wood was now working in a remote Arab country that had no extradition treaty and de Chabris soon returned to Florida. Inevitably information was collected that interrelated with finance and Thorpe of which the natural instincts of police officers would wish to pursue but were denied access. The usual procedure in law was that if further charges were believed to be justified they would be added to existing charges, but in this case officers were told to wait and see what would happen in the pending murder conspiracy trial.

Understandably all that was being revealed was quite devastating to Liberals who had nothing to do with the events. Thorpe made an uninvited attendance to the Liberal Party Conference and sat on the platform in full view of the media. As he did so he was cheered by some of the delegates who still believed he might be innocent but the majority just sat in silence hoping that he would go away, which after a short while he did.

Considering the circumstances, David Steel had tried hard to work with Callaghan's Labour Government to curb the greed of powerful union officials who had become increasingly unpopular with strikes and hyper inflation. He entered what was called the Lab Lib pact but Mrs Thatcher was growing in confidence and was expected to win and become Britain's first woman prime minister. In North Devon one candidate walked round the district with a Great Dane dog reminding everyone of the shooting incident. Of the M.P.s only John Pardoe (who was an M.P. from a neighbouring constituency) campaigned alongside Thorpe in his constituency. Inevitably both these M.P.s were to lose their seats and Mrs Thatcher was to become Prime Minister.

The die was cast for what the media described as the trial of the century. Jeremy Thorpe was predicted by many as a future British Prime Minister. Under his leadership the Liberal Party had more than doubled its vote from two and a half million votes to over six million votes in the 1974 General Election. He was the Godfather of Royal children and had persuaded one man to donate over a quarter of a million pounds to the Liberal Party. He was also approaching numerous companies to either donate to the Liberals or if they insisted on giving to the Conservatives, ensure that it was conditional that they should support proportional representation. He was charming, witty and quite brilliant and was popular with Liberal activists.

It was hardly surprising that so many party activists could not believe that he should, but for the grace of God, be a cold hearted murderer. The prosecution case was that he had persuaded up to at least eight men to either kill or cover up a murder. Originally even Prime Minister Harold Wilson believed that he had been set up by the intelligence agency of South Africa; Thorpe was hated by the racist regime for his and the Liberal Party's opposition to apartheid. I know that the Pencourt team would have loved it if that had been true but their investigative journalism uncovered the dreadful truth.

After the judge had heard the testimony and cross examination of Bessell, Newton and Scott, Colin Lambert gave his evidence and the judge declared 'He is the first credible witness to be presented by the prosecution.' Our lunch at the Royal Horse Guards Hotel had delivered some light on the proceedings.

The defence lawyers constantly tried to discredit the prosecution by mentioning cheque book journalism with the implication that witnesses were lying for money. The big difference between the Pentagon Papers and Watergate Tapes revelations was that in those cases newspaper proprietors supported a team of investigative journalists to discover the truth: the New York Times and the Washington Post. In Britain no newspaper proprietor or broadcasting corporation put all of their resources into revealing the truth with the possible exception of Private Eye. It was left to individual journalists such as Barry Penrose and Roger Courtier to dig for information. In hindsight, the gross sum of monies paid to witnesses was not nearly as much as had been suggested and I just wondered how much was earned by all the top lawyers involved in the case.

Before the Old Bailey trial I had been invited to spend a weekend with friends, who included a film producer. He was planning to produce a movie based upon the saga if Thorpe was found guilty. I bluntly told him that I believed he would be acquitted. It came as no surprise to me when watching the news on television the 'Not Guilty' verdict was delivered. Within minutes the phone rang and it was a senior police officer. I will always remember his words, 'I thought a bent cop was the lowest of scum but I was wrong. A bent politician is far worse.'

Another police officer, Detective Chief Superintendant Michael Challes is on record as saying 'Sir Joseph Cantley's summing up was the worst I have ever heard. The judge failed in his public duty.' Within two years of the trial David Holmes, one of the key defendants admitted that there had been a conspiracy to kill Norman Scott. His account was printed in the News of the World and he insisted that he would not be paid for the article but a contribution would be made to charity.

Although Thorpe had been acquitted, few people believed that he was innocent and though some sycophantic friends tried to promote him in a senior position within Amnesty International and the United Nations Association, public outcry prevented him from doing so. He was to live in a state of denial with diminishing social contacts and prevented from playing any part of political life. He had tried to enter the House of Lords but David Steel would not agree to this.

It's possible that after the shooting he may have been better off if he had pleaded guilty. He could have spared himself from the lurid details of his sex life and presented mitigating circumstances and possibly spoke of the hideous treatment of gays. After serving two or three years in jail on his release he could have started again by writing his memoirs and even promoting his altruistic ambitions for Britain. Then he might have spent a happy retirement in the South of France.

On the other hand if Scott had been killed and the matter successfully covered up what would that have done for the future political life of our country? There must surely be some kind of moral code for those who wish to lead us or we will all sink into the abyss. Of all our institutions I believe that generally the police force came out of it very well whilst politics, law and media was all tarnished.

As a lifelong Liberal I was saddened that the Liberal Party never really recovered from this sorry saga. There was profound disillusionment with numerous good activists distancing themselves from the Party. Some like Peter Hain and Simon

Hebditch joined the Labour Party; a few helped to create the Green Movement whilst others became involved with charities or law but the majority simply turned their backs on political aspirations. Even those who inherited the National Liberal Club were to part with the most valuable part of the premises, such as the bedrooms for a lucrative sum of £1,600,000. This was ironic as I had once prevented the selling of the Club for a much lesser sum, and at the time when I first became involved, I was told that the Club was worthless and about to close.

Turmoil was not exclusive to the Liberal Party but a defeated Labour Party now led by Michael Foot was divided. Though I had great respect for Michael Foot for speaking out against American carnage in Cambodia and Vietnam, economic policies of the seventies when shop stewards appeared to rule the government and stagnate business was not something that I could subscribe to. Labour still retained a block vote system that put huge policy decisions into the hands of union leaders; they still had clause four which indicated a dominant and ever increasing role for nationalised industries and were too bureaucratic and centralised, stifling community values and small business.

Four prominent members of the Labour Party created the Social Democratic Party breaking away from Labour and linking up with kindred spirits in the Liberal Party. Of the four, I believe that Shirley Williams would have had a heavy heart breaking with Michael Foot as she had a strong peace heritage. Roy Jenkins was the senior member of the group. He was popular for bringing about reform for gays and divorcees and ending censorship in literature and the theatre when he had served as Home Secretary. He was also a very strong supporter of the

European Community. David Owen was a confident and strident member of the team. Overnight the policy of Grimond, Thorpe and Steel on nuclear deterrence of the Liberals, which was there should be a comprehensive deterrent with NATO and the Americans but not duplicating it with a British one, was changed to accept a so called independent deterrent.

Roy Jenkins was to play a prominent role within the new partnership with the Liberals but he was dismissive of Jo Grimond's brand of Liberalism calling it Luddite or Poujardist economics. At first I associated the Social Democrats in a favourable light with examples of two great statesmen, Willy Brandt and Olaf Palme, who bravely had invited Vietnam draft dodgers to live in Sweden. Though I liked the grass roots democracy of the Liberals I recognised that it did require a more structured approach: however the rigid approach of the Social Democrats was just too centralised and eventually too elitist. At the height of the Alliance I was asked what would happen if they won power. I replied "it would be somewhere between a Heath and a Callaghan government" and then I yawned.

Mrs Thatcher won popular acclaim after her stand against the Falkland Island invasion and was to win landslide victories in 1983 and 1987. She had the advantage of North Sea oil, the benefit of a thaw of the Cold War, and the gradual sale of public utilities, which brought short term gain for new share holders and the economy. The global economy brought some benefit to consumers but the British economy was over dependant on financial services. There was a sharp decline in industrial production throughout Britain, so Friedman Thatcherism brought about brazen affluence alongside dismal poverty. Monetarism was to bring about up to nineteen per cent interest rates on some small businesses which had tried to expand at the wrong time and resulted in a huge loss of small business. The new kings of the economy were the sleazy money lenders, the arms industry and the oil barons. Unlike Norway that invested in its own industry and ensured that North Sea revenues would be safeguarded for future pensioner needs, Britain had reduced rates of tax for big business and far more use of tax havens, which gave them an unfair advantage over home based British competitors. Though it was understandable that old style socialism as in the seventies was rejected by the electorate, all three parties supported the 'flog everything idea' of Friedman Thatcherism. Was there ever a third way that could have been applied? Perhaps a greener way, based upon community values and economics based upon human need.

Chapter 14

Micro and Macro Politics

When I started work in the National Liberal Club it was with great enthusiasm but as I turned my back on a professional political career it was like emerging from a dark tunnel into fresh air. After the Old Bailey trial I had a phone call from Paul Foot, the investigative journalist, who told me that he felt certain that Private Eye would be sued as they intended printing even stronger articles and were even attacking the Judge. He asked 'Can we count on your support to give evidence on our behalf?' My reply was that 'I would be prepared to back anything that I had already said in public in a court hearing.' They printed a strong and assertive article but were never sued on the relevant nuances.

During the next few years I worked in the family company free of party politics but was invited to become the founding chairman of the Federation of Small Business in the Canterbury district. Under the auspices of the Federation I chaired large public meetings in which ministers of Mrs Thatcher's government were the guest speakers. During this period I contributed to a research group of employers and teachers of Canterbury College, to discover which skills would be required in the future to support jobs. I was also invited to a national four day seminar in which union leaders and top bosses of industry participated.

Kent was known as the 'Garden of England' with numerous small holdings and market gardens intensively producing fruit, salad and vegetables. Many of these small farms were worked by tenant farmers who often began as farm labourers but had been trained in various agricultural colleges. Wye Agricultural College lecturers regularly visited the farms and provided advice and assistance with soil analysis and up to date information on the latest chemical advances and marketing techniques. A friendly partnership grew up between the college and the small farmers who were regularly invited to see the workings of the college.

At this time the revenue from agricultural production was six times greater than from our biggest exporting industry which was cars, but the money men came to realise that the dwellings on these small farms were a great asset. Soon so called experts who had never been near a farm were saying that these holdings were too small to be efficient and advocating their sale. As soon as one became vacant through retirement instead of being offered to another tenant they were sold. Soon the land was sold to large and less intensive farms and the dwellings had a ready market. No thought was given to the long term effects of local communities or to the economy.

From the seventies to the present day well paid 'experts' were proclaiming that economies of scale meant that only ever bigger business units could be efficient and a massive campaign was launched to elevate the idea of monetarism and 'Friedman Thatcherism'. Perhaps only the Green Party showed concern at erosion of the communities and ignoring the damage to the environment of food travelling hundreds of miles before reaching the consumer. It was not just agriculture that was being forced to change but small shops gradually disappeared. Also Post offices, residential and nursing homes and even hospitals were closed, despite their close proximity to patients and communities. The great God Mammon became the clarion call of all three major parties. Even the policies of the old Liberal Party which was based upon small business and free trade, abandoned its policy of having a Minister of Small Business with full Cabinet rank.

Following the '70's' during which there were numerous strikes which resulted in piles of uncollected refuse in the streets, as well as bodies left unburied and union leaders dictating to government. The economy stagnated under a great surge of bureaucracy and the electorate turned away from Labour. Mrs Thatcher won some popularity from the privatisation of huge swathes of industry, from those who could afford to pay for shares and also the sale of council houses at vastly reduced prices. When Mrs Thatcher's over riding and strident policies particularly on the poll tax became unpopular, the country turned to Blair and New Labour for a more broad appeal of politics. His toothpaste smile and his friendly personality gave him a start and he struck a positive chord when Princess Diana was killed.

The peace accords in Ireland strengthened his position but he will always be remembered for his support of George Bush's Crusade and starting the war in Iraq which is still rumbling along with an ever growing number of fatalities including innocent women and children. His economic policies were similar to Thatcher's with an over reliance on financial services and the neglect of industry including building, engineering and agriculture.

The financial crisis of 2008 began with the banking establishment overstretching itself in the United States. Countries such as Britain which were over dependant on the City and banking were particularly vulnerable and we were forced to face up to the deficit. That meant we had to either increase our exports or decrease our imports or face the consequences of mounting debt and interest to comply with international banking rules.

The General Election of 2010 included three television debates by the three party leaders. The relatively unknown Nick Clegg gave an excellent presentation and his popularity grew as a result of the first debate. He had successfully analysed the situation and there was hope that in the next two debates he would present some solution to the problems. Sadly he simply repeated what he had stated previously and was lacking in providing relevant policies for the future, so as the election drew closer Liberals even lost a little ground. David Cameron won most of the seats but lacked an overall majority. Either there would be a minority government or possibly a coalition government. Liberal representatives floated from Labour to Conservative representatives as the country waited to see what would happen.

I have heard from those who were involved with negotiations, that Labour representatives accepted that they had lost the election as the numbers did not add up for a left of centre coalition. I understand that they had no stomach for an all party coalition of national unity, for it would have meant serving under the leadership of the party with the most seats; the Conservatives led by David Cameron. I still believe that the Liberal Democrats missed a trick by not calling for an all party coalition to deal with the serious consequences of the deficit before committing to a coalition with the Conservatives. This would have banged the patriotic drum and showed that they were not only serious in facing up to the situation, but that financial problems would not unfairly be placed upon the poorest and most vulnerable.

The electorate could have been reminded that facing the trauma of war in 1939/40 required full cooperation from both the Labour Party; that provided the deputy prime minister and several prominent members of the Cabinet and the Liberal Party, that provided its leader to become the Minister of Air. There was not a more important job in 1940 than overseeing the RAF. People could also have been reminded that post war credits were introduced to pay for the war: this entailed that high earners were compelled to loan the Treasury monies that would be returned either on retirement or when the country could afford it. Another reminiscent and unifying thought would have been that despite the poverty of war the Beveridge Report was commissioned, promising a universal health and benefit scheme.

After such public declarations by the Liberal Democrats, if Labour had still not participated in a coalition government, Liberal Democrats would have captured the high ground and been free to enter negotiations with the Conservatives with a clear conscience, advocating a raise of income tax thresholds and a triple lock for pensioners. Instead the Conservative led coalition were able to reduce the top rate of tax and Liberal Democrats were forced to renege on their student tuition policy. British people were prepared to support the need to reduce the deficit and support policies that would increase exports and reduce imports so long as it was fair, particularly to the vulnerable.

Demoralising policies that affected many grass roots Liberal activists included the privatisation of Royal Mail and the Crown Post Offices. A few years before the 2010 coalition was formed I proposed a motion at the Regional Liberal Democrat Conference, the essence of which, was to transform the Crown Post Offices into Community Banks to finance small businesses and local charities and therefore provide real competition to the big Banks. The aspiration was to create a full blooded co-ownership scheme from Royal Mail. My motion was passed and I hoped that the parliamentary party would support such a policy when in government. I was appalled when Vince Cable implemented a privatisation plan: a policy that even Mrs Thatcher didn't do.

There was a referendum for a change in the electoral system. It was simply an alternative vote in single member constituencies. This would have brought about an increase in the majority of Mrs Thatcher or Tony Blair. For many years the policy advocated by the Electoral Reform Society and the Liberal Party was for a single transferrable vote in constituencies of five or six members, plus a regional list to ensure a Parliament that was based upon proportional representation but still had M.P.s with local links.

Policies advocated by the Liberal Party under the leadership of Grimond, Thorpe and Steel were disregarded, such as a full Cabinet position for the Minister of Small Business. Though there was a democratic vote to support Trident, I doubt if it would have been supported by members at local level.

In recent years on both sides of the Atlantic there is

growing dissatisfaction with political leadership. What was once described as 'decay' in the over-riding sense of purpose had become more cynical, with fear of immigration particularly including Islamic terrorism. This has led to our departure from the European Community. The white working class felt neglected with a growing housing shortage and a lack of jobs paying a reasonable wage. Youngsters who were told that a university degree would enable them to have a well paid job often find themselves in debt with only low paid work found.

The remarkable rise of Jeremy Corbyn against the insults and rebuke of the Blairites and the Conservatives which was compounded by the right wing media had made him the darling of the young. He was almost accused of treason for talking to Sinn Fein during the Irish troubles. As a peace campaigner he was striving to change the military conflict for a peaceful one leading in a democratic direction. Peacemaking is at the heart of Christianity and today the world needs peace makers as much as we needed Winston Churchill for the war in 1940.

As one who is not a member of the Labour Party I believe the five hundred thousand members that they now have is an incredible success. Older citizens may remind the younger generation of the dreadful seventies which helped to prepare the way for Thatcherism. Though a few union leaders may dream of a return to those days, I believe the majority of Labour's new membership is looking for a new sense of direction. They reject more of the soul-less Friedman Thatcherism with ever greater concentrations of wealth in fewer hands and the slogan of 'I'm alright Jack.'

If the Corbyn led movement ever succeeds is an open question. If they are too insular and triumphant, their numerous opponents will defeat them. If on the other hand they can reach out to other progressives in the Green Party and grass roots Liberals, they can have a long lasting effect upon politics. Pragmatic wealth creation alongside social justice and an ethical foreign policy could transform British politics.

I believe that since the First World War and the emergence of the Labour Party the split on the left has led to the electoral pendulum sticking on the right side during the last century. I think that there will always be a Conservative Party just as there will always be a negative to the positive. They should not however be allowed to dominate the next century as they have the last but I believe the best we can hope for is a free flowing pendulum.

Politics in both Britain and the United States is probably more fluid than for many years. The uncertainty of where negotiations between Britain and the European Community will eventually lead is causing a lack of confidence in the future. The sporadic terrorist attacks add to the confusion and the failure of the Muslim community to integrate, is increasing tension in many working class districts.

Sadly just after the end of the Cold War and the Irish troubles we now appear to be engaged in a conflict situation of which few of us understand. Our prime minister waxes lyrical about the merits of the arms trade: we appear to be selling arms to every Al Capone in the terrorist world then wondering why we exacerbate the situation in the Middle East. The great majority of Muslims are peaceful and hard working and I believe we must urgently seek advice and guidance from the moderate ones. When senior politicians urge us to bomb Syria, but don't know which side to bomb first, it does appear to express ignorance of the situation. To overcome any alien ideology we must have a superior one; military means alone is not enough. We must try to understand how a death cult can hypnotise or brainwash youngsters to volunteer for martyrdom and counter the threat to our own people.

If a progressive alliance is to come about, Labour, Liberal and Green activists should seek common ground. I believe an agreement in a change to the electoral system is the only way to bring the three groups together. I was at a loss to understand when Liberal Democrats had a chance to promote a referendum, they should not choose a form of Proportional Representation. Such a system works elsewhere and could be relevant if we are ever to see a progressive alliance that could bring our politicians in line with the aspirations of the people.

I have long believed that over dependence on the financial sector has led to sleazy money lenders, arms dealers and oil barons hijacking participatory democracy and killing off so many entrepreneurs who require investment, research and initial help of development.

For several decades political leaders have spoken of technology and science creating a brave new world in which we will benefit. Back in the sixties Harold Wilson spoke of the white heat of technological revolution creating a world with less need to work and a great deal of leisure. In the age of globalisation and the internet this view is compounded but it is the countries that have developed medium technology and devolution for smaller economic units that have prospered. A small country such as Holland has built economic success upon thousands of small businesses and exports foodstuff whilst Britain imports so much of its needs. In all the arguments about whether we should trade more in or outside the European Community there has been little discussion from either side about how we can create wealth in Britain and though the deficit has been reduced, a balanced budget when we can pay off our debts, looks a long way off. Meanwhile the living standards of Germany and the Benelux nations are far better than ours. Even when we have had the benefit from North Sea oil it has been squandered, unlike in Norway where oil revenues has been ring fenced for future generation of pensioners and for healthcare.

How can we develop an ethical foreign policy that will strengthen and not weaken our security and how can we base our economics upon human need? Such questions should be at the centre of debate, at local as well as national level throughout the country.

During the Second World War leaders declared that everyone had a role to play in overcoming adversity. By developing localism and identifying what can be achieved, must start by encouraging communities to engage with dialogue. We have lots of examples of good practise that can be expanded throughout the country.

In my local village it looked as if we would soon be lacking a post office and general shop. A meeting was called for residents and it was agreed that we should ask for support for a new shop that could be built on to our community hall. Money was raised to build an extension to the hall and eventually a new shop and post office was constructed. A lease holder was chosen and we now have a flourishing general shop together with a post office plus a money machine that saves numerous trips to congested Canterbury. The investment produces a small profit each year which is distributed to local charity and good causes.

I recently took a right wing friend of mine for a lunch to thank him for his help during a recent illness of mine. We enjoyed a good lunch at the Haywain in Bramling. The place was packed and we were lucky to have a table even though it was a mid week day. This was a wonderful example of a community pub with a great landlord and wife who raise thousands of pounds for charity. Afterwards we visited a local farm shop run by Mike Gibson. It is a great venture that employs thirty four staff where meat, fruit and vegetables are locally sourced and a comprehensive range of cakes, pickles and a wide range of Kentish produced food is sold; even local honey. These are two examples of what is possible when community ventures survive, but they have become far too rare for less fortunate districts.

The Treasury and the right wing media praise and support the banking establishment but as a mechanism for converting our savings into positive businesses, the banking establishment has failed lamentably. Our forefathers created building societies which have played a positive role in developing property owning democracy and providing real competition to the big banks. British banks have only invested in 5% of their assets. If the post offices had been allowed to develop as community banks, a far greater investment would have been made in local enterprises. Most of the postmasters and postmistresses are self employed businesses but have never been allowed to play a role in organising the national board.

If we look at the dichotomy of so many of the negatives of our democracy and dare to examine the kind of nation we might have had if many of the policies and vision of Jo Grimond had become a reality, there is a stark jolt to our sensibility. We may have paid off two thirds of our deficit but even when we eventually have a balanced budget we will still have to pay interest on a massive debt. The cost of austerity is that the burden has hurt the most vulnerable and restored a class divide. Britain now has an investment crisis, an income crisis, a productivity crisis and gross inequality. Human dignity has been lost as thousands of small businesses have been lost together with opportunities of grass roots wealth creation.

Politics has become centralised and elitist with few examples of unity and inspiration. There is a massive void in the centre of politics and any form of development is led not by people but piecemeal; new housing estates are built without consideration of community needs and often lack basic infrastructure. In Canterbury, Hitler solved the traffic and congestion problem but the beautiful city of Canterbury is gradually being choked by pollution. Over a decade ago I wrote an article stating that there was a danger that Canterbury could be transformed into a fume filled hell hole. I didn't mince my words! I knew that my intemperate words would upset friends and political foes alike.

I could cite numerous examples of developer led planning decisions that have worsened the situation. A decade or so ago a possible development site was suggested on both sides of the Rheims Way, the main imposing entry into Canterbury. On the one side there was room for a reception centre and the new building of the Marlowe Theatre. On the other side of the road was an ideal site for a coach park. If an underpass had been built connecting the two and the continuance of a foot path to the city centre and cathedral, it would have saved so much pollution. Instead coaches now have to pass to the other side of the city causing a very real threat of pollution.

The idea that bigger units are always more efficient is eroding the common sense within local communities and unfairly affecting small businesses. As a district councillor I questioned the wisdom that officers and the ruling Conservative group, of automatically amalgamating with several other district councils. I knew of several small businesses that efficiently and satisfactorily undertook council contracts but might not be big enough to undertake a contract with a larger district. A question I put in Council was 'Would such businesses still be able to tender for local contracts?' The answer from the officer was that small businesses would still be able to take on local council contracts and that they valued such businesses. Alas once the amalgamation took place a local contractor had been removed from the approved list despite a record of satisfactory work in the past. When I questioned this the officer responsible told me that small businesses should apply to larger contractors to sub contract.

During eight years as a district councillor I was fortunate to work with some good conscientious officers but when the council faced cutbacks the most effective ones often disappeared. I had to fight tooth and nail to ensure that a housing project for the elderly would survive. The building needed either renovation or rebuilding. The officers wished to knock it down and not replace it. I was told that no elderly people wanted to live in a village; then I was told it was not placed in a suitable position for elderly residents. The reality was that a pathway to the rear of the site led first, to the recreation field where residents loved to watch the cricket and football and then directly to the shop, post office, community hall and a bus stop for easy access to Canterbury. A short distance away was the surgery and the local church. After newspaper publicity and support from the parish councils I eventually won an agreement that the project would be rebuilt specifically for the elderly. I then demanded that the residents who were living in the old building would have the first chance to return when the new bungalows and flats were built. The original project was warden assisted which was not the case of the new project so I insisted that there should be somewhere on site that could be used as a social centre so that residents could congregate and look after each other. First I was told that all the residents wanted were to watch television and stay in their homes. Again I fought for that social centre and am pleased to say it is well used by the residents.

Another occasion, when I was dismayed by officers, was when the play area behind a block of flats was compulsorily cleared of a swing, trampoline, garden furniture and plants under health and safety rules. The play area could only be reached by the residents and not the general public and the parents were able to watch the activities of the children. As the police ward officer stated, 'the children would now be out on the streets which makes my work more difficult.'

Education can be a wonderfully liberating influence and the two Universities in Canterbury have had a beneficent effect upon the community but in some ways Kent is a backward county in education. By dividing children with the eleven plus the establishment has conditioned the majority of children to some of the most poorly performing schools that exist alongside some elitist ones. Other districts have developed good comprehensive schools that retain adequate grammar, technical and a sixth form syllabus within them.

In 1945 there was no country in the world more revered by friends and respected universally than Britain. Following such grievous sacrifice suffered by so many, Britain may have lacked military muscle but still had the moral leadership of the world.

A positive role in the creation of the United Nations and the beginning of the transformation from empire to commonwealth strengthened respect. Britain became the world's peace maker with a flexible approach to labour and capital rather than conflict. With some provisos, Britain could today have become as prosperous as any country in the world.

At the birth of the European Community if Britain had joined instead of standing by the wayside it might have helped create an even greater free trade area including the commonwealth. Some of the overpowering anomalies could have been ironed out and it might have been less bureaucratic and more popular at grass roots level.

The implementation of the Liberal idea of full cabinet rank for a minister of small business and for larger businesses that required economy of scale, more co-ownership schemes would promote more participatory democracy and healthier communities. Instead of the reliance of the financial sector, a steady supply of capital and a strict code of practice to check the abuse of banks, would help to create social justice with a healthy wealth creation.

Universities and colleges could play a more inclusive role reaching beyond tuition and leading a moratorium within communities and providing pragmatic help in the innovation and development of commerce. Entrepreneurs, business leaders and community leaders of all ages could be encouraged to tap the knowledge of technology that is available within educational centres.

The creation of new business or expansion of existing ones requires finance and the problem for banks is that their reputation means that a whole generation, plus children, no longer trust the big banks though building societies and the post offices are considered less brutal. Community banks delivered by the Crown Post Offices could still be a positive way to strengthen and rebuild the economy.

It is estimated that two hundred and five billion pounds be spent on Trident. The Liberal Party led by Grimond, Thorpe and Steel advocated a comprehensive nuclear deterrent within N.A.T.O. but not duplicated by a so called independent deterrent. Such a policy would be similar to that of Australia, Canada and Germany and numerous other countries. Like the paranoia of North Korea this policy is crippling the economy and many military leaders together with Mrs Thatcher's Defence Secretary, think money could be better spent.

We need to find a new way to do politics. The common sense and the common purpose of the common man is the greatest force on earth. If fear erodes that purpose it can become a negative force as in the thirties, but if it embraces an ethical or spiritual dimension it can move us to the broad sunlit uplands.

We all want the best of all possible worlds, so if a new discovery in medicine happened or something that positively helps humanity we would wish it to be applied universally. The global economy has been advantageous to millions living in China and India and modern communication has helped us to make friends across the world. For example, the charity that I chaired, the Gurkha Peace Foundation has established twinning between a school in Folkestone and a school in Nepal. Children talk to children through Skype and seeing that the children in Nepal were shivering with cold, the children in Cheriton, Folkestone emptied their money boxes and paid for warm school uniforms for the children in Nepal. The positive advantage of this was that the children could see where their money went and lead to firm friendships being formed. Such forms of communication can become a positive business as well as charity link.

Sadly there is a downside to the wonderful advantages of social media and globalisation. Greedy and clever financiers have created tax havens which have disadvantaged local based firms. This has brought about a wide gap in wealth. Eight men now have as much wealth as half the population of the world. Such brazen affluence alongside dismal poverty does not equate with a healthy democracy and opposes the ethos of the great religions. Freedom is of value in proportion to its universality and the first freedom is the freedom from want. Such disparity of wealth is the root cause of the turmoil throughout the world. Many of the poorest throughout the world now have a glimpse of the wealth of the few and knowledge of injustices.

The moral compass that many of us in the Anglo Saxon world believed that we had, has now faded away despite the effort of altruistic charity workers. When Tim Farron resigned as the leader of the Liberal Democrats in 2017 citing that he found it impossible to practise his Christian faith and remain the Liberal leader, plus having an American President who approves of torture of prisoners as well as a British prime minister who blames Putin for her government's ineptitude, this surely reflects the decline in western values.

Yet there are some great examples to all of us of what can be achieved, but the media fails to give them the light of day.

There is an Israeli rabbi who educates Palestinian and Israeli children together in what is called an 'Oasis of peace': A retired Methodist minister who as a prison chaplain brought about Christians and Muslims to pray together: Sir Tim Smith plans to expand his Eden Project and green the world. There is the Mondragon Project that created a whole town based upon cooperatives and profit sharing. Schumacher economics still has a positive message for community politics and a plan of how we should live together. The words of Gandhi are as relevant as ever; there is enough for everyone's need but never enough for everyone's greed.

Chapter 15

Campaign for Gurkha Justice

I first came across the Gurkhas in the midst of the Vietnam War. I was fairly new to Vietnam and experienced a particularly noisy evening. The rumble of surrounding bombs grew closer; there was the crack of outgoing artillery and the occasional shudder of incoming Viet Cong rockets. A more direct danger was evident with sporadic outbreaks of street fire fights within Saigon and so I decided to retreat to the British Embassy together with other members of the tiny British community where we were guarded by Gurkhas.

I was soon to learn that the Gurkhas had a proud reputation of protecting British Embassies and personnel in trouble spots all over the world. They have a higher opinion of the British than we have of ourselves. I believe they still believe in the Britain of high ideals that existed in the forties. They were always kind and diplomatic but strong and resolute in a war situation and everyone who knew them often said that they are called 'the bravest of the brave.'

Many years later I had a chance conversation with an ex Gurkha who told me how disappointed he was that Gurkhas were being treated so badly. He told me that after serving at least fifteen years in the British Army some of his colleagues were being sent back to Nepal with inadequate pensions and healthcare. Some were even sick or injured and had children who knew no home other than England.

The year was 2004; I was informed that after their dissatis-faction they called upon Michael Howard who was the M.P. for Folkestone where many Gurkhas had settled. At the time he was the Leader of the Opposition and in a powerful position to intervene but again they were disappointed. I suggested to Bhim Raj, the Gurkha I was conversing with that they should call upon Peter Carroll who was standing as a Liberal Democrat candidate for Parliament. They had tried the two big parties so there was nothing to lose by approaching the Liberal Democrats.

Peter Carroll had been a RAF officer and I knew him to be an excellent campaigner with political depth and integrity. I gave Bhim the phone number and address of Peter and also left a message on his answer phone stating that he should expect to be contacted by a little delegation of Gurkhas. I mentioned that I believed that they had a real grievance and I hoped that he could help them.

Three or four days later I turned the television on to see a news item that told of how some local Gurkhas were about to be deported. My first thoughts were of sadness that I had been too late to help but in trooped Peter Carroll with a few Gurkhas. Their case was put on the media and the atmosphere was electric.

Bhim together with Gopal Giri, Prem Limbu and Bidhur Paksrin had knocked on Peter Carroll's door and thus begun what was later called the Campaign for Gurkha Justice. I doubt if there was anyone in the country better than Peter to galvanise what was to become one of the best ever political campaigns, that won over the British public together with media, legal and political activists.

A massive amount of work was undertaken with every news-paper, television and radio centre contacted with letters going directly to every M.P., together with all the appropriate government and military authorities. The message went out to all the Gurkha communities throughout the country, to back the campaign by a peaceful protest outside Parliament.

I arrived with a minibus full of Gurkhas and in a space of a very few minutes Parliament Square was filling up, not only by those originating from Nepal, but by proud Englishmen some wearing military medals of their own and some, medals awarded to their fathers. As we congregated for the first time some police officers were dismayed by yet another protest, as some of them had recently been beaten up by protesting huntsmen who fought their way into Parliament.

As we marched towards Downing Street protesters kept enough space upon the pavement to allow for those walking in the opposite direction. Letters and petitions were handed in to the prime minister's home and the protest was shown on nationwide television.

A contingent of Gurkhas was welcomed at the Liberal Democrat Conference with a standing ovation and Charles Kennedy became the first party leader to publicly support the call for parity of pensions and the right to settle. His comments went far and wide: 'Those who are prepared to die for us should be able to live with us.'

Two formidable ladies were soon to add their support. One came from each of the two big parties; Ann Widdicombe and Betty Boothroyd. We were given a few brochures by the group of lawyers in the Lord McDonald and Mike Mansfield team, which we despatched to key journalists such as Jonathan

Dimbleby. A constant stream of publicity steadily won new friends, with a growing number expressing the view that they were unaware of how badly Gurkhas had been treated.

More mass protests followed in London and our campaign became global. Television crews followed us around from Parliament Square to the Ministry of Defence in Whitehall. I recall just finishing a television interview with a Nepalese crew, to be told that it was to be relayed to fifty two countries. I will always remember the authoritive voice of Betty Boothroyd saying 'You have a meeting in Parliament so hurry along.'

In the early stages I underestimated the role of lawyers who were about to make a massive contribution to the cause. Colleagues had tried to arrange for a Victoria Cross holder to come to Britain for urgently needed medical treatment but had been refused entry, He had been told that he did not have enough association with Britain. This despite having saved over twenty British lives in the Second World War. Eventually he was allowed to enter the country and Martin Howe and his colleagues arranged a lavish welcome for him to which I was invited and I was privileged to be invited to the family home of Pun's children where he was to stay. Pun was the V.C. who had served in the same regiment as the father of Joanna Lumley.

We were all reminded of the cruelty of war when a Canterbury based Gurkha was killed and his widow wished to return to Nepal for the funeral but then return with her two children to England. As a councillor I proposed the motion which was unanimously passed by Canterbury City Council that she should be allowed to return to Canterbury, as she feared that it would be difficult for her. I am pleased to say that the M.O.D. agreed to the request. A little later as Christmas was approaching the Council agreed to distribute sweets to the young Gurkha children who were based at Howe Barracks in Canterbury. As a minor member of the civic team I accompanied the Lord Mayor on this mission of goodwill.

On one of our demonstrations about two thousand people turned up outside the old Bailey to support our legal team. I was a little early and alongside me near the gates to the court was a distinguished lady who told me she was waiting to greet her friend Joanna Lumley. She wanted to support our campaign for the Gurkhas as her late husband had served with them. Well into our conversation, whilst drinking a hot beaker of coffee provided by one of our Gurkha friends, I casually asked if she was a thespian. She modestly replied that she did a little bit of acting. When I asked her name she replied that it was Virginia McKenna. She was indeed a great film actress who had appeared in many iconic films. I immediately remembered her lead role with Gregory Peck and her role in another epic 'A town called Alice' and 'Born Free', in which she appeared alongside her husband Ben Travis.

Joanna turned up and the television journalists soon came to realise that they had two famous celebrities supporting us. Several leading politicians came along but after being photographed soon disappeared, however Joanna Lumley attempted to shake hands with all of the two thousand Gurkhas.

We won a series of victories in the High Court. It was easier to gain human rights for the Gurkhas who had served after Hong Kong had been handed over and when they were based in England, though often they served abroad. The diminishing numbers of elderly ex Gurkhas were the most shabbily treated, abandoned with inadequate pensions and third world healthcare. When they eventually won the right to settle in Britain many of them would have rather stayed in Nepal if their pensions had been a little more reasonable but if they were able to come to Britain they were better off. Many of them came to live near their loved ones and fellow Nepalese. Ashford and Folkestone were popular destinations for them however they found themselves in a country in which they spoke very little English. My Gurkha friends including three of those who knocked on Peter Carroll's door, wished to start a charity to help them integrate in Britain and eventually assist projects in Nepal. The original vision was to start with an equal number of trustees from within the newly settled Gurkha community and indigenous British friends.

There was a need for a base of operations first of all in Ashford and then in Folkestone, where they could congregate at least once a week. They hoped that by providing a blue print for day centres in Kent, the ideas would spread throughout the country. A long term plan was for them to twin projects in Britain with worthy ones in Nepal. Thus began the long tortuous path to create the Gurkha Peace Foundation. For those experienced with small charities and little money, it takes a long time to develop but it was the first charity of its kind to be started and was led by the new Gurkha community that settled in Britain.

Despite our victories in the High Court the M.O.D. appeared to be ignoring the legal ruling so Martin Howe and his team of brilliant lawyers went back to court. I remember being pushed towards the throng with Gurkha colleagues insisting that I should sit on the front bench alongside the lawyers and less than six feet from the deliberating judge, who stood in front of me. A great cheer of approval went up as soon as the judge made his deliberations in our favour.

After this we were dismayed that letters were still being sent to Gurkhas and their families advising them to leave the country. This was quite different to what was being said in public. Joanna Lumley, Peter Carroll and Martin Howe were meeting inside Parliament when Phil Woolas the Minister of Immigration happened to walk through. The Minister tried to evade the group but Joanna chased after him in hot pursuit with the television cameras following them.

Joanna had a letter in her hands that had been sent from Phil Woolas' Immigration department and she diplomatically confronted him with it and asked a few straightforward questions. He nodded his head in agreement when asked if these letters would cease to be sent and if his department would make it clear to those who had received them that they had been rescinded. The Minister had given his word on television which cleared up any misunderstanding. Within such a change of atmosphere Joanna invited the Minister to come back to her flat for a fish and chip supper.

On a sweltering day in July I was invited to a party hosted by Martin Howe and his colleagues. With a glass of wine in my hands David Cameron joined us and I introduced him to a Gurkha whose life had been saved by our campaign. He needed a kidney transplant and his sister had flown to Britain to volunteer being a donor. My conversation was soon joined by a Minister in the Labour Government. Joanna Lumley was surrounded by admirers as she could charm the birds from the trees and was probably more popular than any politician. A little later Nick Clegg arrived with his wife Miriam. They apologised for being late as they wanted to put the children to bed. Social occasions with a cross section of political activists can be very pleasant and lack personal malevolence.

After chatting to Joanna, Peter, Martin and a number of lawyer and political friends as well as Gurkhas, I worked my way to the rear of the room which opened onto a large balcony. This was a welcome relief for the open air was a shade cooler than the inner room. Here was Simon Hughes and further along, Virginia McKenna. Eventually it was time to depart from a full and pleasant party and when I reached home I switched on the television hoping to catch the news. There appeared a young Virginia McKenna swimming between two lions. Having just been chatting to her I found it strange that films could stand still in time. Thespians must be used to it but for most of us it is like seeing another person. It reminded me what an incredible woman Virginia was, spending a lifetime campaigning for animal welfare. Of course Joanna Lumley being a vegetarian, shared that common interest.

In April 2009 there was to be a motion in Parliament moved by Nick Clegg in support of the Gurkha cause. I didn't think it had much chance of defeating the government but it promised to strengthen our objectives, so together with around two thousand others we congregated in Parliament Square just opposite where we expected the debate to be, probably lasting for four or five hours. Only that day did I learn that David Cameron and the Conservatives were going to support the Liberal Democrat motion. There was growing excitement which was shared by the public demonstration opposite the Commons.

I was passed a loudspeaker by a Gurkha friend and invited to speak to the multitude. I climbed onto the base of the statue to say my piece. Speaking to such a multitude is different to any other speech. Even though addressing an audience on television or radio may reach more people, the only way to approach it is to speak from the heart without notes or hesitation. I gave my speech and it was well received. The first to greet me was Bill Cash who shook my hand and congratulated me as he introduced himself. He told me that he was soon going over the road to vote when the division came. I was pleased that our campaign had reached across the political spectrum.

I was about to join a judge and a lawyer for a jar in the local pub, as I was told it would take some time for the debate in Parliament to be concluded. On my way I was approached by a large police officer. I thought he was about to tell me off for using a microphone but instead he put his face close to mine and whispered 'we support you.' I was then approached by an ex Gurkha who told me that he had been given less than ten years to live after being used as a guinea pig for chemical weapons. As he was only about thirty years old I found that pretty shocking and I asked my legal friends if he had exaggerated. They both assured me that there were several cases pending, similar to this, that were being pursued for compensation in the courts.

Shortly after this, a jubilant Joanna Lumley emerged from Parliament alongside Nick Clegg and David Cameron. I had heard, from Lynne, Peter Carroll's wife, via her mobile phone that we had defeated the government. I had just concluded a conversation with Andrew Neil asking him to let one of us, preferably Joanna, Peter or Martin to appear on his show as none of us believed that we were about to win this victory in Parliament. There was a tumultuous cheer as our colleagues walked across the road with television cameras following them.

In triumphant mood we planned the creation of our charity. Charlotte McCaul was the Canterbury City Sheriff and at the annual dinner chose her two charities for the event. Peter Carroll spoke about our campaign and the children of Gurkhas entertained the diners with traditional Nepalese dancing. A thousand pounds was raised, and half of it went to a project supporting local handicapped children and the other half enabled us to open an account for the proposed charity.

Providing a good curry, together with Nepalese hospitality and entertainment by the children of Gurkhas performing traditional dancing and singing, was a positive way to raise funds. We filled halls all over Kent with this formulae and it started a steady build up of supporters, paying monthly sums to the Gurkha Peace Foundation by standing orders. With the support of Mr and Mrs Goodman, an annual Gurkha Walk has since been held at the delightful Eastwell Manor near Ashford.

With the help of the Bishop of Dover, Trevor Wilmot, we were introduced to St Francis Church in Ashford where it has been possible to hire the hall each week. This was to become the first day centre in 2013 where veterans gathered for help and advice. Soon a smart television was provided that relayed news directly from Nepal. The veterans also enjoyed playing bingo and celebrating special holidays and participating in summer barbeques which were hugely successful.

Following the success of the day centres in Ashford, Gopal Giri found a suitable hall in Folkestone to repeat the weekly events. With the steadily growing Gurkha Peace Foundation there was a desire to begin altruistic work in Nepal so several of us planned to visit Nepal in the hope of identifying up to ten projects worthy of support. The vision was the twinning ideal of linking with local schools or clubs so that monies given could be clearly identified.

Five of the ten trustees including myself, paid out of our own pockets for the trip to Nepal in 2014. The flight would take us from Heathrow to Delhi where we would catch the next flight to Kathmandu in Nepal. I found it a long, tiring journey but we were soon whisked through the Nepalese airport to be greeted with traditional garlands on our arrival. I was pleased to set my feet on the ground but being driven through the streets of the city, the congestion and pollution was stifling. It was a welcome relief to reach a shower and comfortable bed.

Charlotte McCaul and I were the two trustees who went on this fact finding trip, where the schedule was planned by Bhim Raj and Prem Limbu and later by Deb Pun. The temperature in February was similar to a summer's day in Britain and we were to experience a little rain which surprised me as it was not the monsoon season. For the first few nights we stayed in a centre run by a Christian relative of Prem. We discovered though that the main religions of Nepal were Hindu and Buddhist and there was a multi faith philosophy including a strong Christian tradition.

One remarkable sight that surprised me was the number of dogs that slept on the streets. In many countries I had visited in the past I would be wary and keep my distance from them. Here they were different for they were happy well fed dogs usually with their tails up. When they defecated they chose an appropriate place and then covered it up by kicking the dust and soil with their back legs. Throughout our trip I also noticed that there was not the usual sight of vermin seen in many poor countries.

There were obvious signs of poverty but there were no aggressive signs of begging and when I noticed a youngster who drew very close to Bhim when we were in the food market, I mentioned it to him as I suspected he might be a pick pocket. Bhim replied that this was not possible as the youth was Nepalese and they simply did not do such things. I had to agree, for a poor country there was little sign of crime.

I learnt that historically Nepal had a proud tradition of spawning peace movements. This was a far cry from the almost blood thirsty claims of the M.O.D. made on behalf of the Gurkhas. Of course like a brave police officer who faces danger, it's possible to be a courageous soldier combined with diplomacy and compassion. Indeed these are the special qualities of the Gurkhas who are renowned for being peace makers in a troubled world.

Unfortunately I suffered stomach disorders that prevented me visiting the birthplace of the Buddha however I was able to visit the Buddhist centre in Kathmandu where we were reminded that the plight of lepers still continued to this day. We were also taken to witness the continuous stream of Hindu funerals taking place by the river. The feet of bound bodies, were always dipped into the river to ensure that the deceased really were dead. Then the bodies were burnt which resulted in a horrible smell of burning flesh wafting across the river where we were standing.

In the West we are spared such experiences but here funerals took place within a day or so of death. I was happy to move on from the funeral site, to witness more pleasurable scenes of dancing and dining within the streets.

Soon we were to travel on the mountain road to Dhahran. My

Gurkha friends had organised a suitable vehicle together with a brilliant driver. I had driven in Saigon during the Vietnam War, as well as London and Paris but nothing prepared me for motoring in Nepal. I was grateful that I was not in the driving seat as we journeyed on roads that became more like tracks with more stones and boulders than road. We climbed mountain sides but had to stop on several occasions due to rocks falling from the mountains. If we had been underneath them we would have been crushed. As we proceeded, driving down the mountain side, the wheels of our mountain range car were only a few inches to the sheer drop down the mountainside. It was most dangerous when an oncoming vehicle driving far too fast around the bend of the mountainside nearly pushed us over the side. The bumps and grinds as we drove over boulders made this ride uncomfortable but eventually we reached our destination of Dhahran towards the east of Nepal.

This city became my favourite city in Nepal with less traffic pollution and some pleasant hotels and houses. After a good meal and night's sleep we visited a centre run by the Welfare Trust. The veterans who resided here were the luckiest in Nepal. We were greeted by Captain Limbu who introduced us to two young ladies who had no arms. One in her early teens had walked for two days and nights with her mother and neighbours just to visit us. The Welfare Trust had a mandate to help servicemen and their families but we had a wider brief and we could assist those who were not associated with the military.

These two ladies had learnt to write with their toes and managed to write and speak English better than I could ever have managed to speak Nepalese. I told these ladies that we would never forget them and my colleagues and I said we hoped to offer a little extra assistance in education as soon as we were able to. How could we ever forget the look in their eyes as we sat with a cool drink in these comfortable surroundings before it was time for us to depart?

Our next heart rending visit was to the one and only blind school in Nepal. As we entered the premises over a hundred children lined up to greet us. They stood in a straight line in order of age and the youngest presented us with a floral ring to place around our necks. They must have been ages making these tributes to us. They had so little but were clean and received regular meals and appeared pleased to see us. Their food was adequate but reminded me of the gruel in Dickensian Britain. The Principal, Keshari Thapa lived inside the compound with her husband and was like a mother to the children. She was assisted by several teachers who resided nearby.

I was amazed to learn that children not only learnt Braille in Nepalese but also in English, which the older ones spoke quite well. We were shown around the premises and entertained by a small orchestra formed by the older children and a prayer for peace was recited by a twelve year old boy. I managed to get a copy of his prayer and was later able to arrange for it to be relayed by the daughter of a Gurkha at the United Nations World Peace Day Service held in Canterbury Cathedral.

We were told that the older children had a white stick but the younger ones could no longer have one as they used them to hit each other. The Principal told us how much she encouraged the mothers of the children to keep in touch with their children but had to fight a traditional idea that any handicap was caused by wrong doing in a previous life.

I felt there was so much help that we could provide if we were able to find a twinning link in England. The children had a love of music and I thought they would appreciate recordings of popular English music as well as Nepalese ones and perhaps would appreciate some audio recordings of classic children's stories. My fellow trustees did not come prepared with available funds but we all had a little spending money which we gave to the blind school.

Unbeknown to me my Gurkha friends had collected monies independent of the charity for the purpose of saving the life of a Gurkha who was due to be executed in Saudi Arabia. Though he had proclaimed his innocence unless a sum of cash was paid to the relatives of a victim of a killing, the execution would go ahead. I was passed a sum of money to be presented to the wife of the man due to be executed. What was called blood money, I gave to the grateful wife in front of newspaper reporters and photographers.

Early one morning we started to drive to the mountain town of Taplejung which was in sight of the Himalayas and Mount Everest. It was situated to the north of Dhahran and when we reached our destination, we had created a great deal of media interest as newspapers were interested in our objectives. They wondered if we had any association with political machinations for Nepal to form a new coalition government. This was something that we strenuously denied, insisting that we simply wished to identify projects worthy of support. Only later on would we learn how this rumour originated.

Our next destination was to visit Antu village in the Ilam district where we were shown a tea plantation that belonged to the family of one of our trustees, Gopal Giri. We were greeted

293

by his brother. We were shown the large processing plant that had recently been built and then attended the district school. The children were fascinated by seeing themselves in the reflective camera of our photographer and their thirst for learning was impressive.

The next night we spent in a jungle area in a wooden built hostelry. Just before, I had read that in the last few months six unfortunate men had been killed by wild animals: Two by tigers, two by elephants and two by rhinoceros. Yet here we were sleeping on the ground floor protected only by a slender wooden wall and surrounded by rainforests.

We were soon to travel to Tethathum District where some of Bhim's family resided. As ever the hospitality was warm and the children in the two schools appreciated our presence. Unfortunately I suffered from dysentery which limited my ability to fully participate in various activities. For those of us who have been brought up with modern conveniences it is often the fate of travellers to suffer from stomach problems. As in common with numerous countries, lavatories within the Himalayan villages comprise of holes in the floor with buckets of water and a communal ladle used to substitute pulling the chain. I would have liked to spend more time in Bhim's district but ill health prevented it.

Our next destination was the Sankhuwawasawa District, the ancestral home of Prem Limbu where our charity had donated several surgical beds for a newly built health centre. The community was hugely ambitious and hearing of how Prem's father had been responsible for the first school and the first health centre, I understand the motivation.

I was personally pleased to return to Dhahran where my

colleagues took me to the local hospital where I was promptly treated for what I knew was a familiar medical problem for foreigners. When I had partially recovered we started to travel on the longer southern road all the way to Pokera, to the west of Kathmandu. After resting here we set out on the northern road towards Baglung. Ex Major Deb Pun joined us and guided our group along the mountainous road to Shree Shitalpati, his original community where some of his relatives still lived. I had hoped the mountain tracks would be better than some of those we experienced but in fact they were worse. I was amazed that we were able to drive over boulders where any sign of a road almost disappeared but still we continued on our journey.

As we arrived a great noise broke out of cheering and clattering of instruments. The community had turned out to greet us so we dismounted from our vehicle and walked towards the village centre. Floral tributes were hung around our necks and the cheering and clatter of the instruments continued unabated.

Chapter 16

Swords to Ploughshares

The enthusiasm of the community at Shitalpati, high in the Himalayan Mountain range, made its school an easy choice for a possible twinning scheme with a British school. Over the next few years the regular contact with former Major Deb Pun would make this a blue print for twinning, using modern technology such as Skype linking the two communities.

We came across the eldest residents in this community still recalling their time during the Second World War. Since that time most of them had not seen any English men so they were thrilled at seeing our team. Dancing and celebrating our presence would continue for several hours. Our visit was ideal for developing a cohesive strategy with the teachers and ex Major Deb Pun who would dedicate himself to a future twinning scheme.

All too soon it was time to depart and head towards Kathmandu. Eventually we arrived back at the congested capital where we concluded our trip. Our thinking about charity and politics was always to try and help those to help themselves, so we were pleased to visit a project stewarded by a former Lt Col Philip Holmes where abused youngsters were busy working on silver jewellery such as necklaces, ear rings and brooches. They were steadily building an export business as their work improved.

During our trip we identified ten projects that would gradually be twinned with schools and colleges in England. We were to spend the final few days of our trip learning what we could of the current and fast moving events within Nepal. It had often been argued by those who opposed the campaign for Gurkha Justice that the cost of living in Nepal was so much cheaper than in Britain, so there was no injustice to the eldest retired Gurkhas. A visit to the market contradicted this and I was surprised at how expensive food was including meat, fruit and vegetables. Indeed it was almost as expensive as back in Britain. Incomes were much lower but the cost of living was not.

Many families tried to scratch a living by growing basic vegetables and keeping a few chickens around their wooden dwellings. There were basically no pensions or healthcare and just a little education with the wealthier families paying for it out of their meagre budgets. Despite this there was very little crime and the income from those working abroad in security or soldiering in the British or Indian Army would help support whole families still living in Nepal.

We were joined for an evening meal by a famous Nepalese film star called Rajesh Hamal. He was a good looking man and the son of a diplomat who spoke impeccable English. Someone described him as a kind of Nepalese equivalent of Hugh Grant and his sex appeal drove all the girls present at the restaurant including the waitresses, to ask him for his autograph or have a photograph taken with him. He was in great demand but promised to work with our charity in the future.

Nepal is a peace loving country which has spawned several peace movements and is proud to claim to be the birthplace of Buddha. It became a member of the United Nations in

1955 and since then has been an active participant of many support operations. The Nepalese Army and Police have been deployed in conflicting areas under the flag of the United Nations including Kosovo, Lebanon, Somalia, Congo, Sierra Leone, East Timor, Liberia, Ivory Coast, Haiti, South Sudan, and Darfur. It also played a part in Afghanistan where four Nepalese guards courageously fought and died defending a United Nations compound that was attacked by an armed mob. It was said by officials that they were overwhelmed and were killed trying to defend three workers.

The ethnic origin of the Nepalese and shared deprivation unites them with countries with a strong desire for political, economic and social progress. In a spirit of neutrality and peace, the Nepalese Gurkhas have established a positive role in the post imperialist era and they have gained invaluable experience and understanding of transforming swords into ploughshares. Recently the government has provided support for establishing an international standard training centre.

To understand why Nepalese Gurkhas are in a unique position to play such a pivotal role in global affairs, the history and events within the last two or three decades in Nepal itself, is similar to that of other war strewn and poor countries in which they serve. Between 1996 - 2006 Nepal was in a state of civil war with Mao insurgencies in the rural regions. Until 2001 the King of Nepal allowed a very gradual number of reforms leading to a partial democracy.

There was then a bloody massacre of the King and his family. His brother became the King and the reforms ceased and the civil war grew in intensity. The official line was that the late King's entire family had been killed by his son who, having killed his own mother and father, committed suicide. Few people believed this version and there was growing suspicion that the new despotic king was the real murderer. Eventually there was a revolt by leading politicians and the first Constituent Assembly kicked out the unpopular king and attempts were made to end the bloody civil war and bring about a parliamentary election. Understandably this took a long time and our stay in Nepal was in the aftermath of an election which had been held and attempts were ongoing to form a coalition.

The Congress Party became the leading party but was eager to work with the opposition which was the Communist Party. The Maoists came third in seats won but the consensus was that for peace and harmony it was right to encourage participation in the running of the country. A meeting was arranged for us to visit the home of Sujata Koirala who was considered Nepal's leading lady: she had played a positive role in bringing the three parties together and developing a parliamentary democracy. She told us that she was keen to develop devolution as Kathmandu was far too congested with little chance of wealth creation.

Sujata had been the Foreign Minister and was currently the Head of International Relations Department in the Nepali Congress. Our next meeting was with a former prime minister, Jhalanath Khanal. Despite enormous difficulties we felt that there was a mutual interest in working together even with former enemies. I believe that the Communist Party was not Stalinist but more like Clem Atlee's Labour Party. As Winston Churchill once said 'jaw jaw is better than war war!'

I tried to put myself in the place of Nepali political leaders; however much they might wish to raise the standard of living of their people, how on earth could they deliver improvements?

There was no natural asset unlike the oil producing regions of the Middle East. Adventurous tourists could be attracted to the Himalayan mountain range and Everest in particular but it was not a major tourist favourite. The pollution of Kathmandu and the dreadful roads and sanitation within the mountain regions would deter visitors. It might be possible to assist food production and possibly develop fish farming with U.N. agencies but there were no quick and easy solutions. Nepal stood between the two giants China and India but apart from tea plantations there was little chance of being able to export anything.

There was a special quality that could assist the country's economy; the resilient and tough people themselves. The fusing of Hindu, Buddhist and Christian values into a kind of humanist religion made the mountain people ideal to play the role of world policemen. Though serving abroad, the Gurkha soldiers serving in the British and Indian Army together with various security forces did not turn their back on families and communities, but helped to provide assistance in healthcare and education. Their reputation meant that they were in great demand, even as bodyguards in some Muslim countries.

Britain to its credit now gives considerable sums of money to Nepal to assist with the development of water supplies and sanitation. To assist a country that was trying so hard to develop a fledgling democracy would make sense economically, for exporting technology and education could bring financial benefits to Britain. One example of a beneficial effect of a liberal policy is produced by an old friend of mine Chris Jolly. He produces books for those learning to speak and write English throughout the developing world. His successful publishing company called 'Jolly Learning' pays considerable sums into the British Treasury. There could be a long term benefit for exporting science and technology to developing countries which could create a win win situation rather than the selling of yet more arms.

We were interested in the political dialogue including a Deputy Prime Minister Prakashman Singh. In all we spoke to the representatives of all three parties. What I found interesting was that even a Communist leader said that he thought Britain was a leading ally to Nepal. There are huge problems to be resolved and my Gurkha friends in line with the general views of most Nepalese public were impatient and wished to see positive results. I believe the beneficial effects of democracy takes a long time but the desire for change is positive and Nepal has the right approach to succeed.

Before our departure from Nepal we visited other charities with a view to cooperate rather than compete with them. They included the Welfare Trust, UNICEF and a small charity called Rural Assistance for Nepal, run by an English woman called Marianne Heredge who specialised in bringing doctors on sabbaticals and advising in remote health centres in the Himalayas. The tasks in a developing country such as Nepal are so great that each charity, large and small, have a role to play.

On our return to Britain there was a long delay sat in the aircraft in Kathmandu waiting for the thick fog to lift. Eventually we arrived in Delhi where lengthy but necessary delays were made for security reasons. It was a very tiring journey but my Gurkha friends had organised a people carrier which was waiting for us at Heathrow. I was so glad to jump into bed after being driven home.

Back in Kent several of us visited Cheriton Primary School where a number of children of serving Gurkhas together with the children of indigenous British soldiers studied together. With the guidance of a progressive headmistress Angela Maxted and a few teachers originating from Nepal, there was a harmonious spirit. Some of the local children asked if they could learn a few words of Nepalese so that they could communicate with their friends. The children asked some provocative and intelligent questions. I recall one being 'What about the wives left behind when the men go off to war?' Our inadequate reply was that we loathed war and the objective of the Gurkha Peace Foundation was to try and prevent war and build a peaceful world.

After several visits to and fro by Major Deb Pun we organised a Skype connection between the school in Cheriton and with Shitalpati School in the Himalayas. When the children spoke to each other on Skype they noticed that the Nepalese children were shivering with cold. The children from Cheriton emptied their money boxes and this paid for the children in Nepal to have school uniform for the first time, which helped them to keep warm.

Alongside other altruistic organisations such as Amnesty the Gurkha Peace Foundation was invited to participate in the World Peace Day celebration held in Canterbury Cathedral. The bright colours of girls and ladies saris were a wonderful and inspiring sight as they joined in the parade.

There existed some injustices particularly of elderly Gurkhas still living in Nepal and we had to fight a number of court cases to establish the rights of the children to settle here. Some children were then denied access to a Student Loan despite winning their rights to live here. Bhim and I appeared before more judges than many habitual criminals!

Some well intentioned ex Gurkhas campaigned for parity in their treatment and began to starve themselves to death near to the entrance of Downing Street. We were pleased when this particular protest came to an end resulting in an opportunity for all organisations and charities such as our own to present the case to a Parliamentary Inquiry. This we did with a team which included one of the barristers from the Martin Howe group. We were delighted that Raphael Jesurum, who had defended the rights of Gurkha children was able to contribute to our presentation. We were able to state that the cost of living in Nepal was much higher than the M.O.D. had stated. We stated unequivocally that if the elderly ex Gurkhas were given a modest increase in their pensions it would save the Treasury money because they would then be content to stay in Nepal.

We were asked if the payments that the Department of Overseas Development made to Nepal were justified. I replied that the people of Nepal richly deserved support but to avoid any risk of corruption every charity that assisted Nepal should be invited to two meetings a year in Parliament to advise the government.

At this time some reactionary voices in the M.O.D. were suggesting that now we had won parity for current Gurkha soldiers, Britain could no longer afford them. My reaction to this was that the threat to our national security came from various forms of terrorism and experienced personnel were more important than nuclear weapons or battleships.

At this time, when for a brief period I became the vice chairman of Canterbury United Nations Association I became

deeply involved in the dialogue for creating peace and reconciliation. The Canterbury U.N.A., had a positive vibe due
to the influence of the church and the two universities. The
chairman Geoff Meaden was an academic and leading Green
activist and had helped to give advice on fish farming in South
East Asia and had recently been asked to assist Iran with their
programme. He has some interesting ideas on how to gradually
create a peace securing United Nations element rather than just
a peace keeping role. His vision was to prevent conflict situations before they occurred and to persuade countries to donate
one or two percent of their military budget for this cause.

As a first step to such an altruistic objective I believe the
future of policing a troublesome world might include a
Standing Force for the United Nations and the Gurkhas could
do the job with a rapid response rescue and emergency role. It
has often been the Gurkhas who have fought against the fiercest
enemy. In Sierra Leone they were sent to pacify the rebels in the
diamond mining region where the military commander had
his stronghold. When the rebels were told that the Gurkhas
were coming they somewhat reluctantly accepted the situation.

The U.N.'s representative stressed that its forces were being
deployed in a spirit of peace. The strategy was to send peacemakers from outside the region to the most sensitive parts of
the country. The reason being that the mainly Nigerian West
African troops who make up the bulk of U.N. force, had been
fighting the rebels for years as part of a regional intervention
army. This would make them open to accusations that they
were not neutral. It was predicted that the rebels might test the
resolve of the United Nations force but though the U.N. came
in peace they were prepared to deal with such a test.

I believe that the thought of conflict between the super powers is so awful that it no longer is the greatest threat to peace. Increasing trade and improved communication between the large nations despite the usual bluster is easing tensions. I also believe that the deterrent factor of nuclear war may have been relevant when there was a rational opponent but now that is simply a suicide weapon. The real threat of war now comes from the Islamic world and suicidal terrorism from extremists.

Since the end of the Cold War military forces of the United Nations have been increasingly called upon to intervene in trouble spots around the world. While there is no shortage of goodwill in reaction to atrocities in places such as Rwanda, too often international action is too little or too late. Without a swift and decisive response from outside, a crisis arising from a breakdown of civil authority can easily lead to humanitarian catastrophe.

Inaction by the world community may be unintentional but failure to deal with such situations often lead to growing refugee problems that lead to further trouble spots. The problem stems from the lack of a standing military force under U.N. command. A solution would be to put together a contingent of Gurkha professional soldiers from Nepal who are particularly well suited for such missions.

The Gurkhas are experienced and superb professional soldiers used to service on behalf of an authority other than leaders of their homeland. They have served with great distinction in the British Army and for the last half century with the Indian Army. A minimum of 5,000 troops would be needed for the force to be credible and to give it the flexibility to answer more than one call at a time.

The neutrality of Nepal situated between China and India and retaining a parliamentary democracy in which the Communist Party is able to act as a leading opposition group strengthens the moral authority of Gurkhas. The fact that poverty is an ever present problem makes the Gurkhas a kindred spirit of poor people throughout the world. The presence of Nepalese soldiers would also be unlikely to provoke antagonistic reactions based on nationality. Indeed the formidable reputation of Gurkhas as impartial fighters might help to defuse tense situations.

Such a proposal raises challenges that many governments are reluctant to face. If a Gurkha force is assembled and used, the United Nations would be taking a large step toward acting as an independent supranational body. The force could only be used if the major powers on the U.N. Security Council supported its intervention. The United States is the only nation capable of providing the airlift the force would need to reach trouble spots. The hope of many is that the U.S. is tired of being a world policeman and might welcome a gradual decline from such a responsibility and accept the role of Nepalese Gurkhas.

Once the job was done the United Nations would have to take control of the territory in question for an indeterminate time. This raises fundamental issues about the role of the United Nations in building a new world order. Perhaps the world is ready to confront these questions. Improvised multinational military contingents are simply too slow to assemble and pose too many political and operational problems. A viable alternative must be found. Pragmatism must be allowed to outweigh cynical objections that Western governments seek the political benefits of putting Gurkhas at risk in chaotic situations in place of their own soldiers.

Our fascination with war is difficult to understand. I must confess that I have spent many hours watching war films. I recall a visit to a Vietnamese family during that war where I discovered that they were watching a film based upon the Second World War. At a reunion of doctors and nurses recently, the question was posed; why did we volunteer to spend time in the midst of the Vietnam War? I expected the answer to be that there was a great deal of altruism but the honest reply was that we were adventurous and curious. Much of our culture and history is based upon killing, with our literature rich in dealing with individuals caught up in conflict through the ages.

What a wonderful world we would have if there was no more threat of war or if violence became as remote as suffering from major crime in peace time. It appears that every few decades one threat of destruction ends and another replaces it. With fascism defeated and the Cold War over, we are reminded by the atrocity of 9/11 that another conflict with extremists from the Islamist world is now with us and few of us really knows the reasons.

Most wars are caused by large countries bullying smaller ones for their resources. After the Second World War the European Empires gradually came to an end. The British held on to Kenya, Cyprus and even attempted to control Suez and the French fought in Algeria and Vietnam. Both eventually faced reality. Large nations attempted different forms of imperialism; Russia in Eastern Europe, China in Tibet and the United States in a form of economic and military control, where they needed resources or a global strategy. With self reliance on imported oil there are signs that the U.S. is less inclined to commit troops to present conflicts such as Syria.

There are positive indications that numerous countries wish to live in more liberal and democratic environments; even the abortive Arab spring is evidence of that. Yet suicidal terrorism has un-nerved Western civilisation. When nineteen men engaged in an operation to hijack four aircraft and killed themselves and the passengers in a most horrific way, it begs the question that if nineteen men are prepared to commit such an act why not ninety or even nine hundred.

After defeat on battle fields in Syria and Iraq it is estimated that over four hundred British Muslims trained in the art of suicidal terrorism are returning to Britain and several thousand similarly trained men are returning to Europe. We lack the resources to monitor all of them and the Minister of Defence stated that they should be killed. We must try to understand the motivation of potential suicidal terrorists if we are to overcome the growing threat.

To explain the brain washing or hypnotic state, potential terrorists are in, some years ago after returning from Vietnam I was speaking to a group of around forty five people when I experienced a strange and unexplained incident. It was towards the end of my speech when I noticed that almost all of the group were listening in an almost zombie like way. It was as if I had hypnotised them and to check on my own sanity without saying anything, I concentrated my thoughts on one man who was sat with his arms leaning on a desk. I willed him to raise his arms three times. This he did, so I willed the whole group to break with any spell that I might have on them. Every speaker wishes to influence an audience but not to bypass the reasoning process. One of my core values is the sanctity of individual freedom for everyone.

Since that incident I have spoken to several friends within the medical profession and they all insist that any form of hypnosis can only be applied with the profound agreement of the individual. For example, someone who wishes to give up smoking, drinking or taking drugs may benefit from the strengthened will that hypnosis provides. I hope my medical friends are right but I remember seeing a young and beautiful girl who had been told to sit on Michael Parkinson's lap, on his weekly TV show start kissing him passionately, until the spell was broken and she shot up amazed at her own actions; did her inner thoughts really wish to embrace Michael Parkinson?

There are numerous examples in war when men are conditioned to be more afraid of being afraid than inevitable destruction; men going over the top in the First World War or the Japanese kamikaze pilots. Men who face death and their close relatives are always encouraged to believe in life after death. Air Marshall Dowding was a spiritualist who held séances for the relatives of killed or missing pilots. A Scottish spiritualist, Isabella Duncan, became Britain's last witch to be imprisoned. She had a remarkable record of accurately telling families who had not received news from loved ones at sea, that they had been killed. This did not please naval intelligence as they would often hold back news when a ship was sunk and only release information once there was some more favourable news of enemy losses. Ian Fleming was concerned just before D-day that Isabella Duncan would give information that would damage morale.

I believe that those wishing to brainwash Islamic terrorists would instil in them, a terrible hatred of infidels. Pictures of women and children being burnt or blown apart; prisoners being tortured in Guantanamo Bay or information about Israeli expansion in the West Bank or foreign take-overs of oil refineries in Iraq, would all help. They would then be constantly told that those who became martyrs would find great gratification in paradise where beautiful girls would greet them and they would be gifted with an eternal libido and spend eternity with continual orgasms. Constant prayers to repeat these ideas would strengthen such beliefs.

The only way to defeat an alien ideology is with a superior one. Perverted religion is used to promote the cause of war but I believe true religion based upon universal love and the brotherhood of man can be the powerful way to build a new world order. An essential element of the Christian faith states 'Thy Kingdom come as it is in heaven.' In other words we should attempt to build a better world here on Earth. I believe that other major religions also contain such a vision. Another biblical quotation states 'However you treat the least of these you also treat me.' This is a clear rejection of the greedy materialist world in which we live. An ethical foreign policy is as important as any other politics for the security of the nation and this determines that we only enter just conflicts. This has an effect upon all of us morally and economically.

Most of us who have experienced war are often the most powerful voices for peace. It is time for soldiers, charity workers, reporters, diplomats and church leaders to raise their voices against the cruelty and selfishness of war and poverty.

Mainstream media in Britain and the United States is so controlled by corrupt financiers with vested interests in the arms trade and oil, that truth is rarely printed or heard. Perhaps now that new means of direct communication are possible the cry of 'liberty, fraternity and egality' may be heard again.

The world needs leadership and a new moral compass. It is obscene that eight men have more wealth than half of the world's population. The Western democracies used to call themselves the free nations of the world, but freedom is of value in proportion to its universality. The first freedom is the freedom from want: it simply doesn't exist for a starving child. The frustration of those who used to be called working class in Britain, the United States and southern Europe, grows with the despair of declining living standards in healthcare, education, jobs and housing. History has shown that such situations often lead to disadvantaged people turning against minority groups. It happened in Germany in the thirties when the Jews were associated with bankers and is beginning to happen here with growing resentment of refugees.

Even in a global economy I believe it's more important to build self sustained countries than welcoming refugees in a mass exodus. For this purpose the various U.N. agencies play a crucial role and could contribute much more with increased resources.

Since the 1940's when Britain transformed its Empire into a Commonwealth, it has been revered by friends and respected everywhere. Throughout the Vietnam War I heard the familiar call from moderate peace campaigners that Britain was in a strong position to help end the bloodshed as it retained strong friendship with the U.S. and China in Hong Kong. The English language, culture, history and its reputation for charitable work, places Britain in a strong position to provide a positive role in a troubled world.

To strengthen participatory democracy, major constitutional change is required in Britain. Such a system would encourage everyone to participate in national and local politics and bring about more innovative ideas.

Alongside the recharging of democratic institutions there is a need to refinance British industry. To overcome the deficit we must export more or import less. If tiny Holland can export foodstuff why does Britain need to import almost a third of its requirements? It may be fine to import mangoes or oranges but why is it necessary to import vegetables such as cabbages, cauliflowers and potatoes when our own crops are being ploughed in?

A big unit of production leads to more food miles which must be environmentally wrong. To require social justice, community values and economics based upon human need, it may be necessary to launch a national moratorium. Serious research at local level is required to ask how to build wealth creation and provide future jobs within the caring professions, services and production.

After experiences in the seventies during a Labour Government many were disillusioned by hyper inflation and a stagnant economy. Bureaucracy was rife and small businesses were over charged by banks. This prepared the way for what was known as Friedman Thatcherism, an idea that penetrated the minds of all three parties. People are now tiring of both State Capitalism and Friedman Thatcherism. The long term effect on the economy is that such ideologies are centralist and elitist and widened the class divide.

I believe that community values are second only to family values and can provide far more pleasant and greener environments. The common sense and the common purpose of the common man can be the most powerful force on earth if it is tempered by prudence and ethics.

Some of those mentioned in the book

American

Larry Burrows, photographer for *Time Life*.

Corrine Collins, niece of third man to visit the moon.

Tom Dooley, doctor who started a healthcare project in Laos.

Foster Dulles, Secretary of State in the nineteen fifties.

Jane Fonda, actress and peace campaigner.

James William Fulbright, Chairman of Senate Foreign Relations Committee.

Shaun Flynn, son of Errol Flynn and journalist.

Ted Kennedy, younger brother of President Jack and Bobby, both of whom were assassinated.

John Kerry, Democrat Candidate for the Presidential Election in 2004.

Henry Kissinger, Secretary of State under Nixon.

Eugene McCarthy campaigned for Democrat candidature in early 1968.

George McGovern, Democrat Presidential candidate in 1972.

Richard Nixon, President from 1968 till 1974.

Ross Perot, Independent Candidate for the Presidency.

Mark Pratt, leading man in charge of the Indochina desk in Paris.

Oliver Stone, film producer and peace campaigner.

Don Tate, Pulitzer Prize Winning journalist.

General Westmoreland, Supreme Military Commander.

British

Frank Allaun, Chairman of the Labour Party and Vice Chair of the Peace in Vietnam Committee.

Dr John Bass, Member of British Medical team in Saigon.

John Biggs-Davidson, Member of Conservative Party Foreign Affairs Committee.

Melvyn Bowler, technician serving the British Medical Team in Saigon.

David Cameron, Prime Minister from 2010 until 2016.

James Cameron, journalist and TV broadcaster.

Peter Carroll, organiser of the Campaign for Gurkha Justice.

Campbell Bannerman, Prime Minister elected in 1905.

David Crouch, Conservative M.P. for Canterbury.

Rev Michael Counsel, protestant priest in Saigon.

Michael Challes, Detective Chief Superintendent investigating the Thorpe murder inquiry.

David Davis, Conservative M.P.

George de Chabris, Canadian donor to the Liberal Party.

Basil Goldstone, President of the Liberal Party.

Fenner Brockway, Member of the House of Lords and Chairman of the Peace in Vietnam Committee.

Jo Grimond, Leader of the Liberal Party from 1957 until 1967.

Michael Foot, Leader of the Labour Party.

Paul Foot, Investigative journalist who worked with Private Eye.

Douglas Grey, medic who started the Polio Centre for orphans.

Sir Jack Hayward, donor to the Liberal Party.

Ted Harrison, journalist and TV broadcaster.

Martin Howe, Leader of lawyers presenting the Campaign for Gurkha Justice.

Charles Kennedy, Leader of the Liberal Party.

Lloyd George, the last Liberal to become Prime Minister.

Eric Lubbock, Chief Whip of the Liberal Party.

Joanna Lumley, actress and campaigner for the Campaign for Gurkha Justice.

Angela Maxted, Headmistress of Cheriton Primary School and pioneer of twinning scheme with Nepal.

Charlotte McCaul, former Sheriff of Canterbury and trustee of the Gurkha Peace Foundation.

Dr McCaully, Leader of the medical team in Saigon.

Brian McConnell, feature editor of the Sun.

Virginia McKenna, film actress and supporter of the Campaign for Gurkha Justice.

Tim Page, war photographer.

Dr Adrian Pointer, member of Medical Team in Saigon.

Verdun Perl, peace campaigner.

Frank Rushworth, Detective Chief Inspector of the serious crime sector of Scotland Yard.

Ray Small, Chief Detective Superintendent of Scotland Yard.

Cyril Smith, Chief Whip of the Liberal Party.

Leonard Smith, Chairman of the National Liberal Club.

Peggy Stanley, anaesthetist with W.H.O. in Laos.

Sir Robert Thompson, right wing military writer.

Sir Julian Thompson, senior military officer.

Jeremy Thorpe, Leader of the Liberal Party 1967 until 1976.

Charles Wheeler, BBC investigative journalist.

Harold Wilson, Prime Minister.

Richard Wood, Member of Conservative Party Foreign Affairs Committee.

Phil Woolas, Minister of Immigration.

International

Gennady (Genner), Russian diplomat.
Sir Keith Holyoake, New Zealand Prime Minister.
Catherine Leroy, French war photographer.
La Norrinne, P.A. to Lao Prime minister.
Prince Sihanouk, Prime Minister of Cambodia.
Souvanna Phoumma, Prime Minister of Laos.
U Thant, United Nations Secretary General.

Nepalese

Bhim Raj, Chairman of trustees of Gurkha Peace Foundation and founding supporter of the Campaign for Gurkha Justice.
Deb Pun, trustee of Gurkha Peace Foundation and coordinator of twinning scheme linking schools with Nepalese projects.
Gopal Giri, Vice Chairman of Gurkha Peace Foundation and founding supporter of the Campaign for Gurkha Justice.
Jhalanath Khanal, former Prime Minister of Nepal.
Sujata Koirala, former Foreign Minister and Head of Senate International Relations.
Prem Limbu, founding supporter of Campaign for Gurkha Justice and Gurkha Peace Foundation.
Prakashman Singh, Deputy Prime Minister of Nepal.

Vietnamese

Ung An, Uncle of deposed Emperor Bao Dai.
Madam Bhin, Leader of the Viet Cong (N.L.F.) during the Paris Peace talks.

Monsignor Bhin, senior Catholic prelate in South Vietnam.
Lieutenant Bhin, Military spokesman for South Vietnam.
Van Bong, Member of South Vietnamese Peace Delegation in Paris.
Prince Buu Loc, Prime Minister of Vietnam under the French.
Le Chanh, diplomat representing North Vietnam.
Trang Dinh Dzu, Peace candidate in the 1967 Presidential Election.
General Tran Van Don, last Prime Minister of President Thieu's.
Duc, film producer and teacher.
Le Van Hao, Spokesman for North Vietnam in Paris.
Big Minh, President of South Vietnam during last days of the regime.
Ho Chi Minh, President of North Vietnam and father of the nation.
Deputy Ham, Social Democrat and peace campaigner.
Major Hoang, Leading officer at the Officer Training School at Nha Trang.
Vice President Hoang became the leader when Thieu departed.
Ky, Became Vice President following Presidential Election in 1967.
Tran Ngoc Lieng, leading lawyer and nominated Vice President of Big Minh in 1967 Presidential Election.
Nhan, Viet Cong diplomat based in Paris.
Tran Thoung Nhon, architect of the Kissinger Tho Agreement.
Nhin, Catholic teacher who worked in the International School.
Nhie, Buddhist and peace activist.
Pham Nam Sach, former chairman of the Senate.
Pham Khac Sum, Chief of State of South Vietnam 1963-4.
Pham Dung Sum, diplomat for Viet Cong in Paris.

Le Van Sao, Viet Cong diplomat and adviser to Madam Bhin.
Madam Ngo Ba Thanh, Lawyer and peace activist.
Nguyen Thai Son, journalist.
Thieu, President of South Vietnam 1967 to 1975.
Vo Van Truyen, Chair of Senate Cao Dais.
Nguyen Than Vinh, Chair of Constitutional Assembly.
Thaung, President of North Vietnam, 1969 following death of Ho Chi Minh.
Tri Quang, Buddhist peace leader.
Xuan, music teacher working at the International School.

***